Critical Essays on
GEORGE BERNARD SHAW

CRITICAL ESSAYS
ON
BRITISH LITERATURE

Zack Bowen, General Editor
University of Miami

Critical Essays on

GEORGE BERNARD SHAW

edited by

ELSIE B. ADAMS

G. K. Hall & Co./New York
Maxwell Macmillian Canada/Toronto
Maxwell Macmillan International/New York Oxford Singapore Sydney

G.K. Hall & Co.   Maxwell Macmillan Canada, Inc.
Macmillan Publishing Company   1200 Eglinton Avenue East
866 Third Avenue   Suite 200
New York, New York 10022   Don Mills, Ontario M3C 3N1

Macmillan Publishing Company is part of the
Maxwell Communication Group of Companies.

Library of Congress Cataloging-in-Publication Data

Critical essays on George Bernard Shaw/edited by Elsie B. Adams.
        p.   cm.—(Critical essays on British literature)
    Includes bibliographical references and index.
    ISBN 0-8161-8858-0
    1. Shaw, Bernard, 1836-1950—Criticism and interpretation.
    I. Adams, Elsie Bonita, 1932-   . II. Series.
    PR5367.C68   1991
    822'.912—dc20   91-13072

The paper used in this publication meets the minimum requirements of
American National Standard for Information Sciences—Permanence of Paper
for Printed Library Materials, ANSI Z39.48-1984.   ∞™

10 9 8 7 6 5 4 3 2 1

Printed in the United States of America

Contents

◆

General Editor's Note

♦

The Critical Essays on British Literature series provides a variety of approaches to both classical and contemporary writers of Britain and Ireland. The formats of the volumes in the series vary with the thematic designs of individual editors and with the amount and nature of existing reviews and criticism, augmented, where appropriate, by original essays by recognized authorities. It is hoped that each volume will be unique in developing a new overall perspective on its particular subject.

In both her introduction and her selection of essays Elsie Adams concentrates on the continuity of the major critical and philosophical issues that have surrounded Shaw's plays over the years: his political ideology, his methodology in presenting arguments, and the openness of his work to change and interpretation. The selected criticism, arranged chronologically, covers the ongoing debate over a period of more than 75 years, concluding with Richard Dietrich's deconstructionist assurance that "post-modern criticism seems tailor-made for Shaw" and the sense that the playwright's work remains as vital a source of critical energy as ever.

ZACK BOWEN
University of Miami

Publisher's Note

◆

Producing a volume that contains both newly commissioned and reprinted material presents the publisher with the challenge of balancing the desire to achieve stylistic consistency with the need to preserve the integrity of works first published elsewhere. In the Critical Essays series, essays commissioned especially for a particular volume are edited to be consistent with G. K. Hall's house style; reprinted essays appear in the style in which they were first published, with only typographical errors corrected. Consequently, shifts in style from one essay to another are the result of our efforts to be faithful to each text as it was originally published.

Critical Essays on
GEORGE BERNARD SHAW

Introduction

ELSIE B. ADAMS

A history of the criticism of George Bernard Shaw (1856–1950) would reveal that there has never been a consensus about the ultimate value of his dramatic work or about the efficacy of his opinions. He is generally conceded to be the greatest playwright of the English-speaking world in the twentieth century, yet detractors insist that his "drama of ideas" led to a theatrical dead end and that the ideas themselves belong to an age, not to all time. Shaw began writing in the 1870s and continued writing to the end of his long life. His first novel was written in 1879; his last play was written more than 70 years later, in 1950. Few literary figures of the twentieth century have attracted more critical attention: the three-volume bibliography of writings about him published in 1986–87 contains more than 9,000 entries.[1]

Critical Essays on George Bernard Shaw attempts not to present a history of this criticism but instead to provide a glimpse at the variety of approaches to, opinions about, and assessments of Shaw. The collection focuses on Shaw the dramatist, without attempting to include criticism of Shaw the art critic, music critic, or drama critic—except insofar as these affect his drama. Shaw's philosophy of Creative Evolution, especially as formulated in his concept of the Superman and as dramatized in his "Metabiological Pentateuch," Back to Methuselah (written 1918–20), is examined, and his Fabian socialist politics are assessed as they relate to his dramatic art. Most of the essays treat—as the title of Eric Bentley's essay states—"The Theory and Practice of Shavian Drama."

Shaw began his literary career after arriving in London from his native Ireland in 1876. He at first tried his hand at writing novels—five of them, all rejected by London publishers. In an appendix to the fifth, An Unsocial Socialist, Shaw's hero advises the author to abandon the outmoded novel form—advice the young Shaw followed. The success denied him as a fiction writer came in the 1880s and 1890s through his book reviews, art criticism, and music criticism for London newspapers: he began to gain recognition for his journalism, especially the music criticism written for the Star (as "Corno di Bassetto"— basset horn) and for the World (as "G.B.S."). In the meantime, his conversion to socialism in 1882 contributed not only to a changed direction in his art but also to his increasing fame as a platform orator and pamphleteer.

Shaw's career as a dramatist began alongside of and was nourished by his drama criticism of the 1890s. In 1891 he wrote a defense of Ibsen's drama that was to serve as an anchor for Shaw's own dramatic practice. In *The Quintessence of Ibsenism* Shaw created the categories of idealist, philistine, and realist to describe central character types in Ibsen—types that were to appear over and over in Shaw's own plays—and his full-scale attack on "the womanly woman" prepared the way for the magnificent Shavian woman. Shaw's three years as drama critic for the *Saturday Review* (1895–98)—with his attacks on the fashionable "well-made" play and on the "Bardolatry" of Shakespeare on the late Victorian stage—helped pave the way for the "New Drama," including the drama of Shaw, that emerged at the end of the nineteenth century.

For an analysis of the development of Shaw's drama the reader is referred to Bentley's "The Theory and Practice of Shavian Drama" (included in this volume). Bentley divides the plays into prewar (First World War) and postwar plays, seeing *Heartbreak House* (written 1916–17) as the pivotal play, in which and after which Shaw's socialist optimism and Life Force philosophy are seriously brought into question as Shaw sees civilization drifting like a ship onto the rocks. In addition to writing more than 50 plays and playlets,[2] Shaw continued to speak and write on political issues, frequently preaching, like Sidney Trefusis (his "unsocial socialist"), a sermon on "Socialism or Smash." Shaw was a tremendously prolific writer—of art, music, drama, and social criticism; of political and economic tracts; of fiction and drama. It is of course the last that has elicited most criticism of Shaw.

The selections in *Critical Essays on George Bernard Shaw* illustrate a variety of interpretations and approaches to Shaw, beginning with H. L. Mencken's *George Bernard Shaw: His Plays* (1905). Mencken points "By Way of Introduction" (his title) to the themes and techniques governing all Shaw's plays. He defines the central dramatic conflict in Shaw as orthodoxy versus heterodoxy brought about by basically two character types: "the worshipers of old idols"—that is, the ordinary folk, the majority—and the iconoclasts. Mencken describes Shaw as a realistic dramatist rather than a sermonizing preacher and provides a useful starting place for a study of Shaw: "if we divest ourselves of the idea that Shaw is trying to preach some rock-ribbed doctrine in each of his plays, instead of merely setting forth human events as he sees them, we may find his dramas much easier of comprehension."

Another early critic of Shaw, G. K. Chesterton, offers a contrary opinion, arguing that Shaw tends toward fanaticism in his writing of propaganda plays. In *George Bernard Shaw* (1909) Chesterton attacks three popular generalizations about Shaw: that Shaw is a writer of problem plays, that he is paradoxical, and that he is a socialist writer. Chesterton's refutation of each "misconception" depends on his own specific definition of "problem play," "paradox," and "socialist." Calling a problem play one that presents two points of view, neither of which is endorsed by the writer, Chesterton asserts that Shaw "cannot really divide his mind and let the two parts speak independently to each other." Chesterton finds Shaw's dialogue like a religious tract in that it loads the case for Shaw's point of view and fails to do justice to the opposition. Chesterton sees the same failure in Shaw's inability to recognize paradox (defined as "truth inherent in a contradiction"); using Shaw's attitude toward the education of children and the institution of marriage as examples, Chesterton argues that Shaw single-mindedly carries an idea to its logical conclusion without recognizing the "paradox of childhood" (that the more perfect being must be controlled by the less perfect adult) or the "paradox of marriage" ("that the woman is all the more the house for not being the head of it"). Chesterton points to Shaw's attacks on convention and tradition in stating that Shaw is anarchist, not socialist. More evidence against Shaw as socialist is that he "dislikes men in the mass" and has "no respect for collective humanity."

Chesterton's highly idiosyncratic definitions and his traditionalist bias make his commentary a suspect, though very lively, assessment of Shaw. In dealing with the three popular "misconceptions" (as Chesterton describes them), he introduces questions that have plagued Shaw criticism from its beginning. Is Shaw's theater of ideas effective drama or merely talk, talk, talk? Does he use the stage as a platform for propagandizing or preaching sermons? Is he capable of fairly representing more than a single point of view? What relationship—if any—has his socialism to his art? Did he abandon his socialist principles in advocating the Shavian Superman and repudiating, as Chesterton says, "men in the mass"?

A controversy about the effect of Shaw's theater of ideas found expression in the pages of the *New Statesman and Nation* in 1950. Calling for a "theatre that deals with people and stories instead of with ideas and theories," Terence Rattigan set off a debate that ran for two months. In "Concerning the Play of Ideas" Rattigan blames Shaw for "fifty years of completely stagnant thought and theory concerning the drama"—the legacy of Shavian-Ibsenite "sociologically significant" drama. Rattigan assumes, as Chesterton did years before, that Shaw's plays are closer to tracts than to representations of flesh-and-blood people in real-life situations. Sean O'Casey, answering Rattigan, argues that Shaw and Ibsen brought "a dead drama back to a serious and singing life again." In "The Play of Ideas" O'Casey observes that drama cannot exist without ideas and that the greatest works of literature contain not only ideas but ideas of social significance. Furthermore, a drama of ideas does not preclude the interweaving of idea, character, and plot—Rattigan's "theatre that deals with people and stories."

Shaw himself contributed an essay to the controversy,[3] aligning the technique of his theater with that of the masters of drama: "The truth was that I was going back atavistically to Aristotle, to the tribune stage, to the circus, to the didactic Mysteries, to the word music of Shakespeare, to the forms of my idol Mozart, and to the stage business of the great players whom I had actually seen acting." This passage suggests that Shaw intended to combine entertainment and didacticism, with an eye to the practical exigencies of the stage. He asserts that the quality of ideas—the "mental capacity" of the author—determines the difference between a masterpiece and a trivial play that deals only with the surface of life. "The quality of a play is the quality of its ideas," says Shaw.

In addition to the ongoing debate about the quality of drama produced by the Shavian theater of ideas is a continuing controversy about the degree of Shaw's commitment to socialism. For example, Edmund Wilson in "Bernard Shaw at Eighty" (an excerpt of which is reprinted here as "The Themes of Bernard Shaw") argues that Shaw's idea of the Superman allowed him to escape from the implications of his socialism. By the time of *Back to Methuselah,* Wilson says, Shaw's socialism had been replaced by his religious faith in the power of the human will and in the necessity of freeing the human spirit from flesh. The long-lived Ancients in *As Far as Thought Can Reach* are not examples of people living rich, fulfilled lives in a classless society; instead, they are "Shavian super-prigs" separated from any social context and specializing in the art of verbal cruelty. Continuing his theme of Shaw's abandonment of socialism, Wilson makes a connection between the Labour government of Ramsay MacDonald in the 1920s and Shaw's portrait of Proteus in *The Apple Cart* (1929), noting that Shaw placed the blame for the failed socialism not on Fabian tactics but on "democracy." Finally, Shaw offered as an alternative "not socialism of a more thoroughgoing kind, but the super-constitutional-monarch, King Magnus." Though he finds Shaw's politics confused in this play and others, Wilson praises Shaw's power of comic invention, his incisive social criticism, and his realistic reporting. He concludes that, though Shaw "has not acted a straight role as a socialist," his plays "have been a truthful and continually developing chronicle of a soul in relation to society."

For a student of literature the most interesting commentaries on Shaw's socialism are those which examine the relationship between Shaw's politics and his art. In *Bernard Shaw: Art and Socialism* (1942) Erich Strauss discusses how Shaw's socialism permeates his dramatic work in the form of a tension between art and life, between thought and action. In the chapter entitled "Masks and Characters" Strauss offers the hypothesis that Shaw's disappointment with practical politics led him "to merge the Socialist propagandist in the dramatic artist." Shaw's socialism, Strauss says, gave him both a subject—the conflict between his socialist convictions and the world's resistance to them—and a point of view for his drama. Strauss traces the increasing skepticism of Shaw toward both his men of words and his men of action, resulting in political heroes (like King Magnus and Sir Arthur Chavender) who are "miserable failures" and in preachers (Aubrey in *Too True to Be Good* is an example) without a creed and without an audience. Strauss concludes that Shaw's "work is at least as much a document of doubt as of belief": Shaw was disappointed in political action and turned to words; eventually, the disillusionment extended to the words as well.

In an essay on "The Novels of Bernard Shaw" Claude T. Bissell, like Strauss, sees a direct connection between Shaw's socialism and his art, with the socialism producing a sharper comic vision and a more powerful style. Bissell contrasts the serious tone and the formal, studied style of the first three novels—*Immaturity, The Irrational Knot,* and *Love among the Artists*—with the comic invention and the self-assured, original style of the last two. Both of the last two novels—*Cashel Byron's Profession* and *An Unsocial Socialist*—combine comic extravagance with social criticism and anticipate both the satiric technique and the rhetorical prose of Shaw's plays. The movement from "didactic problem novel" with a rationalist hero to "comic extravaganza" with a romantic individualist hero Bissell attributes to Shaw's conversion to socialism. Like Strauss, Bissell believes that socialism gave Shaw a consistent point of view in his artistic depiction of the cultured, leisured class—a point of view lacking in the early novels. Furthermore, the ideal of a Communist utopia satisfied romantic longings while the inequities of the economic system provided matter for Shaw's comic genius.

One of the most interesting—and most challenging—analyses of Shaw's socialism is Alick West's *George Bernard Shaw: "A Good Man Fallen among Fabians"* (1950). Whereas Strauss and Bissell see Shaw's socialism leading not to socialist change in the actual world but to better art in the realm of fiction, West sees Shaw as using his art to slur over socialist issues. Thus for some critics Shaw's socialism feeds the art; for West his art is used to evade his socialism. In the chapter entitled "Debate and Comedy" West attacks Shaw for not giving his rebels a voice in the plays, for repressing his revolutionary creative energy, and for retreating from conflict "lest its intensity should make his position of compromise untenable." Clearly West, like Wilson before him, is objecting to the gradualist Fabian policy of interpenetration of the political mainstream rather than revolutionary action, and he finds Shaw's Fabianism governing his dramatic technique. Wilson had observed that "Shaw's comedy . . . is almost as much dependent on a cultivated and stable society as the comedy of Molière." West adds that Shaw's true rebels against the stable society—Louka (servant breaking the class barrier), Gloria (New Woman), Brassbound (pirate), Anderson (preacher-turned-soldier), etc.—are unfairly set up against Shaw's "realists" (reflecting bourgeois values). Therefore "the plays are haunted by voices which never speak out." After an appreciative and insightful analysis of Shaw's comedy, West concludes that Shaw uses laughter (e.g., the "universal laughter" at the end of *Man and Superman* at Tanner's expense) as an avoidance strategy, just as he retreats behind mysticism and the Life Force to avoid confronting real issues facing real people: "Shaw will not give full freedom to his comic vision, because he will not fully trust in the people." One is reminded of Chesterton's early charge that Shaw does not like "men in the mass."

Though Chesterton's attack on Shaw as a writer of problem plays and on Shaw as socialist anticipated later criticism, his insistence that Shaw cannot recognize paradox is shared by few subsequent critics. For example, Frederick P. W. McDowell in his 1953 *PMLA* study of *Heartbreak House* disagrees with Chesterton, asserting that "Shaw adopts paradox as basic" in his approach to truth. McDowell sees at the thematic center of *Heartbreak House* the paradoxical idea that "the apparently mad are in reality the sane." Like the best of contemporary Shaw critics (and contrary to Chesterton, who believed that Shaw was incapable of seeing multiple perspectives), McDowell stresses the fluid, changing, exploratory nature of Shaw's view of reality and truth: reality for Shaw is "a dynamic mosaic of conflicting forces," and the truth is "that there is no final truth." McDowell offers the characters of *Heartbreak House* as illustrations of these points; though the characters can be seen as tending toward the allegorical and representing the archetypical, they nevertheless have psychological depth, combining human strengths and weaknesses. The marriage of Ellie Dunn and Captain Shotover is a union of the ideal and the pragmatic, of "youthful dream and aged wisdom," a resolution of opposites instead of the pursuit of a single idea.

McDowell argues that *Heartbreak House* is central (not only chronologically but also thematically and technically) in the Shaw canon. It is a "conversion" play like the early plays; it depicts learning through disillusionment, like the middle plays; and it looks forward to the late plays in the abandonment of the concept of the Superman as savior of society and in its dreamlike structure. In *Heartbreak House* Shaw moves beyond realism, and beyond the admitted Chekhovian influence, by using dramatic effects that suggest the disjunction, exaggeration, and grotesquerie of dream.

Shaw's use of the dream vision—a literary type that looks back to medieval religious poetry and forward to twentieth-century surrealism—is fully discussed in Stanley Weintraub's article on "The Avant-Garde Shaw: *Too True to Be Good* and Its Predecessors" (first published in 1966). Speaking of *Heartbreak House,* Weintraub says that the play is perhaps the dream of Ellie Dunn, "who falls asleep in the Hushabye (Heartbreak) House before the play is two pages old." Shaw had earlier used dream vision in the "Don Juan in Hell" episode of *Man and Superman* (1901–1903), and he uses it in the dream fantasy that constitutes the epilogue of *Saint Joan* (1923). As Weintraub observes, *Too True to Be Good* (1931) may also be the dream of the Patient in act 1 fantasizing her escape from her sickbed. In these plays the dream motif allows Shaw to move outside time and space for contemplation of an otherwise socially oriented, realistically conceived dramatic situation.

As its title suggests, Weintraub's essay isolates other avant-garde techniques in Shaw, including those which belong to the theater of the absurd. Examples of absurdist dialogue and action—irrational, nonsensical, uncommunicative—are found in the early playlet *Passion, Poison and Petrifaction* (1905), in *Too True to Be Good,* and in *Village Wooing* (1933). Shaw also creates self-conscious characters, actors who are aware of the audience (as in the "Don Juan in Hell" scene); this shattering of stage illusion makes empathetic identification with characters difficult, producing, Weintraub notes, the effect of Brechtian "alienation." At times Shaw "makes the audience well aware that it is an audience and that the play is a play," as in the god Ra's address to the audience in the prologue to *Caesar and Cleopatra*. Or Shaw pulls the audience into the action of the play: the final stage directions of *Too True to Be Good* begin with "The audience disperses," while the eloquence of the preacher continues after the curtain goes down. The nonrealistic, intensified rhetoric that Weintraub finds characteristic of Shaw at points of crisis, along with absurd dialogue and action, allows Shaw to break out of "the confines of realism" and puts him closer to the contemporary stage than some critics have admitted.

Other critics who find a place for Shaw in avant-garde theory and practice are Barbara Bellow Watson, in "The New Woman and the New Comedy" (1977); J. L. Wisenthal, "Having the Last Word: Plot and Counterplot in Bernard Shaw" (1983); and Richard F. Dietrich, "Deconstruction as Devil's Advocacy: A Shavian Alternative" (1986). These essays not only argue for Shaw's currency at the end of the twentieth century but also shed light on his basic philosophy of life and art.

Watson sees the comic structure of Shaw's theater of ideas tied directly to his ideas on women: whereas comic writers have traditionally ended their plays with the assimilation of lovers into society and its values (thus promising a recurrence of the conflict in later generations), Shaw "sees society, and even nature, as capable of genuine evolution, of an escape from recurrence," and portrays this viewpoint through women characters whose primary object in life is *not* marriage, whose major struggle is "the born self against the assigned self." Traditional comedy treats woman as an element of the plot, frequently as a sexual object; Shavian comedy, on the other hand, makes woman "primarily an element in the thought of the play." Finally, the resolution of traditional comedy comes about through the recognition of human folly and through various pairings off. In Shavian comedy, however, "[w]eddings and matings recede from the center of interest and take their place along with other human concerns including social change and the survival of the species." Unlike Wilson and other critics who see Shaw's comedy as ultimately dependent on a stable, cultured society, Watson sees Shaw's comedy generating from an evolutionary, revolutionary belief in the necessity for social change.

Shaw shifted the focus of drama from the traditional man of action to "the woman of awareness." Instead of seeing woman as mysterious and enigmatic, Shaw considered her—as the title of one of his feminist essays has it—"man in petticoats." Frequently, as in the case of Lady Cicely in *Captain Brassbound's Conversion* (1899), Shaw's heroine escapes from marriage with a sense of relief. Sometimes, as in *The Millionairess* (1935–36), she is the "Boss incarnate," independent and sexually self-assured. She rebels against the role that society tries to force on her (Joan is an example) and teaches men to likewise rebel against social constraints that work against self-realization. Watson's final assessment of Shaw's attitude toward women and the reflection of it in his female characters gives him a place as "a patron saint of the woman's movement."

Another perceptive analysis of Shaw's break with traditional drama is Wisenthal's study "Having the Last Word: Plot and Counterplot in Bernard Shaw." Beginning with Shaw's account of the origin of *Widowers' Houses* (William Archer provided a plot and Shaw "used it all up" by the middle of the first act) and with Shaw's rewriting of the ending of Shakespeare's *Cymbeline* in *Cymbeline Refinished,* Wisenthal asserts that Shaw typically refuses to allow the demands of plot or the requirements of genre to govern his playwriting. In both *Widowers' Houses* (1885–92) and *Cymbeline Refinished* (1937) the outcome of the plot depends on the characters' understanding of their situation; each play ends with questions raised and problems unresolved. It was Shaw's way, Wisenthal argues, of "giving human will ascendancy over the revelations of plot." Ideology is wed to technique, and provides Shaw with a dramatic strategy: he frustrates the audience's expectations and leaves the resolution of the plot in the hands of the audience. For example, in *Pygmalion* (1912) Eliza Doolittle refuses to accept her transformation from flower girl to duchess, stating that she was better off as a flower girl. Furthermore, the romance that the plot demands between Higgins and Eliza is averted: the marriage that occurs at the end of the comedy is that of Eliza's father, the *senex* of traditional comedy. By disappointing expectations, Shaw forces the audience to reevaluate the way it views love and life, "to think about human problems in a direct and original way."

Surveying the entire dramatic corpus of Shaw, Wisenthal illustrates Shaw's technique of counterpoint, achieved through a "double perspective" offering a competing point of view to the text as read or performed. Examples are Trefusis's letter to the author at the end of *An Unsocial Socialist* criticizing the failure of the novel to present real life, the "Revolutionist's Handbook" appended to *Man and Superman,* and the epilogue to *Pygmalion* discussing Eliza's marriage to Freddy. Behind the plot of the novel or play is a counterplot, frequently suggested by an epilogue, appendix, or final discussion after the "plot" is over.

For the philosophical underpinning of Shaw's dramatic technique, Wisenthal points to Shaw's Hegelian view of history as an unending process ("every dialectical resolution is merely a resting place or jumping-off point") and quotes Shaw's statement that "The beginning of one of my plays takes place exactly where an unwritten play ended. And the ending of my written play concludes where another play begins." Sometimes the process is dramatically realized by a play that begins where a traditional comedy might end (e.g., *Candida* begins with a happy marriage); sometimes the process is implied in the "unwritten play that follows the ending" (e.g., the play about the woman of action needed to save the world alluded to in the final stage direction of *Too True to Be Good*). Wisenthal's thesis that "Shaw's plays are open, living, growing structures" is carefully argued and well supported. In contrast to Chesterton's view (echoed by other Shaw critics over the years) that Shaw's vision was single minded, Wisenthal makes a convincing case for the multiple perspectives offered and for process as a structural principle in Shavian drama.

Nothing is fixed and nothing is "finished" in Shaw: "For Shaw there is always something to add," Wisenthal concludes. Richard F. Dietrich, in "Deconstruction as Devil's Advocacy: A Shavian Alternative," agrees. Dietrich argues that Shaw uses devil's advocacy—verbal shock—as a conscious deconstructive strategy both to challenge "attempts at closure" and to point "to fissures by which new ideas may enter." As part of his deconstructive activity, Shaw attacks conventional ideas through inversion of plot and character and through verbal inversion, "revealing the contradictions within and between creeds, and between creed and actual behavior." Consequently, truth in Shaw is hard to locate because it lies in the contradictions in the text, "embedded in the interplay between propagandists and competing ideologies."

In light of Derrida's definition of "the general text" as "everything in the realm of language . . . , whether graphic, spoken, thought, or suspended in the structures of the mind," Dietrich discusses Shaw's Shakespeare criticism and his biblical criticism in the preface (1915) to *Androcles and the Lion*. Shaw's attack was not on Shakespeare texts but on " 'Shakespeare' as a construct of 'the general text,' " that is, the Shakespeare of popular imagination and thought. So too the biblical criticism aimed primarily at the sociopolitical context of "the general text" (i.e., popular ideas about Christ and Christianity), at the same time balancing opposing hierarchies of skepticism and belief and finding in this very opposition an emotional unity.

Dietrich contrasts Shavian idealists and realists: the idealists believe that language and life ("the play of signification" and the "favored text") can be stopped, fixed—made "sacrosanct, absolute, and unified"; the realists love "the play of signification" and hold "no text so authoritative or unified that it cannot be deconstructed." Like his realists, Shaw distrusts absolutisms, and challenges conventional hierarchies—inverting them, replacing them with new hierarchies, calling attention to their arbitrariness. He holds polar opposites in "dialectical tension," with new meaning generated by "the play of polarization." (One is reminded of Erich Strauss's contention that Shaw's disillusionment with politics led to "the powerful tension" in his art between his socialist ideals and "the unyielding resistance of reality.") The strength of Shaw, Dietrich finds, is in "modifying the moorings that anchor [humankind's] being" (the phrase is from Lacan) through linguistic change. In other words, Shaw disturbs and unsettles his audience through his art.

Dietrich's closely argued essay ends with the "Shavian alternative" suggested by the title. Out of the oppositions and contradictions in a text (e.g.,

Shaw's New Testament criticism in the *Androcles* preface) Shaw is able to find a literary unity: though he undercuts Christianity as understood and practiced by many, he nevertheless affirms religious values—values largely based on New Testament study. It is, Dietrich says, "a high-wire act that balances between heterogeneity and orthodoxy, the open mind and the closed mind, tilting at the end in favor of establishing and following a dogma." Without such a tilt, deconstruction ends either in reductionism or in paralysis. Perhaps Shaw's ability to transcend the disintegrative effects of deconstruction can serve, Dietrich suggests, as an alternative to current practice: Shaw "sought out a metaphysic that would explain the conflict and contradiction as part of a larger unity, that would make conflict and contradiction cause for rejoicing rather than cause for despair." Though the approach is new, the idea is not. Compare, for example, Chesterton's description of "the first and finest item of the original Bernard Shaw creed": "if reason says that life is irrational, life must be content to reply that reason is lifeless; life is the primary thing, and if reason impedes it, then reason must be trodden down."

It should be clear from this brief introduction that, throughout the history of Shaw criticism, certain areas of agreement and certain points of controversy have prevailed. From Mencken (1905) to Dietrich (1986) there is general agreement that at the heart of Shavian drama is the conflict between orthodoxy and heterodoxy. Whether the resulting tension arises out of Shaw's disappointment with socialist politics, as Strauss believes; out of a philosophical commitment to pragmatic pluralism, as Bentley believes; or out of a deliberate deconstructive strategy, as Dietrich believes, this conflict is seen as central in Shaw. There is less critical agreement about the nature of Shaw's theater of ideas. Rattigan deplores the influence of a drama void of character and plot; other critics insist that Shaw's plays have story (parable) and situations and that discussion does not preclude dramatic character and action. Recent criticism tends to disagree with the perspective (expressed by Chesterton and by West) that Shaw represents only one point of view as a way of making his propagandistic point. Shaw's reality is described as a "mosaic of conflicting forces" (McDowell, 1953); as an evolutionary, revolutionary force (Watson, 1977); and as multiple perspectives presented in both text and subtext (Wisenthal, 1983).

The criticism published in recent years suggests that Shaw's work lends itself readily to contemporary approaches. As Dietrich says, "Post-modern criticism seems tailor-made for Shaw." In this statement Dietrich is referring to both criticism *of* Shaw and criticism *by* Shaw. Shaw is seen as more complex and less doctrinaire than formerly. He does not attempt to resolve the oppositions that govern his drama. Instead, he allows those very contradictions to feed his view of reality and truth in a fluid, changing "multiverse." In this contemporary view of Shaw, his drama and his ideas have not only survived a century of criticism but remain current and alive.

Notes

1. *G. B. Shaw: An Annotated Bibliography of Writings about Him,* ed. J. P. Wearing, Elsie B. Adams, and Donald C. Haberman (Dekalb: Northern Illinois University Press, 1986–87). For a history of Shaw criticism, see the introduction to each of the three volumes of this work.

2. The definitive Bodley Head *Bernard Shaw. Collected Plays with Their Prefaces* (London, Sydney, and Toronto: Max Reinhardt, The Bodley Head, 1970–74; also New York: Dodd, Mead, 1975) includes 51 plays in the Shaw canon.

3. "The Play of Ideas," *New Statesman and Nation,* n.s. 39 (6 May 1950): 510–11.

ESSAYS

◆

By Way of Introduction

H. L. Mencken

Popular opinion and himself to the contrary notwithstanding, Shaw is not a mere preacher. The function of the dramatist is not that of the village pastor. He has no need to exhort, nor to call upon his hearers to come to the mourners' bench. All the world expects him to do is to picture human life as he sees it, as accurately and effectively as he can. Like the artist in color, form, or tone, his business is with impressions. A man painting an Alpine scene endeavors to produce, not a mere record of each rock and tree, but an impression upon the observer like that he would experience were he to stand in the artist's place and look upon the snow-capped crags. In music it is the same. Beethoven set out, with melody and harmony, to arouse the emotions that stir us upon pondering the triumphs of a great conqueror. Hence the Eroica Symphony. Likewise, with curves and color, Millet tried to awaken the soft content that falls upon us when we gaze across the fields at eventide and hear the distant vesper-bell—and we have "The Angelus."

The purpose of the dramatist is identical. If he shows us a drunken man on the stage it is because he wants us to experience the disgust or amusement or envy that wells up in us on contemplating such a person in real life. He concerns himself, in brief, with things as he sees them. The preacher deals with things as he thinks they ought to be. Sometimes the line of demarcation between the two purposes may be but dimly seen, but it is there all the same. If a play has what is known as a moral, it is the audience and not the playwright that formulates and voices it. A sermon without an obvious moral, well rubbed in, would be no sermon at all.

And so, if we divest ourselves of the idea that Shaw is trying to preach some rock-ribbed doctrine in each of his plays, instead of merely setting forth human events as he sees them, we may find his dramas much easier of comprehension. True enough, in his prefaces and stage directions, he delivers himself of many wise saws and elaborate theories. But upon the stage, fortunately, prefaces and stage directions are no longer read to audiences, as they were in Shakespeare's time, and so, if they are ever to discharge their natural functions, the Shaw dramas must stand as simple plays. Some of them,

From *George Bernard Shaw: His Plays* (Boston and London: John W. Luce, 1905).

alackaday! bear this test rather badly. Others, such as "Mrs. Warren's Profession" and "Candida," bear it supremely well.

It is the dramatist's business, then, to record the facts of life as he sees them, that philosophers and moralists (by which is meant the public in meditative mood) may deduce therefrom new rules of human conduct, or observe and analyze old rules as they are exhibited in the light of practice. That the average playwright does not always do so with absolute accuracy is due to the fact that he is merely a human being. No two men see the same thing in exactly the same way, and there are no fixed standards whereby we may decide whether one or the other or neither is right.

Herein we find the element of individual color, which makes one man's play differ from another man's, just as one artist's picture of a stretch of beach would differ from another's. A romancist, essaying to draw a soldier, gave the world Don Cesar de Bazan. George Bernard Shaw, at the same task, produced Captain Bluntschli. Don Cesar is an idealist and a hero; Bluntschli is a sort of refined day laborer, bent upon earning his pay at the least possible expenditure of blood and perspiration. Inasmuch as no mere man—not even the soldier under analysis himself—could ever hope to pry into a fighting man's mind and define and label his innermost shadows of thought and motive with absolute accuracy, there is no reason why we should hold Don Cesar to be a more natural figure than Captain Bluntschli. All that we can demand of a dramatist is that he make his creation consistent and logical and, as far as he can see to it, true. If we examine Bluntschli we will find that he answers these requirements. There may be a good deal of Shaw in him, but there is also some of Kitchener and more of Tommy Atkins.

This is one of the chief things to remember in studying the characters in the Shaw plays. Some of them are not obvious types, but a little inspection will show that most of them are old friends, simply viewed from a new angle. This personal angle is the possession that makes one dramatist differ from all others.

Sarcey, the great French critic, has shown us that the essence of dramatic action is conflict. Every principal character in a play must have a complement, or as it is commonly expressed, a foil. In the most primitive type of melodrama, there is a villain to battle with the hero and a comic servant to stand in contrast with the tearful heroine. As we go up the scale, the types are less strongly marked, but in every play that, in the true sense, is dramatic, there is this same balancing of characters and action. Comic scenes are contrasted with serious ones and for every Hamlet you will find a gravedigger.

In the dramas of George Bernard Shaw, which deal almost wholly with the current conflict between orthodoxy and heterodoxy, it is but natural that the characters should fall broadly into two general classes—the ordinary folks who represent the great majority, and the iconoclasts, or idol-smashers. Darwin made this war between the faithful and the scoffers the chief concern of the time, and the sham-smashing that is now going on, in all the fields of human inquiry, might be compared to the crusades that engrossed the world in the middle ages. Everyone, consciously or unconsciously, is more or less directly engaged in it, and so, when Shaw chooses conspicuous fighters in this war as the chief characters of his plays, he is but demonstrating his comprehension of human nature as it is manifested to-day. In "Man and Superman," for instance, he makes John Tanner, the chief personage of the drama, a rabid adherent of certain very advanced theories in social philosophy, and to accentuate these theories and contrast them strongly with the more old-fashioned ideas of the majority of persons, he places Tanner among men and women who belong to this majority. The effect of this is that the old notions and the new—orthodoxy and heterodoxy—are brought sharply face to face, and there is much opportunity for what theater goers call "scenes"—*i.e.* clashes of purpose and will.

In all of the Shaw plays—including even the farces, though here to a less degree—this conflict between the worshipers of old idols and the iconoclasts, or idol-smashers, is the author's chief concern. In "The Devil's Disciple" he puts the scene back a century and a half because he wants to exhibit his hero's doings against a background of particularly rigid and uncompromising orthodoxy, and the world has moved so fast since Darwin's time that such orthodoxy scarcely exists to-day. Were it pictured as actually so existing the public would think the picture false and the playwright would fail in the first business of a maker of plays, which is to give an air of reality to his creations. So Dick Dudgeon in "The Devil's Disciple" is made a contemporary of George Washington, and the tradition against which he struggles seems fairly real.

In each of the Shaw plays you will find a sham-smasher like Dick. In "Mrs. Warren's Profession," there are three of them—Mrs. Warren herself, her daughter Vivie and Frank Gardner. In "You Never Can Tell" there are the Clandons; in "Arms and the Man" there is Bluntschli, and in "Man and Superman" there are John Tanner and Mendoza, the brigand chief, who appears in the Hell scene as the Devil. In "Candida" and certain other of the plays it is somewhat difficult to label each character distinctly, because there is less definition in the outlines and the people of the play are first on one side and then on the other, much after the fashion of people in real life. But in all of the Shaw plays the necessary conflict is essentially one between old notions of conduct and new ones.

[Shaw the Philosopher]

G. K. CHESTERTON

Now it is an irritating and pathetic thing that the three most popular phrases about Shaw are false. Modern criticism, like all weak things, is overloaded with words. In a healthy condition of language a man finds it very difficult to say the right thing, but at last says it. In this empire of journalese a man finds it so very easy to say the wrong thing that he never thinks of saying anything else. False or meaningless phrases lie so ready to his hand that it is easier to use them than not to use them. These wrong terms picked up through idleness are retained through habit, and so the man has begun to think wrong almost before he has begun to think at all. Such lumbering logomachy is always injurious and oppressive to men of spirit, imagination or intellectual honour, and it has dealt very recklessly and wrongly with Bernard Shaw. He has contrived to get about three newspaper phrases tied to his tail; and those newspaper phrases are all and separately wrong. The three superstitions about him, it will be conceded, are generally these: first that he desires "problem plays," second that he is "paradoxical," and third that in his dramas as elsewhere he is specially "a Socialist." And the interesting thing is that when we come to his philosophy, all these three phrases are quite peculiarly inapplicable.

To take the plays first, there is a general disposition to describe that type of intimate or defiant drama which he approves as "the problem play." Now the serious modern play is, as a rule, the very reverse of a problem play; for there can be no problem unless both points of view are equally and urgently presented. *Hamlet* really is a problem play because at the end of it one is really in doubt as to whether upon the author's showing Hamlet is something more than a man or something less. *Henry IV* and *Henry V* are really problem plays; in this sense, that the reader or spectator is really doubtful whether the high but harsh efficiency, valour, and ambition of Henry V are an improvement on his old blackguard camaraderie; and whether he was not a better man when he was a thief. This hearty and healthy doubt is very common in Shakespeare; I mean a doubt that exists in the writer as well as in the reader. But Bernard Shaw is far too much of a Puritan to tolerate such doubts about points which he counts essential. There is no sort of doubt that the young lady in *Arms and the Man* is improved by losing her ideals. There is no sort of doubt that Captain

From *George Bernard Shaw* (London: The Bodley Head, 1909).

Brassbound is improved by giving up the object of his life. But a better case can be found in something that both dramatists have been concerned with; Shaw wrote *Caesar and Cleopatra;* Shakespeare wrote *Antony and Cleopatra* and also *Julius Cæsar.* And exactly what annoys Bernard Shaw about Shakespeare's version is this: that Shakespeare has an open mind or, in other words, that Shakespeare has really written a problem play. Shakespeare sees quite as clearly as Shaw that Brutus is unpractical and ineffectual; but he also sees, what is quite as plain and practical a fact, that these ineffectual men do capture the hearts and influence the policies of mankind. Shaw would have nothing said in favour of Brutus; because Brutus is on the wrong side in politics. Of the actual problem of public and private morality, as it was presented to Brutus, he takes actually no notice at all. He can write the most energetic and outspoken of propaganda plays; but he cannot rise to a problem play. He cannot really divide his mind and let the two parts speak independently to each other. He has never, so to speak, actually split his head in two; though I dare say there are many other people who are willing to do it for him.

Sometimes, especially in his later plays, he allows his clear conviction to spoil even his admirable dialogue, making one side entirely weak, as in an Evangelical tract. I do not know whether in *Major Barbara* the young Greek professor was supposed to be a fool. As popular tradition (which I trust more than anything else) declared that he is drawn from a real Professor of my acquaintance, who is anything but a fool, I should imagine not. But in that case I am all the more mystified by the incredibly weak fight which he makes in the play in answer to the elephantine sophistries of Undershaft. It is really a disgraceful case, and almost the only case in Shaw, of there being no fair fight between the two sides. For instance, the Professor mentions pity. Mr. Undershaft says with melodramatic scorn, "Pity! the scavenger of misery!" Now if any gentleman had said this to me, I should have replied, "If I permit you to escape from the point by means of metaphors, will you tell me whether you disapprove of scavengers?" Instead of this obvious retort, the miserable Greek professor only says, "Well then, love," to which Undershaft replies with unnecessary violence that he won't have the Greek professor's love, to which the obvious answer of course would be, "How the deuce can you prevent my loving you if I choose to do so?" Instead of this, as far as I remember, that abject Hellenist says nothing at all. I only mention this unfair dialogue, because it marks, I think, the recent hardening, for good or evil, of Shaw out of a dramatist into a mere philosopher, and whoever hardens into a philosopher may be hardening into a fanatic.

And just as there is nothing really problematic in Shaw's mind, so there is nothing really paradoxical. The meaning of the word paradoxical may indeed be made the subject of argument. In Greek, of course, it simply means something which is against the received opinion; in that sense a missionary remonstrating with South Sea cannibals is paradoxical. But in the much more important world, where words are used and altered in the using, paradox does not mean merely this: it means at least something of which the antinomy or apparent inconsistency is sufficiently plain in the words used, and most commonly of all it means an idea expressed in a form which is verbally contradictory. Thus, for instance, the great saying, "He that shall lose his life, the same shall save it," is an example of what modern people mean by a paradox. If any learned person should read this book (which seems immeasurably improbable) he can content himself with putting it this way, that the moderns mistakenly say paradox when they should say oxymoron. Ultimately, in any case, it may be agreed that we commonly mean by a paradox some kind of collision between what is seemingly and what is really true.

Now if by paradox we mean truth inherent in a contradiction, as in the saying of Christ that I have quoted, it is a very curious fact that Bernard Shaw is almost entirely without paradox. Moreover, he cannot even understand paradox. And more than this, paradox is about the only thing in the world that he does not understand. All his splendid vistas and startling suggestions arise from carrying some one clear principle further than it has yet been carried. His madness is all consistency, not inconsistency. As the point can hardly be made clear without examples, let us take one example, the subject of education. Shaw has been all his life preaching to grown-up people the profound truth that liberty and responsibility go together; that the reason why freedom is so often easily withheld, is simply that it is a terrible nuisance. This is true, though not the whole truth, of citizens; and so when Shaw comes to children he can only apply to them the same principle that he has already applied to citizens. He begins to play with the Herbert Spencer idea of teaching children by experience; perhaps the most fatuously silly idea that was ever gravely put down in print. On that there is no need to dwell; one has only to ask how the experimental method is to be applied to a precipice; and the theory no longer exists. But Shaw effected a further development, if possible more fantastic. He said that one should never tell a child anything without letting him hear the opposite opinion. That is to say, when you tell Tommy not to hit his sick sister on the temple, you must make sure of the presence of some Nietzscheite professor, who will explain to him that such a course might possibly serve to eliminate the unfit. When you are in the act of telling Susan not to drink out of the bottle labelled "poison," you must telegraph for a Christian Scientist, who will be ready to maintain that without her own consent it cannot do her any harm. What would happen to a child brought up on Shaw's principle I cannot conceive; I should think he would commit suicide in his bath. But that is not here the question. The point is that this proposition seems quite sufficiently wild and startling to ensure that its author, if he escapes Hanwell, would reach the front rank of journalists, demagogues, or public entertainers. It is a perfect paradox, if a paradox only means something that makes one jump. But it is not a paradox at all in the sense of a contradiction. It is not a contradiction, but an enormous and outrageous consistency, the one principle of free thought carried to a point to which no other sane man would consent to carry it. Exactly what

Shaw does not understand is the paradox; the unavoidable paradox of childhood. Although this child is much better than I, yet I must teach it. Although this being has much purer passions than I, yet I must control it. Although Tommy is quite right to rush towards a precipice, yet he must be stood in the corner for doing it. This contradiction is the only possible condition of having to do with children at all; anyone who talks about a child without feeling this paradox might just as well be talking about a merman. He has never even seen the animal. But this paradox Shaw in his intellectual simplicity cannot see; he cannot see it because it is a paradox. His only intellectual excitement is to carry one idea further and further across the world. It never occurs to him that it might meet another idea, and like the three winds in *Martin Chuzzlewit,* they might make a night of it. His only paradox is to pull out one thread or cord of truth longer and longer into waste and fantastic places. He does not allow for that deeper sort of paradox by which two opposite cords of truth become entangled in an inextricable knot. Still less can he be made to realise that it is often this knot which ties safely together the whole bundle of human life.

This blindness to paradox everywhere perplexes his outlook. He cannot understand marriage because he will not understand the paradox of marriage; that the woman is all the more the house for not being the head of it. He cannot understand patriotism, because he will not understand the paradox of patriotism; that one is all the more human for not merely loving humanity. He does not understand Christianity because he will not understand the paradox of Christianity; that we can only really understand all myths when we know that one of them is true. I do not underrate him for this anti-paradoxical temper; I concede that much of his finest and keenest work in the way of intellectual purification would have been difficult or impossible without it. But I say that here lies the limitation of that lucid and compelling mind; he cannot quite understand life, because he will not accept its contradictions.

Nor is it by any means descriptive of Shaw to call him a Socialist; in so far as that word can be extended to cover an ethical attitude. He is the least social of all Socialists; and I pity the Socialist state that tries to manage him. This anarchism of his is not a question of thinking for himself; every decent man thinks for himself; it would be highly immodest to think for anybody else. Nor is it any instinctive licence or egoism; as I have said before, he is a man of peculiarly acute public conscience. The unmanageable part of him, the fact that he cannot be conceived as part of a crowd or as really and invisibly helping a movement, has reference to another thing in him, or rather to another thing not in him.

The great defect of that fine intelligence is a failure to grasp and enjoy the things commonly called convention and tradition; which are foods upon which all human creatures must feed frequently if they are to live. Very few modern people of course have any idea of what they are. "Convention" is very nearly the same word as "democracy." It has again and again in history been used as an alternative word to Parliament. So far from suggesting anything stale or sober, the word convention rather conveys a hubbub; it is the coming together of men; every mob is a convention. In its secondary sense it means the common soul of such a crowd, its instinctive anger at the traitor or its instinctive salutation of the flag. Conventions may be cruel, they may be unsuitable, they may even be grossly superstitious or obscene; but there is one thing that they never are. Conventions are never dead. They are always full of accumulated emotions, the piled-up and passionate experiences of many generations asserting what they could not explain. To be inside any true convention, as the Chinese respect for parents or the European respect for children, is to be surrounded by something which whatever else it is is not leaden, lifeless or automatic, something which is taut and tingling with vitality at a hundred points, which is sensitive almost to madness and which is so much alive that it can kill. Now Bernard Shaw has always made this one immense mistake (arising out of that bad progressive education of his), the mistake of treating convention as a dead thing; treating it as if it were a mere physical environment like the pavement or the rain. Whereas it is a result of will; a rain of blessings and a pavement of good intentions. Let it be remembered that I am not discussing in what degree one should allow for tradition; I am saying that men like Shaw do not allow for it at all. If Shaw had found in early life that he was contradicted by *Bradshaw's Railway Guide* or even by the *Encyclopaedia Britannica,* he would have felt at least that he might be wrong. But if he had found himself contradicted by his father and mother, he would have thought it all the more probable that he was right. If the issue of the last evening paper contradicted him he might be troubled to investigate or explain. That the human tradition of two thousand years contradicted him did not trouble him for an instant. That Marx was not with him was important. That Man was not with him was an irrelevant prehistoric joke. People have talked far too much about the paradoxes of Bernard Shaw. Perhaps his only pure paradox is this almost unconscious one; that he has tended to think that because something has satisfied generations of men it must be untrue.

Shaw is wrong about nearly all the things one learns early in life and while one is still simple. Most human beings start with certain facts of psychology to which the rest of life must be somewhat related. For instance, every man falls in love; and no man falls into free love. When he falls into that he calls it lust, and is always ashamed of it even when he boasts of it. That there is some connection between a love and a vow nearly every human being knows before he is eighteen. That there is a solid and instinctive connection between the idea of sexual ecstasy and the idea of some sort of almost suicidal constancy, this I say is simply the first fact in one's own psychology; boys and girls know it almost before they know their own language. How far it can be trusted, how it can best be dealt with, all that is another matter. But lovers lust after constancy more than after happiness; if you are in any sense prepared to give them what they ask, then what they ask, beyond all question, is an oath of final fidelity. Lovers may be lunatics; lovers may be children; lovers may be unfit for citizenship and outside human argument; you can take up that position if you will. But lovers do not only desire love; they desire marriage. The root of legal monogamy does not lie (as Shaw and his friends are for ever drearily asserting) in the fact that the man is a mere tyrant and the woman a mere slave. It lies in the fact that *if* their love for each other is the noblest and freest love conceivable, it can only find its heroic expression in both becoming slaves. I only mention this matter here as a matter which most of us do not need to be taught; for it was the first lesson of life. In after years we may make up what code or compromise about sex we like; but we all know that constancy, jealousy, and the personal pledge are natural and inevitable in sex; we do not feel any surprise when we see them either in a murder or in a valentine. We may or may not see wisdom in early marriages; but we know quite well that wherever the thing is genuine at all, early loves will mean early marriages. But Shaw had not learnt about this tragedy of the sexes, what the rustic ballads of any country on earth would have taught him. He had not learnt, what universal common sense has put into all the folk-lore of the earth, that love cannot be thought of clearly for an instant except as monogamous. The old English ballads never sing the praises of "lovers." They always sing the praises of "true lovers," and that is the final philosophy of the question.

The same is true of Mr. Shaw's refusal to understand the love of the land either in the form of patriotism or of private ownership. It is the attitude of an Irishman cut off from the soil of Ireland, retaining the audacity and even cynicism of the national type, but no longer fed from the roots with its pathos or its experience.

This broader and more brotherly rendering of convention must be applied particularly to the conventions of the drama; since that is necessarily the most democratic of all the arts. And it will be found generally that most of the theatrical conventions rest on a real artistic basis. The Greek Unities, for instance, were not proper objects of the meticulous and trivial imitation of Seneca or Gabriel Harvey. But still less were they the right objects for the equally trivial and far more vulgar impatience of men like Macaulay. That a tale should, if possible, be told of one place or one day or a manageable number of characters is an ideal plainly rooted in an aesthetic instinct. But if this be so with the classical drama, it is yet more certainly so with romantic drama, against the somewhat decayed dignity of which Bernard Shaw was largely in rebellion. There was one point in particular upon which the Ibsenites claimed to have reformed the romantic convention which is worthy of special allusion.

Shaw and all the other Ibsenites were fond of insisting that a defect in the romantic drama was its tendency to end with wedding-bells. Against this they set the modern drama of middle-age, the drama which described marriage itself instead of its poetic preliminaries. Now if Bernard Shaw had been more patient with popular tradition, more prone to think that there might be some sense in its survival, he might have seen this particular problem much more clearly. The old playwrights have left us plenty of plays of marriage and middle-age. *Othello* is as much about what follows the wedding-bells as *The Doll's House. Macbeth* is about a middle-aged couple as much as *Little Eyolf.* But if we ask ourselves what is the real difference, we shall, I think, find that it can fairly be stated thus. The old tragedies of marriage, though not love stories, are like love stories in this, that they work up to some act or stroke which is irrevocable as marriage is irrevocable; to the fact of death or of adultery.

Now the reason why our fathers did not make marriage, in the middle-aged and static sense, the subject of their plays was a very simple one; it was that a play is a very bad place for discussing that topic. You cannot easily make a good drama out of the success or failure of a marriage, just as you could not make a good drama out of the growth of an oak tree or the decay of an empire. As Polonius very reasonably observed, it is too long. A happy love-affair will make a drama simply because it is dramatic; it depends on an ultimate yes or no. But a happy marriage is not dramatic; perhaps it would be less happy if it were. The essence of a romantic heroine is that she asks herself an intense question; but the essence of a sensible wife is that she is much too sensible to ask herself any questions at all. All the things that make monogamy a success are in their nature undramatic things, the silent growth of an instinctive confidence, the common wounds and victories, the accumulation of customs, the rich maturing of old jokes. Sane marriage is an untheatrical thing; it is therefore not surprising that most modern dramatists have devoted themselves to insane marriage.

To summarise; before touching the philosophy which Shaw has ultimately adopted, we must quit the notion that we know it already and that it is hit off in such journalistic terms as these three. Shaw does not wish to multiply problem plays or even problems. He has such scepticism as is the misfortune of his age; but he has this dignified and courageous quality, that he does not come to ask questions but to answer them. He is not a paradox-monger; he is a wild logician, far too simple even to be called a sophist. He understands everything in life except its paradoxes, especially that ultimate paradox that the very things that we cannot comprehend are the things that we have to take for granted. Lastly, he is not especially social or collectivist. On the contrary, he rather dislikes men in the mass, though he can appreciate them individually. He has no respect for collective humanity in its two great forms; either in that momentary form which we call a mob, or in that enduring form which we call a convention.

The general cosmic theory which can so far be traced through the earlier essays and plays of Bernard Shaw may be expressed in the image of Schopenhauer standing on his head. I cheerfully concede that Schopenhauer looks much nicer in that posture than in his original one, but I can hardly suppose that he feels more comfortable. The substance of the change is this. Roughly speaking, Schopenhauer maintained that life is unreasonable. The intellect, if it could be impartial, would tell us to cease; but a blind partiality, an instinct quite distinct from thought, drives us on to take desperate chances in an essentially bankrupt lottery. Shaw seems to accept this dingy estimate of the rational outlook, but adds a somewhat arresting comment. Schopenhauer had said, "Life is unreasonable; so much the worse for all living things." Shaw said, "Life is unreasonable; so much the worse for reason." Life is the higher call, life we must follow. It may be that there is some undetected fallacy in reason itself. Perhaps the whole man cannot get inside his own head any more than he can jump down his own throat. But there is about the need to live, to suffer, and to create that imperative quality which can truly be called supernatural, of whose voice it can indeed be said that it speaks with authority, and not as the scribes.

This is the first and finest item of the original Bernard Shaw creed: that if reason says that life is irrational, life must be content to reply that reason is lifeless; life is the primary thing, and if reason impedes it, then reason must be trodden down into the mire amid the most abject superstitions. In the ordinary sense it would be specially absurd to suggest that Shaw desires man to be a mere animal. For that is always associated with lust or incontinence; and Shaw's ideals are strict, hygienic, and even, one might say, old-maidish. But there is a mystical sense in which one may say literally that Shaw desires man to be an animal. That is, he desires him to cling first and last to life, to the spirit of animation, to the thing which is common to him and the birds and plants. Man should have the blind faith of a beast: he should be as mystically immutable as a cow, and as deaf to sophistries as a fish. Shaw does not wish him to be a philosopher or an artist; he does not even wish him to be a man, so much as he wishes him to be, in this holy sense, an animal. He must follow the flag of life as fiercely from conviction as all other creatures follow it from instinct.

[The Themes of Bernard Shaw]

EDMUND WILSON

What are the real themes of Bernard Shaw's plays?

He has not been a socialist dramatist in the sense that, say, Upton Sinclair has been a socialist novelist. His economics have served him, it is true, as anatomy served Michael Angelo; but to say that is to give as little idea of what kind of characters he creates and what his plays are about as it would of the figures of the sculptor to say that they were produced by an artist who understood the skeleton and the muscles. It is quite wrong to assume, as has sometimes been done, that the possession of the social-economic intelligence must imply that the writer who has it writes tracts for social reform.

Shaw is himself partly responsible for this assumption. In his early days, when he *was* a social reformer, he wrote books about Wagner and Ibsen which introduced them to the English-speaking public as primarily social reformers, too. There is of course a social revolutionist, a man of 1848, in Wagner, and a critic of bourgeois institutions in Ibsen. But Bernard Shaw, in his brilliant little books, by emphasizing these aspects of their work at the expense of everything else, seriously misrepresents them. He appreciates Siegfried and Brunhilde in their heroic and rebellious phases; but Wagner's tragedies of love he pooh-poohs; and it is sometimes just when Ibsen is at his strongest—as in *Brand* or *Rosmersholm*—that Bernard Shaw is least satisfactory on him, because the tragic spirit of Ibsen does not fit into Shaw's preconception. In Ibsen's case, Shaw is particularly misleading, because Ibsen disclaimed again and again any social-reforming intentions. His great theme, characteristic though it is of nineteenth-century society, is not a doctrine of social salvation: it is the conflict between one's duty to society as a unit in the social organism and the individual's duty to himself. Ibsen treats this theme over and over but in a number of different ways, sometimes emphasizing the validity of social claims as opposed to the will of the individual (*Little Eyolf*), sometimes showing them as unjustified and oppressive (*Ghosts*); sometimes showing the individual undone by self-indulgence or perverse self-assertion (*Peer Gynt* and *Brand*), sometimes showing him as noble and sympathetic (the hero and heroine of *Rosmersholm*); sometimes dramatizing the two poles of conduct in the career of a single individual, like

From "Bernard Shaw at Eighty." Excerpts from *The Triple Thinkers,* by Edmund Wilson. Copyright 1938, 1948, and renewal © 1956, 1971 by Edmund Wilson. Renewal © 1976 by Elena Wilson. Reprinted by permission of Farrar, Straus & Giroux, Inc.

Dr. Stockman in *An Enemy of the People,* who begins by trying to save society but who later, when society turns against him, is driven back into an individualistic vindication of the social conscience itself with the realization that "the strongest man is he who stands most alone." But the conflict is always serious; and it usually ends in disaster. Rarely—*A Doll's House* is the principal example—does it result in a liberation. Ibsen is hardly ever a social philosopher: he goes no further than the conflict itself.

Now is there any such basic theme in Bernard Shaw? Has he been creating a false impression not only about Ibsen but also about himself? Certainly the prefaces he prefixes to his plays do not really explain them any more than *The Quintessence of Ibsenism* really explains Ibsen.

The principal pattern which recurs in Bernard Shaw—aside from the duel between male and female, which seems to me of much less importance—is the polar opposition between the type of the saint and the type of the successful practical man. This conflict, when it is present in his other writing, has a blurring, a demoralizing effect . . . ; but it is the principle of life of his plays. We find it in its clearest presentation in the opposition between Father Keegan and Tom Broadbent in *John Bull's Other Island* and between Major Barbara and Undershaft—where the moral scales are pretty evenly weighted and where the actual predominance of the practical man, far from carrying ominous implications, produces a certain effect of reassurance: this was apparently the period—when Bernard Shaw had outgrown his early battles and struggles and before the war had come to disturb him—of his most comfortable and self-confident exercise of powers which had fully matured. But these opposites have also a tendency to dissociate themselves from one another and to feature themselves sometimes, not correlatively, but alternatively in successive plays. In *The Devil's Disciple* and *The Shewing-up of Blanco Posnet,* the heroes are dashing fellows who have melodramatic flashes of saintliness; their opponents are made comic or base. *Caesar and Cleopatra* is a play that glorifies the practical man; *Androcles and the Lion* is a play that glorifies the saint. So is *Saint Joan,* with the difference that here the worldly antagonists of the saint are presented as intelligent and effective.

Certainly it is this theme of the saint and the world which has inspired those scenes of Shaw's plays which are most moving and most real on the stage—which are able to shock us for the moment, as even the "Life Force" passages hardly do, out of the amiable and objective attention which has been induced by the bright play of the intelligence. It is the moment when Major Barbara, brought at last to the realization of the power of the capitalist's money and of her own weakness when she hasn't it to back her, is left alone on the stage with the unregenerate bums whose souls she has been trying to save; the moment when Androcles is sent into the arena with the lion; the moment in the emptied courtroom when Joan has been taken out to be burned and the Bishop and the Earl of Warwick are trying each to pin the responsibility on the other. It is the scene in *Heartbreak House* between Captain Shotover and Hector, when they give voice to their common antagonism toward the forces that seem to have them at their mercy: "We must win powers of life and death over them. . . . There is enmity between our seed and their seed. They know it and act on it, strangling our souls. They believe in themselves. When we believe in ourselves, we shall kill them. . . . We kill the better half of ourselves every day to propitiate them." It is the scene in *Back to Methuselah* when the Elderly Gentleman declares to the Oracle: "They have gone back to lie about your answer [the political delegation with whom he has come]. I cannot go with them. I cannot live among people to whom nothing is real"—and when she shows him her face and strikes him dead.

But now let us note—for the light they throw on Bernard Shaw in his various phases—the upshots of these several situations. In *Major Barbara,* the Christian saint, the man of learning, and the industrial superman form an alliance from which much is to be hoped. In *Androcles and the Lion,* written in 1913, in Shaw's amusing but least earnest middle period, just before the war, Androcles and the lion form an alliance, too, of which something is also to be hoped, but go out arm in arm after a harlequinade on the level of a Christmas pantomime. In *Heartbreak House,* which was begun in 1913 and not finished till 1916, the declaration of war by the unworldlings takes place in the midst of confusion and does not lead to any action on their part.

In *Back to Methuselah,* of the postwar period, the Elderly Gentleman is blasted by the Oracle in a strange scene the implications of which we must stop to examine a moment. The fate of the Elderly Gentleman is evidently intended by Shaw to have some sort of application to himself: though a member of a backward community in which people have not yet achieved the Methuselah-span of life, he differs from his fellows at least in this: that he finds he cannot bear any longer to live among people to whom nothing is real. So the Oracle shrivels him up with her glance.

But what is this supposed to mean? What *is* this higher wisdom which the Elderly Gentleman cannot contemplate and live? So far as the reader is concerned, the revelation of the Oracle is a blank. The old system of Bernard Shaw, which was plausible enough to pass before the war, has just taken a terrible blow, and its grotesque and gruesome efforts to pull itself together and function give the effect of an umbrella, wrecked in a storm, which, when the owner tries to open it up, shows several long ribs of steel sticking out. The Life Force of the man and woman in *Man and Superman* no longer leads either to human procreation or to social-revolutionary activity. The Life Force has been finally detached from socialism altogether. In the *Intelligent Woman's Guide,* Shaw will reject the Marxist dialectic as a false religion of social salvation; but the Life Force is also a religious idea, which we have always supposed in the past to be directed toward social betterment, and now, in *Back to Methuselah,* we find that it has misfired with socialism. Socialism has come and gone; the planet has been laid waste by wars; the ordinary people have all perished, and there is nobody left on earth but a race of selected supermen. And now the race of superior human beings, which was invoked in *Man and Superman* as the prime indispensable condition for any kind of progress whatever but which was regarded by Shaw at that time as producible through eugenic breeding, has taken here a most unearthly turn. It has always been through the superman idea that Shaw has found it possible to escape from the implications of his socialism; and he now no longer even imagines that the superior being can be created by human idealism through human science. The superior beings of *Back to Methuselah* are people who live forever; but they have achieved this superiority through an unconscious act of the will. When they have achieved it, what the Life Force turns out to have had in store for them is the mastery of abstruse branches of knowledge and the extra-uterine development of embryos. Beyond this, there is still to be attained the liberation of the spirit from the flesh, existence as a "whirlpool in pure force." "And for what may be beyond, the eyesight of Lilith is too short. It is enough that there is a beyond."

Humanity, in *Back to Methuselah*, has dropped out for the moment altogether. The long-livers of the period of progress contemporary with the Elderly Gentleman are not the more "complete" human beings, with lives richer and better rounded, which Marx and Engels and Lenin imagined for the "classless society": they are Shavian super-prigs who say the cutting and dampening things which the people have always said in Shaw's plays but who have been abstracted here from the well-observed social setting in which Shaw has always hitherto presented them. And the beings of the later epoch are young people playing in an Arcadia and ancients immersed in cogitations, alike— both cogitations and Arcadia—of the bleakest and most desolating description. There is in *Back to Methuselah* nothing burning or touching, and there is nothing genuinely thrilling except the cry of the Elderly Gentleman; and that, for all the pretense of revelation, is answered by a simple extinction.

In the *Tragedy of an Elderly Gentleman*, the Elderly Gentleman is frightened, but his tragedy is not a real tragedy. *Saint Joan* (1924) is an even more frightened play, and, softened though it is by the historical perspective into which Shaw manages to throw it through his epilogue, it was the first genuine tragedy that Shaw had written. The horror of *Back to Methuselah* is a lunar horror; the horror of *Saint Joan* is human. The saint is suppressed by the practical man; and even when she comes back to earth, though all those who exploited or destroyed her are now obliged to acknowledge her holiness, none wants her to remain among them: each would do the same thing again. Only the soldier who had handed her the cross at the stake is willing to accept her now, but he is only a poor helpless clown condemned to the dungeon of the flesh.

Back to Methuselah is a flight into the future; *Saint Joan* is a flight into the past. But with *Heartbreak House* Bernard Shaw had already begun a series of plays in which he was to deal with the postwar world and his own relation to it in terms of contemporary England—a section of his work which, it seems to me, has had too little appreciation or comprehension.

Heartbreak House has the same sort of setting and more or less the same form as such Shavian conversations as *Getting Married* and *Misalliance;* but it is really something new for Shaw. There is no diagram of social relations, no tying-up of threads at the end. *Heartbreak House,* Shaw says in his preface, is "cultured leisured Europe before the War"; but the play, he told Archibald Henderson, "began with an atmosphere and does not contain a word that was foreseen before it was written," and it is the only one of his plays which he has persistently refused to explain. "How should *I* know?" he replied, when he was asked by his actors what it meant. "I am only the author." Heartbreak House, built like a ship, with its old drunken and half-crazy master, the retired adventurer Captain Shotover, is cultured and leisured England; but the characters are no longer pinned down and examined as social specimens: in an atmosphere heavily charged, through a progression of contacts and collisions, they give out thunder and lightning like storm-clouds. Brooding frustrations and disillusions, childlike hurts and furious resentments, which have dropped the old Shavian masks, rush suddenly into an utterance which for the moment has burst out of the old rationalistic wit. For once, where Bernard Shaw has so often reduced historical myths to the sharp focus of contemporary satire, he now raises contemporary figures to the heroic proportions of myth.—An air-raid brings down the final curtain: Heartbreak House has at last been split wide. The capitalist Mangan gets killed, and there is a suggestion that they may all be the better for it.

But in 1924 the Labour Party came to power, with Ramsay Macdonald as Prime Minister. Macdonald had been a member of the Executive Committee of the Fabian Society, and he brought with him two other Fabians, Sidney Webb and Sydney Olivier, who took the portfolios of Minister of Labour and Secretary of State for India. When Macdonald was re-elected in 1929, he was accompanied by no less than twenty Fabians, of whom eight were cabinet members. The Fabians had now achieved the aim which was to have been the condition for the success of their ideas: they had "interpenetrated" the government. But in the meantime the competition of the British Empire with the German had culminated in a four years' war; and in England of after the war, with the top manhood of her society slaughtered and the lower classes laid off from their wartime jobs, and with English commercial domination further damaged by the United States, the influence of the Fabians could do little to bridge over the abyss which had been blasted between the extremes of the British class society. The best measures of the Labour Government were able to accomplish no more than just to keep the unemployed alive; and when the capitalists began to feel the pinch, they openly took over control. Ramsay Macdonald, in 1931, became Prime Minister in a Nationalist government and cleared his socialists out of office.

At the moment of the second accession of the Labour Party to power,

Shaw had written *The Apple Cart,* in which Macdonald is caricatured as Proteus, the Prime Minister of a labor government. This government is represented as really controlled by Breakages, Limited, a great monopoly which opposes industrial progress for the reason that it has an interest in perpetuating the inferior and less durable machinery that requires more frequent repairs. But one finds in *The Apple Cart* no comment on the Fabianism, which, after all, has been partly responsible for Proteus: the blame is laid at the door, not of that socialism by interpenetration which has ended by itself being interpenetrated, but of something which Shaw calls "democracy"; and what is opposed to the corrupt socialism of Proteus is not socialism of a more thoroughgoing kind, but the super-constitutional-monarch, King Magnus. Again, Shaw has given the slip to his problems through recourse to the cult of the superior person.

Yet in 1931, after the final collapse of the Labour Government, Bernard Shaw visited Russia and, by applauding the Soviet system, incurred unpopularity in England for the first time since the war. In the same year, he wrote *Too True to Be Good,* a curious "political extravaganza," in which he turns back upon and criticizes his own career. Here the theme of the bourgeois radical of the eighties, disillusioned with himself under stress of the disasters of the twentieth century, is treated in the same vein, with the same kind of idealist poetry, now grown frankly elegiac and despairing, which Shaw had opened in *Heartbreak House* and which had made the real beauty of *The Apple Cart.*

A rich young English girl of the upper middle class is languishing with an imaginary illness in a gloomy Victorian chamber, fussed over by a Victorian mother. Into this sickroom erupt two rebels: a young preacher and a former chambermaid, who is an illegitimate child of the aristocracy. The chambermaid has been masquerading as the heiress's trained nurse, and she and the preacher have a plot to steal the heiress's pearl necklace. The girl comes to from her megrims and puts up an unexpected struggle. The preacher becomes interested in his victim and says that he has always wondered why she does not steal the necklace herself. Why doesn't she take it and go and do what she pleases, instead of staying home with her mother, moping and fancying herself sick? Why doesn't she let him and his accomplice sell the necklace for her, taking 25 per cent of the price apiece and giving her the other 50? The girl enthusiastically agrees, and while she is getting dressed to go with them, the preacher jumps up on the bed and delivers one of those live-your-own-life sermons with which Shaw, in the nineties, made his first success. Then he is off—in the excitement of his rhetoric, at first forgetting the necklace, which the heiress has to remind him they need.

All three sail away together to an imaginary Balkan country reminiscent of *Arms and the Man,* where they are able to do whatever they like but where their revolt turns out to lead to nothing and eventually to bore them to death. Shaw has evidently put into *Too True to Be Good* a sort of recapitulation of his earlier themes, the shams of bourgeois society: the capitalistic doctor of *The Doctor's Dilemma* is as much a fraud as ever; the pompous British military officer, though retaining an air of authority, has practically ceased even to pretend to be anything other than a fraud and is quite willing to leave the command to a private (drawn from Lawrence of Arabia), if he can only be left in peace with his water-colors; the old-fashioned materialist-atheist who is also the most rigorous of moralists, of the type of Roebuck Ramsden in *Man and Superman,* has lived through into a world where his morality has no power to prevent his son's turning thief, etc. Finally everyone except the preacher sets out for the "Union of Sensible Republics."

The preacher is left alone on the shore, abandoned between two worlds. He had come too late for the old and too early for the new. He had had the courage once to steal a necklace but he hadn't carried through his idea. He had given it back to the owner and they had made common cause together: the liberated bourgois girl had gotten 50 per cent of the price, the radicals only 25 apiece. In this last scene, the darkness comes, the clouds gather; the morale of the preacher breaks down. He can only go on explaining and exhorting, whether or not he has anything to say. A keen wind is blowing in, and it may be the breath of life, but it is too fierce for him to bear.

This, Shaw tells us, is a political fable; and now he is to return to politics proper. In *On the Rocks* (1933), he appears to drive himself into a corner as he has never before done and then comes out with a political position which still manages to be somewhat equivocal.

The first act shows a liberal Prime Minister, hard beset during a period of depression. Pall Mall and Trafalgar Square are full of excited crowds. The Prime Minister, on the verge of a breakdown, can think of nothing to do except to call out the police against them, but he is dissuaded by the Police Commissioner himself and finally induced to go away for a rest. He has just been visited by a labor delegation who have impressed him with the importance of Marxism, and he takes volumes of Marx and Lenin away with him.

When the curtain goes up on the second act, the Prime Minister has read Marx and Lenin; but the effect upon him is unexpected. He has gained an insight into economic motivation, an understanding of the technique of making use of it; but he has not been converted to socialism: he has worked out, on the contrary, an exceedingly clever scheme for preserving the capitalist state through a program, essentially fascist, of partial nationalization and taxation of unearned incomes. He will conciliate the various social groups which would normally be antagonistic by promising a concession to each. The plan seems bidding fair to succeed when it runs aground on Sir Dexter Rightside, the Liberal Prime Minister's Tory colleague in a coalition National Government. Sir Dexter represents the blind conservatism which sticks to the *status quo* through sheer obstinacy and inability to imagine anything else: he threatens to put colored shirts on "fifty thousand patriotic young Londoners" and to call them into the streets against the proposed program of the government. The Prime Minister has to give up his attempt, but he is now forced to face his situation: "Do you think I didn't know," he confesses to his wife, "in the days of my great speeches and my roaring popularity, that I was only whitewashing the slums? I couldn't help knowing as well as any of those damned Socialists that though the West End of London was chockful of money and nice people all calling one another by their Christian names, the lives of the millions of people whose labor was keeping the whole show going were not worth living; but I was able to put it out of my mind because I thought it couldn't be helped and I was doing the best that could be done. I know better now! I know that it can be helped, and how it can be helped. And rather than go back to the old whitewashing job, I'd seize you tight around the waist and make a hole in the river with you. . . . Why don't I lead the revolt against it all? Because I'm not the man for the job, darling. . . . And I shall hate the man who will carry it through for his cruelty and the desolation he will bring on us and our like."

The shouting of the crowd and the crash of glass is suddenly heard outside. The people have broken into Downing Street. The police begin to club them and ride them down. The people sing, "England, arise!"

Sir Arthur Chavender's more or less liberal fascism has been defeated by the reactionary fascism of his Tory colleague in the National Government, with whom he is indissolubly united. (There is no question any longer of the superior man: King Magnus has disappeared from the scene.) There is a third point of view, opposed to both, but this, also, sounds rather fascist. Old Hipney, the disillusioned labor veteran, who speaks for the dissatisfied classes, seems to be looking for a Man on Horseback, too: "Adult suffrage: that was what was to save us all. My God! It delivered us into the hands of our spoilers and oppressors, bound hand and foot by our own folly and ignorance. It took the heart out of old Hipney; and now I'm for any Napoleon or Mussolini or Lenin or Chavender that has the stuff in him to take both the people and the spoilers and oppressors by the scruffs of their silly necks and just sling them into the way they should go with as many kicks as may be needful to make a thorough job of it." But Chavender declines the job; and the people begin throwing bricks.

The conclusion we are apparently to draw is that parliamentary fascism must fail; and that we may then get either a Lenin or a Mussolini. Is this also a final confession of the failure of Fabianism, which depended on parliament, too?

In any case, at the end of this play, we have come in a sense to the end of Shaw. With the eruption of the uprising, we should be plunged into a situation which could no longer be appropriately handled by the characteristic methods of his comedy. He is still splendid when he is showing the bewilderment of the liberal governing-class prime minister: it is surprising how he is still able to summon his old flickering and piercing wit, his old skill at juggling points of view, to illuminate a new social situation—how quick and skillful he is at describing a new social type: the communist viscount, with his brutal language, which shocks his proletarian allies. But with the shouts and the broken glass, we are made to take account of the fact that Shaw's comedy, for all its greater freedom in dealing with social conditions, is almost as much dependent on a cultivated and stable society as the comedy of Molière, who had his place in the royal dining-room and depended on Louis's favor for the permission to produce his plays. Shaw, as much as Molière, must speak the same language as his audience; he must observe the same conventions of manners. And further than *On the Rocks*—in depicting the realities of the present—we feel that he cannot go.

Then we realize that, after a detour of the better part of half a century, of almost the whole of his artistic career, Shaw has only returned to that Bloody Sunday of 1887 when the Socialists had headed a demonstration and been driven away by the police; and we remember, apropos of Molière, that the most celebrated of British dramatists for a long time found it impossible to get a theater in London for *On the Rocks*.

Shaw's most recent pieces are weaker. *The Simpleton of the Unexpected Isles* (1934) is the only play of the author's which has ever struck me as silly. In it, the Day of Judgment comes to the British Empire, and the privilege of surviving on earth is made to depend upon social utility. But, by setting up a purely theocratic tribunal, Shaw deprives this scene of social point: the principle of selection is so general that it might be applied by the fascists as readily as by the socialists, at the same time that the policy of wholesale extinction seems inspired by an admiration for the repressive tactics of both. The play ends with a salute to the unknown future, which, like the vision of infinity of *Back to Methuselah,* seems perfectly directionless. *The Millionairess* (1936) makes a farce out of the notion that a natural boss, deprived of adventitious authority, will inevitably gravitate again to a position where he can bully and control people, and sounds as if it had been suggested by the later phases of Stalin.

Here it cannot be denied that Bernard Shaw begins to show signs of old age. As the pace of his mind slackens and the texture of his work grows looser, the contradictory impulses and principles which have hitherto provided him with drama begin to show gaping rifts. In his *Preface on Bosses* to *The Millionairess,* he talks about "beginning a Reformation well to the left of Russia," but composes the panegyric on Mussolini, with the respectful compliments to Hitler. . . .

Yet the openings—the prologue to *The Simpleton,* with its skit on the decay of the British Empire and the knockabout domestic agonies of the first act or two of *The Millionairess*—still explode their comic situations with something of the old energy and wit; and the one-acter, *The Six of Calais,* though it does not crackle quite with the old spark, is not so very far inferior to such an earlier trifle as *How He Lied to Her Husband.* It is interesting to note—what bears out the idea that Shaw is at his best as an artist—that the last thing he is to lose, apparently, is his gift for pure comic invention, which has survived, not much dimmed, though we may tire of it, since the days of *You Never Can Tell.*

And he has also maintained his integrity as a reporter of the processes at work in his time—in regard to which his point of view has never been doctrinaire but always based on observation and feeling. He has not acted a straight role as a socialist; a lot of his writing on public affairs has been nonsense. But his plays down to the very end have been a truthful and continually developing chronicle of a soul in relation to society. Professionally as well as physically—he has just turned eighty-one as I write—he is outliving all the rest of his generation.

Nor can it be said that the confusions of his politics have invalidated his social criticism. Of his educative and stimulative influence it is not necessary today to speak. The very methods we use to check him have partly been learned in his school.

Masks and Characters

ERICH STRAUSS

If, in great things, it is enough to have willed, Bernard Shaw has done more than enough. That he has failed to realize the great purpose nearest to his heart is obvious enough; but no temptations, intellectual or material, have persuaded him to abandon the quest. The bridging of the great gulf separating his Socialist ideals from the facts of real life was a task that consumed his noblest energies as a politician and as an artist. The obvious way of achieving his ends was not that of artistic creation, but that of political action. Nobody who has come to the conviction that Socialism alone can loosen the hold of want and greed on humanity can be really satisfied without the practical success of the cause which, to him, means the condition of a civilization worth the name. To have abandoned his share in the practical work of bringing about this fundamental change must have been a great and bitter resolution for an active and, in spite of his superior wit, essentially ardent spirit. For Shaw did not desist from political work either from a sense of personal unfitness or from a conviction that this work was in good hands. On the contrary, only the slowly growing realization of the hopelessness of his task induced him unwillingly to merge the Socialist propagandist in the dramatic artist. Frank Harris, a rather violent but very sensitive observer, seems to have hit upon an important truth when he wrote: "I have felt all my life, through all the years that I have known Shaw, and from familiar knowledge of his works and life, that he feels himself defeated."

The downward phase of this process is represented by the first period of Shaw's dramatic work, up to *Man and Superman*. It was followed by a crucial interval leading up to the first World War which found Shaw at the height of his dramatic powers, but curiously aimless and self-contradictory. The paradox, which in earlier years had been mainly a vehicle for the representation of the contrast between the real and the desirable, the true and the plausible, almost became the main theme of his work, and to startle and upset seemed to be its main purpose. A pretended realism often took possession of one whose discredited ideals only managed to maintain themselves in a weak undercurrent of religious yearning and vision.

The war made an end to all attempts at a peaceful arrangement between

From *Bernard Shaw: Art and Socialism* (London: Victor Gollancz Ltd., 1942). Sincere and multiple attempts to locate the copyright holder failed.

the prophet of a new world and the powers of the old one. It accelerated a process not so much of revulsion of feeling, but of re-definition of aims which had apparently lost their point by the hopelessness of realizing them. This phase was followed by a resumption of the struggle against a system which threatens to engulf humanity in a horrid succession of catastrophes, ending with a relapse into barbarism. Whatever exception may be taken to Shaw's diagnosis of the evil and to many of his proposed reforms, looking back on his dramatic career it is impossible to deny that he has lived up to the programme contained in the *Revolutionist's Handbook* of fully forty years ago: "All who achieve real distinction in life begin as revolutionists. The most distinguished persons become more revolutionary as they grow older, though they are commonly supposed to become more conservative owing to their loss of faith in conventional methods of reform."

A survey of Shaw's artistic life-work goes a long way to answer the question as to the part played by Shaw's Socialism in his art. It has given him a first-rate problem to solve, and a standpoint from which to approach it. Translated into aesthetic terms one may say, Shaw's Socialism has endowed his work with the priceless gift of dramatic tension. This is true not only of his social-problem plays which develop around the social conflicts of modern life; it is even more true of those plays which reflect, and partly solve, the personal conflict arising from the failure of Shaw's original Socialist hopes and from the attempt to re-define his attitude to the world. This conflict endows his conversion, religious and political plays with an undercurrent of moral tension of incomparably higher value and emotional power than the often insignificant stories of the plays would seem to warrant. And it is this quality alone which gives Shaw's dramatic work at its best its true greatness. If Shaw sometimes succeeds in bridging the gulf between a dark past and a dim future, if he resurrects great figures of history and finds moving words for visions of a new world, this is, above all, due to the powerful tension between his Socialist convictions and the unyielding resistance of reality.

This fact is also borne out, in a negative manner, by the curious difference in value between Shaw's great efforts and the large number of his *pièces d'occasion*. With the single exception of *The Man of Destiny*, which belongs to the plays of disillusion, all the shorter plays are many grades below the average of his creations. The difference is so striking that it is sometimes difficult to believe that they are the work of the same author. In spite or perhaps because of the dialectic precision of their dialogue, they are surprisingly dull. *How he Lied to her Husband, Overruled*, most of the small war-time plays and many others down to *Village Wooing* (1933) seem to have been constructed with ruler and compasses rather than created by the imagination of a great artist. This contrast may be easily felt by comparing *The Man of Destiny* with the recapitulation of the same plot in the war-time farce *Augustus Does His Bit* (1916). The difference between these two plays is not due to the dramatic charm of the figure of Napoleon, but to the intensity of feeling underlying the character of the man of action who has lost his faith in great ideals, and now means to make his way to material success through filth and blood. This makes the former a genuine work of art, while it is impossible to read the latter, in spite of its shortness, without sustained effort. The lack of interest in these minor pieces, the complete absence of dramatic tension, is entirely due to their irrelevance to Shaw's main attitude. It is not fortuitous that many of them were written during the period between *Man and Superman* and *Heartbreak House*.

Looking back on the pageant of Shaw's dramatic characters, some curious features of considerable importance seem to have been directly due to the impact, positive and negative, of his Socialist ideals. During the downward phase of his dramatized relations to Socialism, the objects of his psychological analysis are, as a rule, men. This does not mean that the part played by women characters is not very considerable. But, with few exceptions, the women in Shaw's earlier plays are set characters who do not undergo essential changes in the course of the dramatic conflict, while his representatives of manhood are not only mercilessly analyzed, but often emerge from the play fundamentally changed. During the following period (1904–14) this relationship is completely reversed, particularly in connexion with the rise of the religious motive. In the great plays of Shaw's later period, girls and women are frequently the main characters, and their psychological analysis is often the main theme.

At the same time, the most beautiful and moving of Shaw's emotions, the longing for a new world, is now increasingly represented by girl and women characters. This change is ostensibly due to the fact that most of his deeply religious characters are women, and the new world is now frequently painted in the form of paradise. Nevertheless it may be regarded as part of Shaw's renunciation of an active rôle in the political struggle of his time. But this is merely a suggestion, and it would be easy to exaggerate the conscious and unconscious importance of so crude a symbolism. Furthermore, this does not mean that Shaw's heroines are themselves essentially passive. Nothing would be farther from the truth. With the exception of Lavinia *(Androcles and the Lion)*, they have, on the contrary, very strong practical instincts. Barbara actually chooses the opportunity of indulging in this instinct of practical management at the expense of her ideal purpose; but in *Saint Joan* both these tendencies unite into a glorious, if tragic, flame of practical enthusiasm. In many ways the most illuminating of these heroines is, however, the Patient in *Too True to be Good*. In this character the spiritual certainty of religious beliefs is replaced by the wish for something worth living for—and this ardent uncertainty, this demand for something sensible to do in a mad world, is the characteristic feature of the best of Shaw's later heroines. The typical woman of *Man and Superman*, whose only purpose was the propagation of the human race, makes room for a woman in whom the same instinct is widened by the motive of maintaining order in the world into which her children are born: "I have the instincts of a good housekeeper: I want to clean up this filthy world and to keep it clean," says the ex-Patient.

This change in the representation of Shaw's womanhood may be regarded with some justification as a real evolution, but it is noteworthy that it corresponds to a change in the general tendency of Shaw's work. Ann *(Man and Superman)* marks the lowest point in Shaw's belief in the realization of Socialism by political methods. Man must be thoroughly transformed by the biological process of better breeding, before there is any hope for Socialism. Woman leaves to man the subsidiary task of bread-winning and the luxury of "talking" about indifferent subjects, and concentrates on the improvement of the race. The change in Shaw's women heroines corresponds to the slow change in Shaw's attitude towards politics. The various stages of this process are marked by a succession of female characters of a kind which is clearly incompatible with the ideals and theories of *Man and Superman*. Lina *(Misalliance)* is proud of earning her own bread and despises the slavery of marriage; Lavinia *(Androcles and the Lion)* prefers martyrdom to a comfortable life and a handsome husband; Savvy *(Back to Methuselah)* is the most outspoken critic of the present parliamentary system and the most enthusiastic advocate of Socialism.

The necessary reverse of this medal is a growing depreciation of Shaw's male characters. Here, again, it is mainly the influence of his Socialism which explains what would otherwise be an arbitrary and anomalous development. The more independent and stronger his girls, the more despicable and weaker are their partners. Both in *Too True to be Good* and *The Millionairess* the leading juveniles are crooks, and in *On the Rocks* the effeminate and supersensitive David Chavender is married—and will probably be maintained—by an energetic woman-politician. These characters are, of course, influenced by the great change in the position of woman since the last war, but the parallel to the change in Shaw's attitude to politics is too close to be disregarded.

There is in general no reason to assume that the leading male characters in Shaw's plays are intended as self-portraits, but in some plays he has himself suggested this interpretation. This is true at least of *The Philanderer, The Man of Destiny* and *Man and Superman,* in all of which Shaw has given unmistakable clues for the identification of their heroes. But this is a minor matter as compared to the great issue which determined Shaw's artistic problems almost from the beginning—the choice between art and life, between thought and action. From an early time Shaw's creations vacillate between these extremes of the man of action and the man of ideas, whom he frequently identifies with the artist. Shaw was undoubtedly fascinated by the great doers of things, but it is difficult to resist the conclusion that he must have slowly become convinced that he was not one of them. The temporary solution of this conflict in *Man and Superman,* where the man of action is transformed into a mere talker, and depreciated in favour of the artist, would be strongly reminiscent of sour grapes but for the redeeming grace of Shaw's self-caricature in the character of Tanner.

During the following period the rise of girl characters to the first place in Shaw's drama is matched by the depreciation of practically all male characters. These are, again, easily recognizable as either men of action or artists. The men of action are from the beginning marked as black sheep by the fact that they are almost always identified with capitalism. Although Shaw nowhere approaches so nearly as in these plays to an acquiescence in the capitalist system as a fact, to all intents and purposes unalterable, he never goes so far as to identify himself with it. If Broadbent, Undershaft and Tarleton are impressive business men, they are emphatically not Shaw—and the last play of this period returns to the traditions of his youth by offering in Mangan a thoroughly despicable specimen of the capitalist.

But if the men of action appear to be greatly deflated, the men of sensibility and imagination fare hardly any better. Doyle, Cusins, Dubedat, Sinjohn Hochkiss (*Getting Married*)—even Shakespeare (*The Dark Lady of the Sonnets*)—Bentley (*Misalliance*) and Professor Higgins (*Pygmalion*) are all of them ineffective, and in one respect or another tainted. The last spokesman of this group, Hector Hushabye (*Heartbreak House*), is at the same time a perverted and utterly useless man of action. In him Shaw draws his final conclusion and gives his considered verdict. Hector is wise and sincere enough to know, and brave enough to say, that he and his kind are "useless, dangerous and ought to be abolished."

After the failure of Shaw's long-drawn-out attempt to make his peace with the world as it is, he returned to the attack on it. But the dramatic artist differs from the theoretical writer in the need for imaginary characters who are able to represent his ideas in dramatic conflicts. The Socialist needs arguments for Socialism and against capitalism, the playwright needs, apart from that, figures who can act as credible representatives of his arguments. But while Shaw easily succeeded in creating excellent representatives for the powers he attacked, he failed conspicuously in the creation of suitable representatives of his own views. This may have been largely due to the warping of his political vision by the will-o'-the-wisp of the "great man." But however this may have been, there is hardly room for disagreement on the simple fact that Shaw's political heroes are miserable failures. Both King Magnus and Sir Arthur Chavender are amiable, sincere and exceptionally intelligent persons. Both are pictured in situations where their professed principles ought to be put to the final test of a deadly conflict with the spokesmen of the pseudo-democracy which Shaw detests. Yet both fight shy of the struggle and end by compromise or defeat.

Clearly, this is a result of great importance for the understanding of Shaw's political development and his final position. The only positive result of his last attempt to solve the political problem of our time on the stage is the exposure of the protagonists of his own ideas as mere talkers. This result obviously contradicts the dramatic logic both of *The Apple Cart* and *On the Rocks,* and it must be due to a powerful force behind the scenes. The most plausible assumption to account for it is probably Shaw's disappointment not only with the general trend of development, but particularly with his own rôle as a mere talker at a time when action is imperative.

Such an assumption cannot be proved with anything like mathematical exactness, but it is supported by weighty internal evidence. The mere fact that the brilliant talkers of these political plays express some of Shaw's salient ideas, and that he is himself a professional talker, does not suffice for this purpose. It is, however, more important that Shaw's opinion of the talker as compared to the man of action considerably deteriorated in the course of time. There was a time when Shaw not only extolled the artist and the philosophical man but went so far as to suggest that the most powerful and resolute men of action were actually warped writers—whereas the course of this study has accumulated materials for the conclusion that the successful writer may have been a frustrated man of action.

The Napoleon of Shaw's youth (*The Man of Destiny*) has suffered "repeated failure as a would-be author," and his namesake of the year A.D. 3000 (*Back to Methuselah*) is in the same predicament: "Yet only as a slayer can I become a ruler. I cannot be great as a writer. I have tried and failed." Here Shaw in all seriousness contrasts "slaying," i.e., political and military power, and "writing" as the main forms of "rule"—and the emphasis suggests that he is ready to prefer writing in which he is himself supreme. Yet the contrast is only superficial because in essence Napoleon *is* Shaw. Just as *The Man of Destiny* has been introduced in a manner which can only be described as candidly autobiographical, the later Napoleon, too, is merely a variation on the theme Shaw. If he boasts of possessing "the only imagination worth having: the power of imagining things as they are," he only repeats a claim made by Shaw for himself as early as 1898. In the preface to his *Plays Unpleasant* Shaw explained that he was the lucky possessor of the rare phenomenon of normal sight "conferring the power of seeing things accurately, and being enjoyed by only about ten per cent of the population. . . . My mind's eye, like my body's, was 'normal': it saw things differently from other people's eyes, and saw them better."

This illusion of the "ruling" position of the writer could be maintained intact only as long as Shaw was content to grapple with imaginary problems, however beautiful and important. It broke down as soon as he returned to the problems of real life, after having found out by experience that he could not avoid them by imaginary solutions in the field of religious and biological speculation. But this return was at the same time a confession of personal failure. If the field of politics was the only one where the battle was to be fought and won, Shaw had spent irretrievable years on a fruitless venture.

This failure colours the leading characters and determines the inconclusive outcome of the two political comedies; but the full force of Shaw's disappointment is felt, curiously enough, neither in *The Apple Cart* nor in *On the Rocks,* but in *Too True to be Good,* which Shaw describes, without apparent reason, as "a political extravaganza." Its most remarkable character is the young housebreaker-clergyman with a divine gift of eloquence and a complete lack of conscience: "my gift of preaching is not confined to what I believe: I can preach anything, true or false. I am like a violin, on which you can play all sorts of music, from jazz to Mozart." This is simply a paraphrase of Shaw's description of himself given at about this time to Frank Harris, when he explained that people like himself and Shakespeare have no soul: "We understand all souls and all faiths and can dramatize them because they are to us wholly objective: we hold none of them."

It is not suggested that this is true, but it is clear that what is true of Aubrey is also true of Shaw. It is, therefore, very surprising that, after a final speech which is, in spite of its inordinate length, one of the greatest that Shaw has ever written, this character is attacked by its artistic father and spiritual brother in the most brutal manner: "any rascal who happens to be also a windbag can get a prodigious volume of talk out of it [*sc.* a rushing mighty wind]. . . . The author, though himself a professional talk maker, does not believe that the world can be saved by talk alone. He has given the rascal the last word; but his own favourite is the woman of action, who begins by knocking the wind out of the rascal, and ends with a cheerful conviction that the lost dogs always find their way home. So they will, perhaps, if the women go out and look for them."

If the woman of action ought to go out and look for the lost dogs, why does not Shaw use his play for imparting this message to the audience? If the clergyman is such an infernal rascal, why in all the world does Shaw give him the last word? Clearly, the theorist and the artist Shaw are again at loggerheads, and the one harbours emotions which are by no means acceptable to the other. Furthermore, though the spectator is asked to take Shaw's word for it that the young clergyman is a rascal without conscience, Aubrey's record and his speeches in the play do not bear out this indictment, except for the artificially inserted housebreaking episode. But a man without conscience would not have been moved by his father's atheism to become a clergyman. He would probably never have joined up at the outbreak of war, and he would certainly not have gone through a spiritual crisis as a result of his war experiences. Add to this the fact that the ideas which he expresses during and particularly at the end of the play are Shaw's most cherished property. Why then the author's violent attack on him, why his attempt to blacken Aubrey's character by all means? The real reason for this surprising state of things is probably to be found in the position of *Too True to be Good* (1932) between *The Apple Cart* (1929) and *On the Rocks* (1933). In both these works Shaw's protagonists fail owing to the fact that they are mere talkers. By representing the talker as a criminal, Shaw was enabled to attack him to his heart's content, though his strictures were really meant for the non-housebreaking and otherwise honourable political leaders who are content with talking where they ought to act.

But this condemnation included, above all, its author. Looking back on a long life of extremely successful and important writing and talking, Shaw sees himself truly and bitterly as "a professional talk maker," and is keenly conscious of the insufficiency of this contribution for the task which was always nearest his heart. The *quondam* admirer of philosophical man "does not believe that the world can be saved by talk alone." It is, perhaps, this background which explains the extreme bitterness of Shaw's attack on the exponent of his own characteristic qualities; and this reflection alone can explain the great and solemn words which he puts into the mouth of this unworthy creature: "I am ignorant: I have lost my nerve and am intimidated: all I know is that I must find the way of life, for myself and all of us, or we shall surely perish. And meanwhile my gift has possession of me: I must preach and preach and preach. . . ."

It is in the guise of the preacher of a great ideal, which determines his thoughts even when he wants to forget it, which gives the supreme power of moral tension to his works even when he tries to repress it, that Shaw appears at his best and truest. He has been not only, nor even mainly, a preacher; and his work is at least as much a document of doubt as of belief. Were it otherwise, Shaw would not be the great realist he is; for it would be idle to pretend that the great hopes of his youth have been fulfilled. His work is living proof of the power which his times exercise even over the strongest intellect. Every attempt to break this power only demonstrated it anew. And there is no denying the fact that his times, though helpful for the thinker, were extremely unfavourable for the artist. Had he been able to overcome the resistance to the realization of his ideals, he would perhaps never have become an artist. His artistic work has remained incomplete, because not even the highest art suffices for the solution of problems which can be decided only by real struggles. And if his art is incomplete, his character is not free from contradictions; yet both his personality and his work bear the stamp of true greatness, which comes from an unceasing and relentless struggle for mastery over the elemental forces of life and society.

The Theory and Practice
of Shavian Drama

Eric Russell Bentley

When a few years ago Thomas Mann said that reality is today seen in political terms, he was quickly pounced upon by many acute critics. Yet he was not talking nonsense, and Friedrich Hebbel had applied a comparable insight to the drama almost a century earlier. Hebbel wrote:

> The new drama, if such a thing comes into being, will differ from the Shakespearian drama, which must now be definitely abandoned, in that the dramatic dialectic will be injected not only into the characters but also directly into the idea itself, so that not alone the relation of man to the idea is debated but also the validity of the idea itself.

Hebbel's words bring us to the threshold of Shavian drama.

What is Shaw's theory of the drama? What has he said on the subject? A great deal, almost everyone would be inclined to say. Yet in fact only a very small portion of Shaw's thirty odd volumes is devoted to dramatic criticism and little of that to dramatic theory. From the earliest prefaces to the preface to *Saint Joan* (1924) we find complaints of a lack of seriousness in contemporary theatre and in criticism and we find discussions of censorship and the like, but for more general judgments one must go to two chapters added in 1912 to *The Quintessence of Ibsenism,* to Shaw's Preface to *Three Plays of Brieux,* and to Archibald Henderson's inexhaustible Shaviana. From such sources one can piece together a body of dramatic theory somewhat as follows.

The nineteenth-century theatre, consisting of the rags and tatters of Shakespeare and the cheap new feathers of Eugène Scribe, is decadent. It presents not life but day-dream, not thought but sentiment, not experience but conventional surrogates. Two men—Ibsen and Wagner—have struggled against the tide, and their efforts have been so successful that it can be said: ". . . there is, flatly, no future now for any drama without music except the

From *Accent* 5 (Autumn 1944): 5–18; reprinted in chapter 5 of *The Playwright as Thinker: A Study of Drama in Modern Times,* copyright 1946 and renewed 1974 by Eric Russell Bentley; reprinted by permission of Harcourt Brace Jovanovich, Inc.

drama of thought." Receptively, Shaw was probably more moved by Wagner; as a creative artist, however, he was to follow in the footsteps of Ibsen.

For Shaw the quintessence of Ibsen was that he was pre-occupied with morality, and that morality was in Ibsen something to be discussed and worked out, not something given. Morality is not only to do right but to discover what *is* right; immorality is not only the doing of certain things, but the deception of self in refusing to see what should and should not be done. In the drama of fixed morality there is no moral questioning at all. Hence the need of much outward action. We must see the hero in many situations, facing right and facing wrong. He must be put to tests of fire and water. Such is the nature of what Shaw calls "the tomfooleries called action" or, more explicitly, "vulgar attachments, rapacities, generosities, resentments, ambitions, misunderstandings, oddities, and so forth." Once the moral problem is one of sincerity and conscience and not merely a test of one's power to live according to the moral law, outward eventfulness becomes superfluous and therefore vulgar. Shaw denounces "crimes, fights, big legacies, fires, shipwrecks, battles, and thunderbolts" as "mistakes in a play, even when they can be effectively simulated."

Since morality is not given, we do not know who is a villain and who is a hero. This fact is both true to life and dramatically interesting. The villain cannot only be—what he always was—plausible and apparently virtuous. He can actually *be* what most people do think virtuous. This too is true to life, and it is dramatically striking because it establishes between author and audience the unusual, ironic, and Shavian relationship of antagonism. It is true that most of the audience will, after a time at least, make exceptions of themselves and assume that Shaw means everybody else. But Shaw does not mean everybody else, and the irony is redoubled. We must therefore conclude that there is more to the shock-technique of Shavian drama than high spirits or even reformism. Shaw's preaching has aesthetic as well as moral point, for it is the preacher who chides his audience and who must not pretend to sympathize with their faults. When Shaw proposed a drama of ideas he did not mean a drama deprived of all dramatic elements except witty conversation. He meant, in his own words, "the substitution of a forensic technique of recrimination, disillusion, and penetration through ideals to the truth, with a free use of all the rhetorical and lyrical arts of the orator, the preacher, the pleader, and the rhapsodist."

The theory of Shavian drama is, on the negative side, a defence of the drama of discussion and, on the positive side, an assault upon all other drama, for when the artist turns literary critic he always generalizes his personal positions and arraigns all the traditions with which he is not in rapport. Shaw was not averse to arraigning Shakespeare. The arraignment was partly unashamed self-advertisement, but partly also it was an attempt to establish that non-Shakespearian drama of which Hebbel had spoken, an attempt to weaken the Bardolatry which was hindering a true understanding of Shakespeare as much as it was hampering the efforts of all who tried to make a drama which would be as expressive of our time as Shakespeare had been of his. As objective evaluation Shaw's Shakespeare criticism is unimportant. As polemic, as part of his own theory, it is consistent and significant. If he has ridiculed some plays which had been thought sacrosanct, he called attention to the fascination of some plays, such as *Troilus and Cressida,* which modern critics would later claim to have "discovered"; he observed that *Hamlet* was laudably un-Shakespearian in that here was real moral doubt and questioning of conscience and inner tragedy; he was privately a great Shakespeare fan and in Shakespeare discussion resembles an atheist who in religious discussion turns out to know and relish the Bible more than the godly.

But Shaw's major critical offensive was against the pre-Ibsenite drama of the nineteenth century. The shadow of Scribe darkened the scene. Shaw fumed. He would annihilate this *infame!* If this was technique, he would annihilate technique! Hence his polemics against the "well-made play": "Your plot construction and art of preparation are only tricks of theatrical talent and shifts of moral sterility, not the weapons of dramatic genius." Or again: "The writer who practises the art of Ibsen therefore discards all the old tricks of preparation, catastrophe, dénouement . . ." Once the mode of these polemics is understood, Shaw's disparagement of dramaturgy in his own work can also be understood for the blarney that it is. Shaw boasts of using the comic tricks of the 'sixties in *Arms and the Man;* in *The Devil's Disciple* he declares he has used those of the next generation; what the critics take for brilliance and originality, he explains, consists only of the "tricks and suspenses and thrills and jests" which were "in vogue when I was a boy." How little these remarks describe the Shavian dramaturgy we shall see in a later section of this essay.

What is the gist of Shaw's case against the Shakespearian and the Scribean traditions? It is that both are Romantic. In the Shavian use of the term, Romanticism means hocus-pocus, pretentious and deceptive artifice, the substitution of flattering but unreal and foolish conventions for realities. The theory is that Zola, Ibsen, and Shaw (and perhaps one should add the later Dickens and Samuel Butler) had made it their business to destroy Romanticism by laying bare the realities. Zola made a fine beginning, says Shaw, by trying to replace Romantic or stagey logic with a correct natural history, but unfortunately he formed a Romantic attachment with morbidity. Ibsen made a monumental contribution, but unhappily retained the catastrophic ending in his plays. The natural historian of modern society knows that the real tragedy of Hedda Gablers is precisely that they do not commit suicide. Shaw gives Chekhov some credit for this insight, and emulates his method in *Heartbreak House.* Eugène Brieux he appears to regard as the most thorough-going exponent of "natural history."

This brings us to the positive side of Shaw's dramaturgy. Shaw's theory, I repeat, is not that everything in traditional drama should be scrapped except talk, and then the residue called the New Drama. "Rhetoric, irony, argument, paradox, epigram, parable," he writes, "the re-arrangement of haphazard facts into orderly and intelligent situations: these are both the oldest and the newest arts of the drama." These words include a good deal more than clever or even profound talk. Attention should be paid to the phrase "the re-arrangement of the facts into orderly and intelligent situations" and to the word "parable." The preface to Brieux contains an assertion that drama does not merely photograph nature but attempts a "presentment in parable of the conflict between man's will and his environment: in a word, of problem." This is indeed an old and new theory of drama, old as the Greeks, new as Ibsen who had characterized his leading theme as "the contradiction between effort and capacity, between will and possibility, the tragedy and at the same time comedy of the individual and of mankind."

II

Shaw's defense of a theatre of idea brought him up against both his great bugbears—commercialized art on the one hand and Art for Art's Sake on the other. His teaching is that beauty is a by-product of other activity; that the artist writes out of moral passion (in forms varying from political conviction to religious zeal), not out of love of art; that the pursuit of art for its own sake is a form of self-indulgence as bad as any other sort of sensuality. In the end, the errors of "pure" art and of commercialized art are identical: they both appeal primarily to the senses. True art, on the other hand, is not merely a matter of pleasure. It may be unpleasant. A favorite Shavian metaphor for the function of the arts is that of tooth-pulling. Even if the patient is under gas, the tooth is still pulled.

The history of aesthetics affords more examples of a didactic than of a hedonist view. But Shaw's didacticism takes an unusual turn in its application to the history of the arts. If, as Shaw holds, ideas are a most important part of a work of art, and if, as he also holds, ideas go out of date, it follows that even the best works of art go out of date in some important respects and that the generally held view that great works are in all respects eternal is not shared by Shaw. In the Preface to *Three Plays for Puritans,* Shaw maintains that renewal in the arts means renewal in philosophy, not in anything artistic; that the first great artist who comes along after a renewal gives to the new philosophy full and final form; that subsequent artists, though even more gifted, can do nothing but refine upon the master without matching him. Shaw, whose essential modesty is as disarming as his pose of vanity is disconcerting, assigns to himself the role, not of the master, but of the pioneer, the role of a Marlowe rather than of a Shakespeare. "The whirligig of time will soon bring my audiences to my own point of view," he writes, "and then the next Shakespeare that comes along will turn these petty tentatives of mine into masterpieces final for their epoch."

"Final for their epoch"—even Shakespearean masterpieces are not final beyond that. No one, says Shaw, will ever write a better tragedy than *Lear* or a better opera than *Don Giovanni* or a better music-drama than *The Niblung's*

Ring; but just as essential to a play as this aesthetic merit is moral relevance which, if we take a naturalistic and historical view of morals, it loses, or partly loses, in time. Shaw has the courage of his historicism, consistently withstands the view that moral problems do not change, and argues therefore that for us modern literature and music form a Bible surpassing in significance the Hebrew Bible. That is Shaw's challenge to President Hutchins and St. John's College.

Such are Bernard Shaw's expressed opinions on dramatic and artistic matters. What are we to make of it? We have seen that most of his critical prose is polemic and is not therefore to be submitted to the same kind of analysis as a more objective criticism. Even when arguing for science and natural history as against Romanticism and artifice, Shaw writes in a prose that is at once artistic, artful, and artificial. He is a poet of polemics, as Einstein seems to have felt when he compared the movement of Shavian dialogue to Mozart's music. His polemics are therefore the more dangerous, for polemics are nothing but the art of skilled deception. Now a prime device of polemics is the either/or pattern, against which so much has been said in recent times, often by great polemicists. Shaw is a great polemicist in his skilled deployment of antitheses. He always forces upon his opponent an alternative which the opponent never wanted to be confronted with and sometimes did not deserve to be confronted with. Watch how he pushes not only the Scribeans but also the Shakespeareans into a corner! He condemns not merely melodramatic action but apparently all outward action as "tomfoolery." Of course the condemnation has some substance (it is the art of the polemicist to avoid untruths, and exploit half-truths) in that not much of the history of the world can be convincingly represented on the stage. Shaw knows that the stage can only show the effect of history on a few individuals and that it is much better suited to talking than to fighting and doing. That is the true half of this remark. But he loads it with a lie in order to attract attention. He feels that the weakness of the well-made play can only be revealed if all plot-construction is ridiculed. The absurdity of melodrama can only be demonstrated by debunking tragedy. Shaw cannot always resist the temptation to remove the unoffending nose with the offending wart.

We cannot, therefore, feel wholly satisfied with Shaw's contributions to dramatic theory brilliant as some of them are. The terms of the theory are too crude. Technique and plot cannot be isolated from the rest of a work of art in so facile a manner. More explanation would be needed to make the antithesis of romantic logic and natural history convincing. Shaw's criticism, which so many think over-explanatory, and which many assumed to be voluminous, is actually reticent to the point of evasiveness. As his pose of conceit hides a considerable shyness about himself, so his volubility is, among other things, a way of avoiding certain issues, chief among them the aesthetic issues. Shaw refuses to lecture on dramaturgy on the grounds that he is a practitioner, and of course he is entirely within his rights in this. Many a creative artist would support him. The peculiar thing about Shaw is that we have the impression that he has explained everything—"I am nothing if not explanatory," he once said—but always stops short in personal and aesthetic matters. Hence we can often learn more from an *obiter dictum* of Shaw's than from an extended statement. When for instance in 1934 Shaw defends one of his plays "simply as a play" we wonder what has happened to the didactic criterion. And we learn much about the art of Shaw when we read of his writing his roles for particular actors, of his own histrionic talent, of his interest in actual production. Plays, he remarks casually, can be considered as exhibitions of the art of acting. Of this conception he says: "As I write my plays it is continuously in my mind and very much to my taste."

These are valuable hints, but they remain hints and are never developed into a critical system. Shaw's critical writing is to some extent camouflage. He has himself, consciously or not, spread the notion, recently reiterated in Hesketh Pearson's biography, that he is most interesting as a person, slightly less interesting as a sage, and least interesting as a playwright. Shaw has said that art must be subordinate to other things, and his readers have applied the theory to Shaw. But the Shavian view is that the subordination of art to morals should make the artist better as an artist. To say that beauty and happiness are byproducts not to be directly aimed at is to alter our method of attaining beauty and happiness; yet beauty and happiness remain the ultimate goal, even though we reach them by doing something else. And the critic is entitled to judge for himself whether beauty has been attained or not. By no amount of polemic can Shaw evade the aesthetic touchstone. Not one exceptional case only, but all his plays must stand or fall as plays.

III

One or two of Shaw's generalizations about drama do help us to an understanding of his plays. One is that there are only two dramatic characters, the long-haired aesthete and the clown. The statement is naughty, for it is either too vague to be exactly applicable or too dogmatic to be true. Yet it opens the door to an understanding of Shaw's characters, at least the male characters, and the way they are contrasted. A still more pregnant remark is that the drama, though now degenerated to a rant and a situation, began as a dance and a story. Shaw has brought dance back into the drama, not directly, to be sure, but in the lively rhythm of his lines and in the musical, rather than "well-made," structure of his scenes; and, precisely by minimizing plot, he has brought back stories to the stage by way of lengthy narratives.

The well-made play, says Shaw, is built on the scheme: exposition, situation, unravelling. *A Doll's House* is built on the scheme: exposition, situation, discussion. Discussion is the crucial technical innovation which accompanies the changes in outlook which Hebbel was one of the first to be aware of. The Shavian play—everyone agrees—is a discussion play. People sit in their chairs and talk everything over. The talk is good. And that, according to many, is Shaw.

But, in the first place, Shaw's plays, though more like each other than any one is like a non-Shavian piece, are not cut to one pattern. Indeed his plays are so various, and there are at least thirty important ones, that classification is extremely difficult even on chronological lines. Yet, though Shaw's dramatic career is not so clearly periodized as, say, Ibsen's, certain groupings do suggest themselves. A major break occurred with the First World War. The plays prior to that compose a single group which in turn may be cut in half at about the turn of the century. Dividing the post-war period also in half, we have two main periods, with two subdivisions:

1892–1899	I. i.	*Plays Pleasant and Unpleasant,* and *Three Plays for Puritans.*
1901–1912	ii.	From *Man and Superman* to *Pygmalion.*
1913–1924	II. i.	From *Heartbreak House* to *Saint Joan.*
1929–1939	ii.	From *The Apple Cart* to *In Good King Charles's Golden Days.*

The plays of the 'nineties are chiefly simple inversions of current theatrical patterns, such as Victorian melodrama (*The Devil's Disciple*), the heroic play (*The Man of Destiny, Caesar and Cleopatra*), and Gilbertian comedy (*Arms and the Man, You Never Can Tell*). But from *Man and Superman* (1901–1903) on, Shaw has his own patterns. These are the years of *Getting Married* and *Misalliance,* which are the extreme instances of Shavian discussion drama, of Shaw's toughest dialectical dramas such as *Major Barbara* and *The Doctor's Dilemma* (two of the most original and the best of Shaw's plays), and of his most controlled and delicate fantasies such as *Androcles and the Lion.* If *Fanny's First Play* and *Pygmalion* are, like the early plays, variants on conventional patterns, they are at once subtler and tougher variants than those of the 'nineties.

The play which Shaw was at work on from 1913 to 1916—*Heartbreak House*—marks a departure in technique and mood. The socialist optimism of *Major Barbara* and the Bergsonian optimism of *Man and Superman* are gone. For the current stage of civilization, Shaw finds a metaphor which was still to be with him in 1933: civilization is a ship on the rocks. From now on, most of Shaw's plays were to be fantasias or extravaganzas in which the disappointment of many liberal hopes is announced and the apartness of Shaw from the new generation is implied. Even *Back to Methuselah,* which so anxiously tries to be optimistic, is most impressive in the extravagant satire against Lloyd George and Asquith and in the pathetic tragedy of the elderly gentleman confronted with a new generation. Even *Saint Joan,* which might seem to be aloof both from the post-war generation and from Shaw, has as its theme the homelessness of genius. Among other things it is a commentary on Shaw's autobiographical remark: "I was at home only in the realm of my imagination, and at my ease only with the mighty dead."

Whether it is fair to stress, to the extent that Edmund Wilson has done, the subjective element in the later plays of Shaw, it is evident that these plays, from *Heartbreak House* to the end of the roster, do compose a separate group which we can now see as a whole. Two of them are called by Shaw Political Extravaganzas, and the name might be extended to the five plays which are a fantastic chronicle of the interim between the two world wars: *The Apple Cart, Too True to Be Good, On the Rocks, The Simpleton of the Unexpected Isles,* and *Geneva.* Are these plays inferior? From a natural tendency to say that what a famous writer does today is not up to what he did twenty years ago, and from a natural feeling that so old a man must be in his dotage, critics have on the whole damned this last cycle of Shavian plays. To be sure, they do not have the galvanic energy of *Man and Superman* or the tough dialectic of *Major Barbara.* But they are not poor stuff. They would be enough to establish a great reputation for any new dramatist. Moreover, the Political Extravaganza is not only a new form in drama, but the form in which Shaw's genius has been most at home. Shaw's career might be regarded as a search for a form which would fully express his genius. The Political Extravaganza is such a form, though Shaw perfected it only after he had passed his prime and written his greatest plays. The Political Extravaganza is definite enough and free enough, fantastic enough and realistic enough, uproarious enough and serious enough. It is Shavian form.

IV

The freshman can see that Shaw is funny. The sophomore can see that he is serious. The junior can see that he is a man of the theatre. To graduate, however, in Shavian analysis we must discover precisely what a Shavian work consists of. I choose for more detailed consideration a play that is probably more characteristic than outstanding in the Shavian canon, a play written while Shaw was still experimenting but was drawing towards the height of his powers: *Captain Brassbound's Conversion* (1899).

Captain Brassbound is a modern version of a pirate king. He roams the seas plotting vengeance on the wicked uncle who has caused his mother's imprisonment and death. But when he has lured the wicked uncle into the Moroccan mountains and is about to hand him over to the tender mercies of a sheikh, there arrives a superior sheikh whose head will be demanded by the British government if Englishmen are kidnapped in his territories. Brassbound is handed over to the American navy, but is finally set free through the intercession of the uncle's kindly sister-in-law. Naturally, the pirate king would like to marry the lady after this, and the lady herself is not hostile; but in the end they agree to part.

This is the simple air on which Shaw plays variations. What is his method? A silent moving picture of a performance would record scene after scene of what the Germans call Kitsch and what Americans call Corn. In a Moroccan setting, all taken, Shaw informs us, from a novel by Cunningham Graham, are enacted corny scenes of pursuit and rescue, spiced with love interest. And there are other conventional ingredients of a graver sort. The plot is unfolded in resolutely Ibsenite fashion, that is, by conversation and innuendo referring to a buried crime about which we only gradually become clear. The play is subtitled: An Adventure.

But only subtitled. The main title is *Captain Brassbound's Conversion,* and of the conversion which is the subject of the play, the narrative pattern gives no inkling. At this point we hit upon Shaw's method of inversion, which in such a play as this is not the simple inversion of *Arms and the Man.* According to the pattern an Englishman and his sister-in-law are rescued by civilization from the clutches of a pirate-villain. According, however, to the interpretation imposed upon this pattern, Brassbound is the hero and protagonist. Yet—and it is such double-twists which are the making of Shavian drama—Brassbound is no hero in Douglas Fairbanks style. He is disreputable and down at heel. He is also no villain, since the person he chiefly imposes upon is himself. He has something of the manner of a Byronic sort of hero; but the Byronic hero is himself an ambivalent figure, compounded equally of strength and weakness. How are we to take Brassbound? In view of the conversion at the end, shall we say that he is a villain converted to virtue as summarily as Edmund in *King Lear?* All possible interpretations are suggested by the play itself, and the method of their suggestion is Shaw's dramatic dialectic. The primary meaning of Brassbound's character appears in the upshot. The real man has been hiding behind the mask of a villain-hero. Degenerating further and further into a shabby tourists' escort, Brassbound, true to his name, shored up the heroic purpose of vengeance against his ruins. He hoarded photographs and newspaper cuttings for purposes of mournful and vengeful contemplation. Then a woman lays bare his soul, and he is converted to realism.

Shaw's technique is not, as has been alleged, to render a serious problem palatable by a silly story. The silly story functions as an integral part of a whole. It is the basis of dozens of ironies, of which the central irony is the contrast between romance and reality, illusion and actuality, silly stories and flinty facts. This irony pervades the whole work. When, for instance, we are told a Kitsch story of crime in the West Indies, and the question is raised why a solicitor was not sent from England, the prosaic but simple explanation is that the value of the estate was less than it would have cost to make it worth a lawyer's while to leave his practice in London. When we are confronted with fighting sheikhs out of pulp fiction, we find that their actions are determined by the plain but significant fact of British imperialism. It may be recalled that Shaw had condemned the staging of fights and crimes as mistakes. This, however, does not mean that he eschews such things. He uses them, but ironically, not naively. They are always ridiculous in Shaw, and their ridiculousness has always a point.

Like the plot, the characters are given ironical meaning. Even the American captain, primarily a tool of the plot, is given a touch of significance as "a curious ethnological specimen, with all the nations of the old world at war in his veins." Every minor character enforces an irony. Hallam, the wicked uncle, is a judge and a pillar of society; conservatism shows its other face in Rankin, the defeatist missionary whose only convert in Morocco is a London slum boy named Drinkwater. Drinkwater is Brassbound on a lower level of culture. Like Brassbound he feasts upon romance—in the pages of the pulps. Brassbound's great theme is his innocent mother punished by Hallam; Drinkwater has been acquitted by Hallam when actually guilty. This contrast shows Hallam as at once ruthless and incompetent.

In this framework of fictions, the problem of romance and realism is thrashed out by violent juxtapositions and confrontations. Rudolph Valentino is, as it were, confronted with Henry Ford. There is irony within irony. If Brassbound does not support his role of villain, Hallam does not support his role of hero. The initial irony of his character is one that Ibsen had rendered familiar: the pillar of society is a scoundrel. Hallam has played a tricky game in the West Indies and Brassbound's mother was driven to her death. The law, moreover, which Hallam administers in England is interpreted by Shaw to be crude vengeance wreaked by a class of crooks masquerading as churchgoers. Yet Hallam is not a villain, for he is more victim than agent. He only does what his class does and what he has been brought up to do. He means well and is privately harmless. Far from battening on his ill-gotten gains, he is finding the West Indies estate more a liability than an asset. Brassbound for his part is no avenging angel. His interpretation of the facts is quite as incomplete and primitive as Hallam's. In fact, his standards are the same: like Hallam, he believes above all in revenge. Pillar of society and Byronic hero are equally guilty because identically guilty.

The conversion of Brassbound is effected by Lady Cicely Waynefleet. The last page of the play, in which the two agree to part, is one of the best illustrations of the achievement of Shavian comedy. It is neither glib nor ponderous, neither flippant nor sentimental. It is a taut, terse, and true ending in which the dialogue, so far from being an independent stream rippling over the stones of a plot, is fused with theme, story, and characterization. Brassbound presses Lady Cicely to marry him to the point where she is about to consent. At that point he withdraws the offer. We infer that Brassbound has found himself anew in the experience of dominating Lady Cicely. "You can do no more for me now," he says. "I have blundered somehow on the secret of command at last." When Brassbound leaves, Lady Cicely says: "How glorious! How glorious! And what an escape!" It is one of the splendid and expressive endings of comedy. It reveals that Lady Cicely herself found the escape from the real to the romantic entirely glorious. The conversion of Brassbound almost caused the apostasy of his savior. That is the ultimate irony. But since Brassbound *was* converted, he could not allow it. The title of the piece is quite inevitable, and it is the only thing in the whole play that is not ironical.

V

What then is to be said for Shavian comedy? What are its merits? What is its nature?

The dialogue of Shavian comedy has always been praised. It was praised by Max Beerbohm and G. K. Chesterton forty years ago, and it is praised by Edmund Wilson, Edgar Johnson, and Jacques Barzun today. But my point in this essay is that Shaw's talent is not merely for conversation but also for dramaturgy. In all justice it should be said that Max Beerbohm pointed this out in a retraction of his earlier view that Shaw was a writer of conversations, not plays. This view, says Beerbohm, collapses when you actually see Shaw in the theatre: "To deny that he is a dramatist merely because he chooses, for the most part, to get drama out of contrasted types of character and thought, without action, and without appeal to the emotions, seems to be both unjust and absurd."

But these words of Beerbohm's, written in 1905, have not been heeded. Bernard Shaw has sometimes been omitted from histories of the drama and more often relegated to a humble role beside Granville Barker and Arthur Pinero. Recent critics who have rediscovered the artistry of Shaw have rediscovered the prose style much more than the dramaturgy. Even Beerbohm's praise is left-handed in its assertion that Shavian drama is "without action, and without appeal to the emotions." It is curious that almost on the same page Beerbohm had spoken of the splendid emotional crisis in the second act of *Major Barbara,* and had shown himself the first critic, so far as I know, to note the vein of spirituality in Shaw. It is curious, because it shows how a critic can revert to the cliché conception of Shaw—"a giant brain and no heart," to cite one of the critics in *Fanny's First Play*—after a momentary escape from it. It has been said of Bertolt Brecht that he thinks with his heart and feels with his head. The same could be said of Shaw. His intellect and his passions are alike all that one could expect of an artist-philosopher. But there is something perpetually unexpected and astonishing about the way they mix.

The allegation that Shaw's plays are "without action" is more plausible but still wrong. Most of the plays from *Arms and the Man* to *The Millionairess* entail every bit as much action as other authors' plays and for the good reason that many of them are other authors' plots. The misapprehension comes about because Shaw *toys* with the plots instead of gratefully accepting them for what they are, because also he has in his prefaces railed so often against the "tomfoolery of action," and because of the interpenetration of action with discussion. Look for a moment at the most actionless of Shaw's plays, *Getting*

Married and *Misalliance*. Even these are not static dramas of a sort to win the approval of a Maeterlinck or a Chekhov. In both there is enough plot for an ordinary Broadway play. (It is amusing that Shaw has to be defended by such an argument.) In *Getting Married* the destiny of a fair number of characters is not merely discussed but settled, and the routine of boy-meets-girl is given a Shavian performance. In *Misalliance*, there is all the violence and tomfoolery that anyone could wish. An aviator—and this in 1910—crashes into the precincts; his passenger turns out to be a lady whom Sidney Hook would have to term at once eventful and event-making. In *Getting Married* there is a coal-dealer's wife who makes love to a bishop through the mails under the name Incognita Appassionata; in *Misalliance* there is a gunman. It is not the lack of action but the presence of intelligent dialogue which is too much for many modern directors, actors, critics, and audiences.

So much for technique. An artist who is a critic of morality and society must also submit to a moral and social criticism. What are Shaw's values? Some will point in reply to the most extended of his philosophic works, such as *Back to Methuselah*. Others will observe that Shaw has chopped and changed. Now he is a social democrat, now an anti-democratic pessimist. Now he is a Huxleyan champion of science against religion, now a metabiological champion of religion against science. He can be represented as merely a disciple of Marx, or of Shelley, or of Samuel Butler. Edmund Wilson concludes that he is just confused.

This might not—though again, it might—be a damaging criticism of a lyric poet, but it is certainly a damaging criticism of a moralist; and one cannot be quite happy about Wilson's approval of Shaw the artist when it is qualified by so strong a disapproval of Shaw the philosopher. Of course it can be maintained that Shaw's argument against the pure artist is a deceptive strategy to trick us into believing that he is a philosopher. Even so a confused satirist is a bad satirist, and thus a bad artist.

But surely Wilson is wrong. What he finds inconsistent—for instance, that Shaw can be at the same time a social democrat and an admirer of Stalin—will not seem inconsistent to everyone. Wilson says that Shaw's thinking is on three levels—the level of everyday life, the level of politics, and the level of metaphysics—and that the three are never integrated. To be sure, it is no answer to retort that *all* men think on these three levels without a successful integration of the three, for Shaw as an artist-philosopher must be expected to succeed where other men fail. The answer, as I have tried elsewhere to demonstrate, is that Shaw's integration is not so incomplete as is supposed.[1] Here is it enough to state that Shaw is sometimes accused of betraying beliefs which he never held. He is often suspected of trying to be much more systematic than he ever intended to be. Indeed he is not utterly systematic but he is roughly consistent; his attitude to beliefs has been, in the main, that of a pragmatist. This is perhaps what most clearly differentiates Shaw from satirists of previous ages, such as Chaucer with his catholic criteria or Voltaire with his deistic criteria. It is at once Shaw's great title to originality as an artist and his great title to represent his age.

Shaw's pragmatic adaptability is not mere opportunism. He has often sponsored an unpopular cause which was later recognized to be right. He has believed in what might as justifiably be called Romanticism as the hocus-pocus of popular novelists, namely, in the continuity of the ideal and the real, the spiritual and the physical, the theoretic and the practical. He is a Marxist in his hatred of hypocritical ideologies, of religions which are opiates; money, he says, is the most important thing in the world, and you are damned without it. On the other hand, Shaw probably agrees with Hotchkiss in *Getting Married:* "Religion is a great force; the only real motive force in the world." The Shavian will see no final contradiction between the two attitudes. Religion is for Shaw a natural fact, not a supernatural fact; just as economics is for Shaw spiritual enough to be the subject of high comedy.

The great problem of Shaw's plays—we have examined one instance in some detail—is the relation between ideals and reality, and thus the relation between idealism and realism. There is, according to Shaw, a wrong realism and a right realism, a wrong idealism and a right idealism. A wrong realism is exemplified in Undershaft, whose realistic vision supports only egoism. Idealism on the other hand may be worse. It may be the conscious mask of a realist, as it is in the propaganda of Undershaft's factory or in the gifts of Bodger the brewer to the Salvation Army. It may be self-deception, as it is in Barbara before she sees quite clearly that she is combatting liquor with a brewer's money. In either case, idealism is painted in more horrible colors by Shaw, as it had been by Ibsen and for that matter by Jesus Christ, than is Machiavellian realism. The conclusion of *Major Barbara* is that the high purpose of the idealist should be linked to the realist's sense of fact, power, and possibility. Where practical genius is found in a lofty mind Shaw approves. His Caesar is a realist with a soul, a realist who values his own life as nothing beside the high destiny of Rome. His Joan is an idealist with a head, an idealist who can see the simple facts better than the soldiers, the politicians, and the clerics put together, a visionary whose hallucinations have more validity than the philosophic ideas of the learned.

Ibsen's Brand, striving to "live the vision into deed," had said:

> Daily drudgery be one
> With star-flights beyond the sun.

Through Ibsen Romanticism came to flower in Scandinavia; through Ibsen, Shaw, and others Romanticism was renewed after a generation of anti-Romanticism. Now the doctrine of religious-materialism or materialist-religion, of idealist-realism or realistic-idealism, is one of the themes of Romanticism from Blake to Shaw. It is a leitmotiv of Shavian drama turning up in the pseudo-flippant form of his late Political Extravaganzas. In *Too True to Be Good* (1929), man is described as having higher and lower centres, as in D. H. Lawrence. But Shaw is not the spokesman of lower centres; nor is he, as many assume, the spokesman of the higher centres. He attributes our troubles to the separation of higher and lower. "Since the war," says his preacher, "the lower centres have become vocal. And the effect is that of an earthquake . . . the institutions are rocking and splitting and sundering. They leave us no place to live, no certainties, no workable morality, no heaven, no hell, no commandments, and no God." Or, as the studious Sergeant in the same play puts it, in speaking of the sexual ethics of the 'twenties: "But when men and women pick one another up just for a bit of fun, they find they've picked up more than they bargained for, because men and women have a top storey as well as a ground floor; and you can't have the one without the other."

Shaw's Romanticism is a more highly developed philosophy than the Romanticism of the first generation. Philosophically one should look for its affiliations less with "mysticism" or "materialism"—the two systems commonly associated with Shaw—than with the pragmatic pluralism of William James. The attitudes of pragmatic pluralism are part and parcel of Shaw's art as well as of his thought. Nowhere in dogmatic communist writing does one have a sense of dialectic and antithesis as keenly as in a Shavian play. Shaw's mind is well-stocked, as everyone knows, and he is famous for the number of things he can mention on one page; but all this would mean nothing if he could not marshal his facts ironically. The chief mark of Shavian prose is its use of ironic antithesis and juxtaposition. Contrary to what one expects from a propagandist, Shaw not only shows the liberal's sense of the other man's point of view. He has a sense of every conceivable point of view, and can pack all the points of view into one long sentence, which climbs by parallelisms and antitheses to a climax, and then sinks with the finality of a conqueror to a conclusion which Shaw will not allow you to evade. In its course the Shavian sentence, still more the Shavian paragraph, looks in all possible directions. For Shaw sees the world as what James called a multiverse, and that is unusual in a satirist, who is customarily something of a monomaniac.

It is a fact of curious interest that William James, who thought Shaw "a great power as a concrete moralist," hit upon one of the essentials of Shaw, to wit, "the way he brings home to the *eyes,* as it were, the difference between 'convention' and 'conscience.'" Such a statement would often be the cue for a discussion of Shaw as puritan and protestant. But there is more to it than that. The difference between convention and conscience is certainly a moral matter, but Shaw is a *concrete* moralist, a master of parable, who has worked out for the presentation of his protestant pragmatist morality a new dramaturgy. Shaw is one of the few artists whose grasp of political, moral, and social forces is really professional; in political, moral, and social territory he is not a mere expropriator. But he is a genuine dramatist in that he brings his matter home to the eyes, which is something that neither the historian nor the sociologist, the poet nor the novelist, need do. All these bring visions before the mind's eye; none, except the dramatist, has to unfold his vision before the physical eye. Appreciators of Shaw's dialogue have explained to us what Shaw has done for the ear; those who appreciate his dramaturgy know that he addressed himself also to the eye, not indeed in giving separate attention to the eye by way of spectacle, but in fusing the elements into the one kinetic picture which is stage production (or screen production, as Shaw's movie audiences will hasten to add). William James' statement that Shaw's genius is much more important than his philosophy is true, if by it we understand that genius is a synthesizing power which obliterates barriers between thought and technique and gives evidence of both in a particular mode of presentation. The Shavian mode is drama.

Note

1. *A Century of Hero Worship*, Part Three, Chapter Two.

The Novels of Bernard Shaw

Claude T. Bissell

In the London of the late seventies, it was inevitable that a young man, determined upon a serious literary career, should try his hand at the writing of novels. For this was an age when the novelist could aim at distinction and, at the same time, reasonably hope for popularity: nobody, it is true, had yet taken the place of Thackeray and Dickens, but George Eliot and Anthony Trollope were still alive, and George Meredith was just entering upon the era of his greatest popular success. In 1879, George Bernard Shaw was a young Irish immigrant of twenty-three, who since his arrival in London three years before had been frequenting artistic and literary circles, and who accordingly felt that his talents and his rich experience of life could find a triumphant issue in the writing of novels. Until 1883 he devoted himself almost entirely to the realization of this purpose. The results were, at least, a tribute to his pertinacity and industry; undeterred by a monotonous succession of refusals from unenlightened publishers, he continued "to fill five pages . . . a day, rain or shine, dull or inspired,"[1] and in five years turned out five novels. Today the novels have taken their place in the Standard Edition, not merely as the *juvenilia* of a great artist, but as works that have considerable merit in their own right. I do not propose, however, to follow those critics who have sought to add another reputation to the many that Shaw has already acquired and have thrust him, belatedly, into the ranks of the great English novelists.[2] It is my purpose rather to show how invaluable these early works are for the understanding of Shaw's intellectual and artistic development.

Shaw's first novel, written in 1879, was called with "merciless fitness,"[3] *Immaturity,* and was, among other things, a conscientious attempt to fulfill Victorian requirements of length and solidity; it is divided into four long books, and it is conceivable that the young author envisaged its inclusion in Mr. Mudie's Select Lending Library of three-volume novels. In *Immaturity* Shaw made his first and only attempt in a novel to come to grips with lower middle class life; the opening book is called "Islington," and the characters are clerks, housekeepers, shopkeepers, and servants, who are driven by the monotonous

From *University of Toronto Quarterly* 17 (October 1947): 38–51. Reprinted by permission of the University of Toronto Press. Copyright, Canada, 1947. All rights reserved. Permission to reproduce in whole or in part must be obtained in writing from the University of Toronto Press.

routine of existence to find emotional release in evangelical religion. But as the novel progresses, these characters receive less and less treatment. We enter a world of wealthy dilettantes, artists, and thinkers. The scene is now set in Kensington, usually in *salons* attended only by those who approve of "felt hats, tweed and velveteen clothes, long hair, music on Sundays, pictures of the nude figure, literary women, and avowals of agnosticism."[4] Along with the change of scene and *dramatis personae* goes a change in literary method. The opening chapters might come from a novel by Gissing; they are written in a tone of sober, detailed realism. But the rest of the novel, with the exception of an incongruous attempt at Dickensian melodrama, strives to maintain a tone of sophisticated social satire.

In spite of publishers' complaints that the novel was innocent of plot, it is obvious that Shaw was doing his best to satisfy the popular demand for intrigue and suspense by introducing a number of complicated romantic entanglements. His real interest, however, was not in plot, not even in social satire, but in what we might call spiritual autobiography. The hero, Robert Smith, is obviously a younger version of the author: "a youth of eighteen, with closely cropped pale yellow hair, small grey eyes, and a slender lathy figure. His delicately cut features and nervous manner indicated some refinement; but his shyness, though fairly well covered up, showed that his experience of society was limited, and his disposition sensitive."[5] It is the study of Robert Smith, who represents Bernard Shaw's "immaturity"—intellect and imagination virtually untouched by emotional insight and experience—that almost gives the novel a leading theme and supplies the chief source of interest for the modern reader.

Until its publication in book form in 1921, *Immaturity* had a reading public consisting exclusively of publishers' critics. Most of them, like George Meredith, reader for Chapman and Hall, merely dismissed the novel without any critical comment. But at least one, in all likelihood John Morley of Macmillan's, found *Immaturity* worthy of a serious appraisal and softened his ultimate refusal with some judicious praise.[6]

In his second novel, *The Irrational Knot,* written in 1880, Shaw made an attempt to remedy the discursiveness and formlessness of *Immaturity.* First of all, he carefully restricts his caste of characters: landladies, clerks, and shopkeeping evangelicals have disappeared; we are throughout, with a few minor exceptions, in a world of wealth and social refinement. True, the hero, Edward Conolly, calls himself a "workman," but he is a workman who speedily amasses a large fortune and a favoured position in society by reason of his enterprise and ingenuity. In the second place, the novel has a carefully worked out structural pattern that springs from the resolution of a conflict between characters who embody two strongly opposed attitudes toward life. On the one side is Conolly, the workman-financier, the apostle of reason, who has forged his ideas of morality and culture on the hard anvil of experience; on the other side is the wealthy and attractive Marian Lind, a creature of instinct and emotion, who accepts the conventions of her social caste. At first, however, neither recognizes that such a cleavage exists between them. Indeed, Marian Lind sentimentally convinces herself that Conolly, with his superior mind and cool self-possession, would make an admirable husband; and Conolly reasons scientifically that Marian Lind, with her wealth, her beauty, and her refinement, would make a desirable wife. The resulting marriage is a dismal failure. Conolly comes to despise his wife for her shallow conventionalism; and Marian finds her husband's condescending assumption of intellectual superiority insufferable. In despair, she elopes with an aristocratic lover, a model of gentlemanly refinement, only to discover that she can no longer tolerate the fatuities of her own class. At the end of the novel Shaw brings the hero and heroine together again. Although they realize that a reconciliation is impossible, they have acquired wisdom from their bitter experiences: Conolly now sees that the dictates of the mind are often cruel and Marian that the promptings of the heart are often foolish.

Rereading *The Irrational Knot* twenty-five years after he had written it, Shaw discovered that "this jejune exploit of mine" was a work of the "first order," in the sense that its morality was original and not secondhand. When *A Doll's House* reached England in translation several years later, Shaw was unimpressed, for had he not already "made a morally original study of marriage, and made it, too, without any melodramatic forgeries, spinal diseases, and suicides. . . ."?[7] It is doubtful whether an anticipation of the "moral originality" of *A Doll's House* establishes a compelling reason for even an academic reconsideration of *The Irrational Knot*. And certainly the publishers, all of whom turned it down, may be forgiven for failing to recognize the genius of the young novelist underneath the stilted dialogue and the unconvincing characterization. But the modern reader will be unable, nevertheless, to accept the Victorian judgment of *The Irrational Knot*; for even in this immature novel he will recognize the first confident signs of those qualities that were to be developed so triumphantly when Shaw turned to the stage—a skill in maintaining a delicate balance between opposing points of view and an intellectual clarity that forbids a sentimental or melodramatic resolution of a dramatic conflict.

Shaw's third novel, *Love among the Artists,* promptly submitted to the publishers a year after he had finished writing *The Irrational Knot,* was, for the most part, a solemnly didactic essay on the nature of art. The characters are all sketchy embodiments of various attitudes toward art, and to each is carefully apportioned an exact measure of approval or disapproval. The highest embodiment of artistic excellence is the great natural genius, in Shaw's novel a sort of cardboard imitation of Beethoven, who answers to no tribunal except his own vision of truth and beauty. From this height we descend through various levels until, at the lowest, we reach the self-conscious academic, for whom art springs, not from an inner necessity, but from a theory of the good and the beautiful.

Love among the Artists is, assuredly, the worst of the five novels and one of the few genuinely dull books that Shaw ever wrote. Fortunately, however, in this novel he exhausted his vein of callow didacticism. *Cashel Byron's Profession,* opus number 4, is a complete contrast in every way to its immediate predecessor.

Cashel Byron's Profession is a comic romance, enlivened by the play of ideas—a variant on the story of how the handsome young beggar lad wins the hand of the rich and beautiful princess. In Shaw's modernized version, the beggar is a prize-fighter, and the princess is an attractive and cultured lady of the world, who has, of course, inherited a large fortune. Along with the fortune, she has received from her father a letter full of considered advice, which concludes with this solemn warning on the subject of marriage: "Beware of men who have read more than they have worked, or who love to read better than to work. Do not forget that where the man is always at home, the woman is never happy. Beware of painters, poets, musicians, and artists of all sorts, except very great artists; beware even of them as husbands and fathers. Self-satisfied workmen who have learnt their business well, whether they be chancellors of the exchequer or farmers, I recommend to you as, on the whole, the most tolerable class of men I have met."[8] When the handsome young prize-fighter proposes to her, the heroine finds it impossible at first to take his avowals of love seriously. Then, with the discovery that this curious suitor is really the long-lost son of a genteel mother and the heir to a fortune of £5,000 a year, she suddenly realizes that she has found the ideal husband described in her father's letter. Moreover, she argues, by accepting the prize-fighter she will be giving a practical and eloquent demonstration of her advanced, scientific views. "I practically believe in the doctrine of heredity," she says, in defending her course before a scandalized friend. "And as my body is frail and my brain morbidly active, I think my impulse towards a man stronger in body and untroubled in mind a trustworthy one. You can understand that; it is a plain proposition in eugenics."[9] After their marriage, the lady and the prize-fighter enter upon a new and richer life: she turns from her books to the pleasant responsibilities of a wife and a mother; he deserts the ring for politics and is elected to parliament in the conservative interest.

In *Cashel Byron's Profession* Shaw's power of comic invention begins to appear for the first time. He exploits with gusto the possibilities of comic incongruity which his theme is constantly offering him. It is not too much to say that one scene anticipates, in conception, at least, the famous situation in *Pygmalion* when Liza Doolittle stuns Chelsea society by marrying an impeccable accent to Billingsgate sentiments. Cashel Byron, the prize-fighter, finds himself in a soirée, where the principal attraction is a lecture by the learned German professor, Herr Abendgasse, on "The True in Art." Cashel, far from being struck by the ridiculous incongruity of his attending such an affair, listens eagerly to the lecture and discovers that his own experiences as a prize-fighter provide a peculiarly lucid commentary on the professor's ponderous generalizations. At the conclusion of the lecture, he is moved to address the astounded assembly:

I made out from the gentleman's remarks that there is a man in the musical line named Wagner, who is what you might call a game sort of composer; and that the musical fancy, though they can't deny that his tunes are first-rate, and that, so to speak, he wins his fights, yet they try to make out that he wins them in an outlandish way, and that he has no real science. Now I tell the gentleman not to mind such talk. As I have just shown you, his game wouldn't be any use to him without science. He might have beaten a few second-raters with a rush while he was young; but he wouldn't have lasted out as he has done unless he was clever as well. It's the newness of his style that puzzles people; for, mind you, every man has to grow his own style out of himself; and there is no use in thinking that it will be the same as the last fellow's, or right for the next fellow, or that it's *the* style, and that every other style is wrong. More rot is talked through not knowing that than anything else. You will find that those that run Professor Wagner down are either jealous, or they are old stagers that are not used to his style, and think that anything new must be bad. Just wait a bit, and, take my word for it, they'll turn right round and swear that his style isn't new at all, and that he stole it from some one they saw when they were ten years old.[10]

Of all Shaw's novels, *Cashel Byron's Profession* attracted the most critical attention and received the greatest popular approval. After the inevitable round of publishers' refusals, it, like the two preceding novels, found a brief existence in a socialist periodical.[11] But it refused to lie buried in these obscure pages and by 1887 had achieved the dignity of book format.[12] Toward the end of the century, it became something of a best-seller in the United States. Shaw, in reviewing the American reception of his novels, tells us that "American ladies were seized with a desire to go on the stage and be Lydia Carew for two thrilling hours. American actors 'saw themselves' as Cashel. Mr. James Corbett has actually appeared on the New York stage in the part."[13] The sudden popularity of the novel stirred Shaw to bring out in 1901 a dramatized version, *The Admirable Bashville or Constancy Unrewarded,* in order to preserve the copyright.

Shaw professed to be annoyed by the preference shown for *Cashel Byron's Profession* over his other novels and attributed its popularity to the deliberate way in which he had pandered to the schoolboy delight in a good fight.[14] Certainly the obvious gusto with which he wrote the prize-fight passages — passages which, he tells us, were solidly founded upon a little personal observation and a considerable amount of research in the British Museum and were conceived in the savagery of his imagination — strengthened the appeal of the novel. But the more reputable reason for its success lay, as Robert Louis Stevenson pointed out, in the tonic mixture of comedy and romance. "It is all mad, mad, mad," wrote Stevenson to William Archer, who had persuaded him to read *Cashel Byron's Profession,* "and deliriously delightful; the author has a taste in chivalry like Walter Scott's or Dumas's, and then he daubs in little bits of socialism; he soars away on the wings of the romantic griffin—even the griffin, as he cleaves the air, shouting with laughter at the nature of the quest—and I believe in his heart he thinks he is labouring in a quarry of solid granite realism—It is horrid fun."[15]

An Unsocial Socialist continues the vein of *Cashel Byron's Profession,* but with an important difference. Whereas *Cashel Byron's Profession,* as we have seen, might be described as a comic romance enlivened by the play of ideas, *An Unsocial Socialist* might be described as a play of ideas with an undercurrent of comic romance. The "little daubs of socialism" in the earlier novel, to which Stevenson referred, have spread to an alarming degree, and the predominating colour of Shaw's canvas is no longer a delicate pink but a bold and dazzling red. For some time now he had been engaged in the study of economics, and he had resolved "to give up mere character sketching and the construction of modes for improved types of individuals, and at once to produce a novel which should be a gigantic grapple with the whole social problem. But, alas! at twenty-seven one does not know everything. When I had finished two chapters of this enterprise—chapters of colossal length, but containing the merest preliminary matter—I broke down in sheer ignorance and incapacity."[16] *An Unsocial Socialist* is, on Shaw's word, the first two chapters of the contemplated *magnum opus.*

Certainly there is no reason to doubt that Shaw had a serious purpose in *An Unsocial Socialist,* that he meant the novel to be an indictment of capitalist society; but we can sympathize with John Morley, reporting on the book for Macmillan's, when he complained that readers "would not know whether the writer was serious or was laughing at them."[17] We are throughout in a world of refined social comedy: the scene shifts from a select boarding-school for girls in the country to West-End London mansions, and thence to the country home of a nobleman. The hero, Sidney Trefusis, may be a thorough-going socialist, but he is also a handsome young man of great wealth, an inveterate philanderer, and a Shelley-like romantic who fancies himself as a latter-day messiah. "With my egotism," he says, "my charlatanry, my tongue, and my habit of having my own way, I am fit for no calling but that of saviour of mankind."[18]

Whether we read *An Unsocial Socialist* as serious social criticism or light romantic comedy, or, best of all, gladly embrace and enjoy the two extremes, we must admit, I think, that this novel reveals an artist who has discovered himself, who writes always with sureness and often with commanding power. It is not surprising, therefore, that *An Unsocial Socialist* is the only one of the five novels, with the possible exception of *Cashel Byron's Profession,* that has found a place in the popular Shaw canon.

From this analysis it can be seen that the first three novels—*Immaturity, The Irrational Knot,* and *Love among the Artists*—have qualities in common that mark them off sharply from the last two novels—*Cashel Byron's Profession* and *An Unsocial Socialist*. The first three novels, for instance, are relentlessly serious in tone; wit of a heavy, intellectual kind there is in plenty, but no escapes into a world of comic fancy. The very reverse is true of the last two novels: they are creations of comic invention, and they are pervaded throughout by a tone of quixotic humour. And if we turn for a while to an examination of prose style, we shall find strong additional contrasts between the two groups of novels.

When he began his brief career as a novelist, Shaw tells us that he deliberately aimed at writing "nothing that should not be intelligible to a foreigner with a dictionary" and that he accordingly avoided idiom.[19] The results of this perverse principle are everywhere present in the early novels. The prose is marked by a self-conscious formality, by a strenuous effort at correctness and elegance that often succeed in being merely awkward and stilted. The sentences have a slow and ponderous movement; they creak painfully from clause to clause. Here, for instance, is an early descriptive passage:

> The pictures [in Mr. Grosvenor's gallery] represented remote incidents, derived from mythology, classic history, early Christianity, or personification of influences. A few of them, by their purity of intention, and evidence of a laborious effort to reach a region where even an honest glorying in technical craft would be too earthy an element, made themselves welcome to the capable spectator by the double appeal of their baffled weakness to his sympathy, and their masterly and hard-earned beauty to his admiration. The rest, bad imitations of these, depicted vacant persons with that vague aspect and indistinct eye, which is in nature the symptom of a bad cold in the head. They were foolishly conceived, and ill executed. At the end of the gallery, opposite to the entrance, the visitor might lift the green curtain and pass into a small apartment formed of dark purple velvet. Here hung a picture of enormous size, painted by Tintoretto, the insolent power of which contrasted as strongly with the works in the adjacent gallery as its luxurious purple surroundings with their faded drapery of green.[20]

Even the dialogue in the early novels fails to escape from the cramping restrictions that Shaw imposed on his style. Indeed, it is often a little less sprightly than the narrative and descriptive passages, for it labours under an additional handicap. In dialogue, Shaw explains, "I had, as the reader will probably find to his cost, the classical tradition which makes all the persons in the novel, except the comically vernacular ones, or the speakers of phonetically spelt dialect, utter themselves in the formal phrases and studied syntax of eighteenth century rhetoric."[21] Without pausing to question Shaw's ascription of literary influences (he might more reasonably have attributed this theory of dialogue to Scott and Thackeray), we need not take issue with his general analysis. The long rhetorical speech, which, as we shall see, becomes in the later novels a triumphant vehicle for Shaw's prose, suffers most under this burden of "formal phrases" and "studied syntax." In the following passage, the young hero of *Immaturity* is rebutting the argument that a certain distinguished contemporary artist derives his power from religious inspiration:

> On the contrary, [his pictures] don't contain one scrap of [religious devotion]. Angelico and Filippo Lippi and the rest of them painted as if they were sent on earth to glorify God. Mr. Donovan Browne paints as if he were self-dedicated to the task of painting beautiful pictures, or, in other words, of ennobling his fellow-creatures; and if we were not tired of the part of his genius which belongs to our own age, and blind to that which belongs to the infinite epoch of the highest art, we should draw a triumphant contrast instead of an apologetic comparison between him and an admirable but obsolete school which owed its concentration to mental narrowness.[22]

Both of the passages I have quoted are from *Immaturity,* and I do not want to suggest that the style of the two succeeding novels shows no development toward a greater flexibility and ease. But it is in *Cashel Byron's Profession* and, above all, in *An Unsocial Socialist,* that we first become aware of a radical change. The prose is now more idiomatic, the straining for elegancy is disappearing, and, above all, the sentences move forward at a greatly increased speed. It is this speed of movement, what Dixon Scott calls "the intoxicating ecstasy of pace,"[23] that most distinguishes the style of the last two novels.

To illustrate the qualities of the later style I have tried to select passages that would be roughly parallel to the two I have already quoted. But, significantly enough, it is difficult to find any extended passage of description in either *Cashel Byron's Profession* or *An Unsocial Socialist.* In his eager pursuit of the comic idea, Shaw seems to have no time to pause and to look around him. Instead of description we have rapid narration and extended passages of argumentative analysis, like the following:

> When Destiny takes nations into new places, it offers them the choice of marching boldly with it and understanding it, or being led like pigs to market, intensely recalcitrant, scuttling in sudden panics or charging in sudden huffs, and using such rests as its leader gives it, to eat, never to ask Whither? How? or What then? Only when Destiny gives the word to stop eating and march, a useless Why? is raised, whereupon Destiny, out of patience, gives the rope a jerk which fetches the poor pig off his trotters. England, observant of the fact that the pig's line of conduct shifted all moral responsibility to his leader, and got the pig finally to his destination without brain worry, adopted it without hesitation in Africa, with the result that when the king of a considerable people there fell, with his territories, into British hands, the conquest seemed useless, troublesome, and expensive; and after repeated attempts to settle the country on impracticable plans suggested to the Colonial Office by a popular historian who had made a trip to Africa, and by generals who were tired of their primitive remedy of killing the natives, it appeared that the best course was to release the king and get rid of the unprofitable booty by restoring it to him.[24]

It is an easy enough matter to find examples of the long rhetorical speech in the last two novels. Indeed, *An Unsocial Socialist* is almost an extended harangue, punctuated occasionally by violent action. In this passage, the hero is attacking the assumption that the artist should have a favoured position in society:

> Now, no men are greater sticklers for the arbitrary dominion of genius and talent than your artists. The great painter is not satisfied with being sought after and admired because his hands can do more than ordinary hands, which they truly can, but he wants to be fed as if his stomach needed more food than ordinary stomachs, which it does not. A day's work is a day's work, neither more nor less, and the man who does it needs a day's sustenance, a night's repose, and due leisure, whether he be painter or ploughman. But the rascal of a painter, poet, novelist, or other voluptuary in labor, is not content with his advantage in popular esteem over the ploughman; he also wants an advantage in money, as if there were more hours in a day spent in the studio or library than in the field; or as if he needed more food to enable him to do his work than the ploughman to enable him to do his. He talks of the higher quality of his work, as if the higher quality of it were of his own making—as if it gave him a right to work less for his neighbor than his neighbor works for him—as if the ploughman could not do better without him than he without the ploughman—as if the value of the most celebrated pictures has not been questioned more than that of any straight furrow in the arable world—as if it did not take an apprenticeship of as many years to train the hand and eye of a mason or blacksmith as of an artist—as if, in short, the fellow were a god, as canting brain-worshippers have for years past been assuring him he is. Artists are the high priests of the modern Moloch. Nine out of ten of them are diseased creatures, just sane enough to trade on their own neuroses. The only quality of theirs which extorts my respect is a certain sublime selfishness which makes them willing to starve and to let their families starve sooner than do any work they don't like.[25]

To analyse passages such as these so as to show how Shaw achieves the effect of dazzling speed is not easy. Shaw himself would discourage even the attempt at analysis, for he has always maintained that his mature prose style is simply the effective statement of clear ideas. But I might draw attention to the close interlocking of clauses, to the way in which balance and antithesis are repeatedly used without sacrificing the idea to a stylized pattern, to the masterly employment of the periodic sentence that carries the reader unprotestingly along to the triumphant conclusion. And I might also draw attention to the kind of word that Shaw uses—words that are chastely devoid of sensuous appeal, that convey information or draw a sharp moral or intellectual distinction and seem to cut through instantaneously to the reader's mind.

The prose that Shaw was developing in his last two novels is certainly a prose of great power and beauty, but it is not, one must admit, an ideal instrument for the novelist. Certainly it is not adapted to the patient analysis of human motivation, to the careful evocation of a mood, nor can it sustain an extended narrative, unless the narrative is made to move with unrealistic speed. It is the prose of the pamphleteer, of the journalist, if you like, provided you admit that the journalist should have an impassioned concern with morals and society. And it is the prose of the rhetorician, prose that is meant to be declaimed from a public platform or from the stage of a theatre.

The direction of Shaw's artistic development during his brief career as a novelist is now clear: he has moved away from the didactic problem novel to what is almost a comic extravaganza, without, in the process, abandoning his role of serious social critic; and he has freed himself from a heavy and imitative prose, at its pedestrian best only in passages of analysis and description, in order to develop a prose that is supple and swift, superbly adapted to the rhetorical speech and the impassioned argument. How can we account for such profound changes? Only in an examination of Shaw's intellectual development during his early years in London can we find a satisfactory answer to this question.

When Shaw arrived in London in 1876 to join his mother and one surviving sister, he knew a good deal, for a young man of twenty, about music and painting and very little about anything else. His education had been almost completely non-academic, acquired, for the most part, by soaking himself in music at home and by frequenting the Dublin art galleries. He was able to make his way socially in London, he tells us, because he could play an acceptable accompaniment and was, therefore, tolerated at polite evening parties.[26] The music that he knew best was romantic music—the operas of Bizet, Gounod, and Verdi; and the literature that he had read most avidly was romantic literature—the poetry of Byron and Shelley, the novels of Victor Hugo, Scott, and Dumas. Chiefly on the basis of these biographical facts, Dixon Scott, whose early essay is still one of the few critical attempts to come to grips with Shaw's work, builds up a picture of the complete romantic who becomes gradually ensnared in a world of hard *isms* and prostitutes his magnificent, poetic talents in the service of intellectual movements to which he is, at heart, profoundly averse. Certainly we must not lose sight of this strong romantic strain; but to understand Shaw, as to understand all great artists, we must be wary of over-simplification. Even as a youth Shaw was a much more complex person than Dixon Scott would have us believe.

If in 1876 he had a romantic temperament and could soak himself "lusciously in the licensed orgies and ecstasies of music," he was also a young man with a restless and inquisitive mind in search of a satisfying intellectual creed. Before he left Ireland, he had already achieved a certain notoriety in family circles for his disposition to question accepted beliefs. Arrived in London, he gravitated inevitably to rationalist and scientific circles and eagerly assumed the complete panoply of ideas that distinguished the advanced Victorian intellectual. In his description of a debating society that he joined in the winter of 1879, Shaw has given us an excellent analysis of the kind of intellectual atmosphere in which he lived during his first years in London:

The Zetetical Society [was] a junior copy of the once well known Dialectical Society which had been founded to discuss Stuart Mill's essay on Liberty when that was new. Both societies were strongly Millite. In both there was complete freedom of discussion, political, religious and sexual. Women took an important part in the debates, a special feature of which was that each speaker, at the conclusion of his speech, could be cross examined on it by any of the others in a series of questions. The tone was strongly individualistic, atheistic, Malthusian, evolutionary, Ingersollian, Darwinian, Herbert Spencerian. Huxley, Tyndall and George Eliot were on the shelves of all the members. . . . Socialism was regarded as an exploded fallacy; and nobody dreamt that within five years it would revive, snatch away all the younger generation, and sweep the Dialectical and Zetetical into the blind cave of eternal night.[27]

Shaw's first novels were written while he was eagerly absorbing the ideas promulgated in societies like these. Especially in *Immaturity* and in *The Irrational Knot* do we see the influence of rationalist and scientific thought. His heroes have exactly the same combination of intense moral earnestness and uncompromising infidelity that distinguishes so many of the "advanced" Victorian writers. Conolly in *The Irrational Knot* might be a portrait of Thomas Henry Huxley before Huxley's immaculate scientific faith was assailed by certain stubborn facts of human experience. Like the early Huxley, he believes that it is possible to mark off an area of life that is "knowable," because subject to undeviating laws of nature, and to dismiss all else as "unknowable," and, therefore, irrelevant. Once this principle is accepted and acted upon, life resolves into a clear and rational pattern. Conolly's wife describes him as a man "never without a purpose, never with a regret, [who] regards life as a succession of objects each to be accomplished by so many days' work; [who] takes [his] pleasure in trifling lazily with the consciousness of possessing a strong brain; [who] studies love, family affection, and friendship as a doctor studies breathing or digestion; [who] looks on disinterestedness as either weakness or hypocrisy, and on death as a mere transfer of your social function to some member of the next generation."[28]

Although the influence of scientific and rationalist thought is strongly evident in the first three novels and, more than anything else, accounts for their similarity of tone, I do not want to suggest that, at this time, the young Shaw had found an intellectual faith that he could embrace with single-minded devotion. Shaw's portrait of himself in *Immaturity* as the young free-thinker and agnostic is done with a half-amused, ironical objectivity. Although Conolly, the rationalist spokesman in *The Irrational Knot,* towers heroically over the other characters in the novel, he does not emerge as a completely sympathetic figure. Often Shaw is happiest with minor characters who are neither free-thinkers nor even intellectuals, but are energetic, successful types who have worked out a practical compromise with life and have embraced a simple gospel of common sense. And in the last novel of this group, *Love among the Artists,* the rationalist hero has disappeared altogether; his place is now taken by the romantic individualist, for whom excellence in art, as in life, can be gauged by emotional sincerity and by devotion to an ideal of beauty.

We must recognize, then, that the writer of these early novels is, in many respects, a complex and mature person. Yet, somehow or other, he fails to make vital the rich diversities in his own mind. His novels give an impression of aridity; they reveal a writer with a great many talents who has not yet learned how to put those talents into triumphant action. We may find one reason for these inadequacies, as I have suggested, in the resolute attempt of the young Shaw to convert the dry bones of rationalism into the flesh and blood of art. For a second and more compelling reason, we must look elsewhere; we must examine the stage Shaw had reached in his speculations about the economic structure of society.

Up until the time Shaw finished *Love among the Artists* and began to write *Cashel Byron's Profession,* his attitude toward the economic structure of society had been determined, not by analysis or theory, but by the hard facts of personal experiences. These experiences, it must be clearly borne in mind, were not of a kind to provide material for a romantic story of the barefoot peasant lad, proud of his honest poverty and haughtily contemptuous of the vulgar ostentation of the rich. The truth of the matter is, of course, that Shaw heartily despised the proletariat and diligently sought out the society of the wealthy and the refined. He gradually became aware of an economic problem not because his poverty made him a social outcast and cut him off completely from sources of emotional and intellectual pleasure but because his income was inadequate to gain him admission to polite society. And the young immigrant felt his plight all the more keenly when he reflected that he came from a genuinely superior family, that his father had aristocratic connections and had unequivocal claims to the title of "gentleman." "If you would know what real poverty is," wrote Shaw in his most revealing autobiographical statement, "ask the younger son of a younger son of a younger son. To understand his plight you must start at the top without the income of the top, and curse your stars that you were not lucky enough to start at the bottom."[29] The economic problem for Shaw was then, at this time, merely a personal problem: how could he, a member of a pathetically small and disorganized group, made up of "the Shabby Genteel, the Poor Relations, the Gentlemen who are no Gentlemen,"[30] ever hope to find a position in society befitting the high estimate of his own worth? The problem was apparently insoluble. He had to resign himself to being an outsider, refusing to descend to the level of the poor and incapable of reaching the level of the rich. Looking back on those unhappy days, Shaw relentlessly recalls that he was "ashamed of his poverty, in continual dread of doing the wrong thing, resentfully insubordinate and seditious in a social order which he not only accepted but in which he actually claimed a privileged part."[31]

It is here—in this picture of the confusion and uncertainty that characterized Shaw's attitude toward the economic structure of society—that we find our second reason for the inadequacies of the early novels. His novels are about the wealthy and the aristocratic; they show an almost morbid consciousness of economic distinctions; and yet he has no consistent point of view toward the society he depicts. He seems to waver between an inclination to idealize a class to which, he is convinced, he rightfully belongs, and a feeling of resentment that wealth and social prestige should so often be accompanied by a cultural development immeasurably inferior to his own.

What Shaw needed, then, both to clarify his own personal problems and to give strength and direction to the works of his imagination was a plausible and consistent critical attitude toward the economic structure of society. The impetus to the development of such a critical attitude came with dramatic suddenness. On the night of September 5, 1882, possibly after he had finished writing five more pages of his fourth novel, *Cashel Byron's Profession,* he wandered into a lecture given by Henry George. George was a radical, but not of the orthodox Victorian stamp: "he spoke of Liberty, Justice, Truth, Natural Law, and other strange eighteenth century superstitions"; he attacked scientific materialism and "explained with great simplicity and sincerity the views of the Creator, who had gone completely out of fashion in London in the previous decade and had not been heard of since."[32] George's radicalism was purely economic; like Ruskin, he felt that man had bound himself to a set of cruel and stupid economic principles. "It flashed on me then for the first time," wrote Shaw, "that 'the conflict between Religion and Science' . . . the overthrow of the Bible, the higher education of women, Mill on Liberty, and all the rest of the storm that raged round Darwin, Tyndall, Huxley, Spencer and the rest, on which I had brought myself up intellectually, was a mere middle-class business. Suppose it could have produced a nation of Matthew Arnolds and George Eliots!—You may well shudder. The importance of the economic basis dawned on me."[33] After hearing George's lecture, Shaw plunged into a course of economic study, which in a few months culminated in his reading Marx's *Das Kapital* and his conversion to socialism.

If we are to understand the significance for Shaw the man and the artist of this espousal of socialism, we must be clear on two points. In the first place, Shaw came to socialism not through his own harsh experience of the economic inequalities of society, and certainly not through the awakening of his humanitarian passion. His conversion was largely an affair of the mind, and it bore fruit in practical activity, not, for instance, in the form of settlement work among the poor in London, but in the form of speeches from the public platform and lectures to groups of intellectuals. In the second place, his socialism is not a fervently revolutionary faith even at this early stage when he is technically a follower of Marx. Indeed, much of the value of socialism consists for him in the solution it offers for his own personal problems. Now that he has a coherent theory, he finds that he can adjust himself with ease to the present economic structure of society while, at the same time, he looks forward to the ultimate communist Utopia of absolute equality.

What are the effects on Shaw the artist of this shift to a socialist analysis of society? Shaw's last two novels, especially *An Unsocial Socialist,* provide the evidence for a preliminary answer to this question. In the first part of this article I have already indicated what the general characteristics of these novels are. It remains now to relate those characteristics to the intellectual development I have been sketching.

As a result of the new direction his intellectual development had taken, Shaw did not become, even faintly, a proletarian novelist. You will find in his last two novels no scenes depicting the harsh sufferings of the workers under capitalism. In only one chapter of *An Unsocial Socialist,* written in the first flush of his conversion, do the oppressed workers, who are presumably never absent from the hero's thoughts since they are continuously present in his speeches, make their appearance; and on that occasion the scene is merely an excuse for introducing a satiric pantomime at the expense of classical theories of economy. Shaw the socialist has not lost his respect for Mammon; indeed he realizes with a new and compelling vividness that the desire for and acquisition of money is the root of all good.

Finally, Shaw's romantic imagination and his power of comic invention, far from being stifled by his immersion in the dismal science, have been gloriously released. The parallel here between Shaw and Samuel Butler is especially striking. Shaw found in *Das Kapital* what Butler, twenty-five years before, had found in *The Origin of Species*—a new and exhilarating explanation of the mystery of experience, and a wealth of fascinating ideas that provided both the inspiration and the materials for literary expression. In the vision of a communist Utopia, Shaw found an ideal that would satisfy his romantic yearnings. In the socialist demonstration of the glaring incongruities underlying the economic structure of society, he found just the material he needed for the exercise of his comic genius. Henceforth he could be a social critic and a moralist without fear of falling into dullness and didacticism; for he now saw that the final truth of a matter reveals itself only to the artist-philosopher who combines a passionate imagination with an exquisite levity of mind.

Notes

1. Preface to *Immaturity,* 37. Quotations from Shaw's works throughout this article are from the Standard Edition (London, 1931–2).

2. Archibald Henderson gives quotations from a number of the more enthusiastic critical comments on the novels. James Huneker maintained that "Shaw could rank higher as a novelist than as a dramatist—always selecting for judgment the supreme pages of his tales, pages wherein character, wit, humour, pathos, fantasy, and observation mingled with an overwhelming effect." Christopher Morley thus concludes a tribute to Shaw, the novelist: "I myself regard him as a great novelist gone wrong." See Henderson, *Bernard Shaw, Playboy and Prophet* (New York, 1932), 112–3; henceforth referred to as Henderson.

3. Preface to *Cashel Byron's Profession,* 9.

4. *Immaturity,* 105.

5. *Immaturity,* 4.

6. See Charles Morgan, *The House of Macmillan, 1843–1943* (London, 1943). In this book Morgan prints generous extracts from the Macmillan reports on all the novels.

7. Preface to *The Irrational Knot,* 18–19.

8. *Cashel Byron's Profession,* 30.

9. *Ibid.,* 223.

10. *Ibid.,* 89–90.

11. *The Irrational Knot* was published in *Our Corner* between April, 1885, and February, 1887, and *Love among the Artists* in the same periodical, between November, 1887, and December, 1888. *Cashel Byron's Profession* was published in *To-day* between April, 1885, and March, 1886. See Henderson, 103, 108–9.

12. For an account of the various editions of *Cashel Byron's Profession,* see Henderson, 103–4.

13. Preface to *Cashel Byron's Profession,* 10.

14. *Ibid.,* 11.

15. *Letters of Robert Louis Stevenson,* ed. Sidney Colvin (New York, 1899), II, 107.

16. "Mr. Bernard Shaw's Works of Fiction. Reviewed by Himself," *Novel Review* (Feb., 1892). Quoted by Henderson, 84.

17. Morgan, *The House of Macmillan,* 127.

18. *An Unsocial Socialist,* 104.

19. Preface to *Immaturity,* 39.

20. *Immaturity,* 103.

21. Preface to *The Irrational Knot,* 8–9.

22. *Immaturity,* 270.

23. "The Innocence of Bernard Shaw," in *Men of Letters* (London, 1916), 19.

24. *Cashel Byron's Profession,* 104.

25. *An Unsocial Socialist,* 74–5.

26. See the preface to *The Irrational Knot,* 11 ff.

27. Shaw to Archibald Henderson, Jan. 17, 1905. Quoted in Henderson, 121.

28. *The Irrational Knot,* 189.

29. Preface to *Immaturity,* 6.

30. *Ibid.,* 8.

31. *Ibid.,* 16.

32. Shaw to Hamlin Garland, Dec. 29, 1904. Quoted in Henderson, 149.

33. Henderson, 151–2.

Concerning the Play of Ideas

TERENCE RATTIGAN

I believe that the best plays are about people and not about things. I am in fact a heretic from the now widely held faith that a play which concerns itself with, say, the artificial insemination of human beings or the National Health Service is of necessity worthier of critical esteem than a play about, say, a mother's relations with her son or about a husband's jealousy of his wife.

I further believe that the intellectual *avant-garde* of the English theatre— or rather, let's be both brave and accurate, and say of the English-speaking theatre, since in my view, the Americans are the worst offenders—are, in their insistence on the superiority of the play of ideas over the play of character and situation, not only misguided but old-fashioned.

It was in 1895 that Shaw began his battle in the *Saturday Review* on behalf of the "New" theatre, the Ibsenite theatre, the "theatre as a factory of thought, a prompter of conscience, and an elucidator of social conduct." In what single respect have the present-day proponents of "sociologically significant" drama advanced one step beyond the standpoint taken up in 1895 by a man whose only aim, as he himself admits, was, by his vituperation of the existing theatre, to "cut his own way into it at the point of his pen"?

That he succeeded brilliantly in that ambition, and that he is still a vital and, happily, living force in our theatre should not blind us to the fact that fifty years of completely stagnant thought and theory concerning the drama is a depressing concept, if not to the *avant-garde,* at least to me. For the history of artistic endeavour is surely the history of change, and our painters are not still urged to paint like Burne-Jones, nor our poets to compose like Swinburne. Why then should our dramatists still be encouraged to write like late Ibsen or early Shaw?

Let us examine Shaw's campaign of the 'nineties and see where it has led the modern theatre.

Nowhere at all, is my belief. In fact, in one most important respect there has been a definite retreat. It is now the practice of the theatrical ideologists (using the word in the general and not necessarily political sense) when confronted with a play which, though an acknowledged world masterpiece, hasn't an idea (in the ideological sense) in it—*Othello,* for instance—promptly

Reproduced with kind permission of New Statesman & Society from *New Statesman and Nation* n.s. 39 (4 March 1950).

to take one of their own ideas, stick it in the play, and then triumphantly discover it. Not so Shaw. That giant, seeing the problem steadily and seeing it whole, scorned such petty tricks of legerdemain. If a play didn't conform to the pattern he had laid down of what a good play should be, then it was just not a good play, and, for that reason, must be attacked. As witness: "*Othello* is pure melodrama. There is not a touch of character that goes below the skin; and the fitful attempts to make Iago something better than a melodramatic villain only make a hopeless mess of him and his motives. To anyone capable of reading the play with an open mind as to its merits, it is obvious that Shakespeare plunged through it so impetuously that he had it finished before he had made up his mind as to the character and motives of a single person in it."

So much for *Othello*. And so much, in these bellicose pages, for *Anthony and Cleopatra* ("To say that there is plenty of bogus characterisation in it—Enobarbus for instance—is merely to say that it is by Shakespeare") for *Julius Caesar* ("rhetoric, claptrap, effective gushes of emotion, all the devices of the popular playwright are employed with a profusion of power that almost breaks their backs") and for many of those other non-ideological works of that non-Ibsenite, but still infuriatingly popular dramatist whom Shaw, correctly and honestly recognised as the arch-enemy of his own pet theory of drama. Finally, in one explosive and oft-quoted sentence Shaw summed up the point at issue. "With the single exception of Homer there is no eminent writer, not even Sir Walter Scott, whom I can despise so entirely as I despise Shakespeare when I measure my mind against his."

That, of course, was bound to be the logical conclusion of the Shavian view of drama—Shakespeare's mind was despicable because it didn't contain the sort of ideas that Shaw would have liked it to contain. Shakespeare's plays were claptrap because they were about people and not about things. Wilde's *Importance of being Earnest* was necessarily an inferior play to the same author's *The Ideal Husband,* for the latter contained an "idea" and the former did not. Ibsen was first, Shaw second, the rest, virtually nowhere. The theatre of ideas, in fact, could not, in Shaw's view, live in peace and amity with any other kind of theatre at all. It had to conquer or die.

Well, it conquered all right, and the theatre it had defeated was condemned to death, without benefit, even, of a Nuremberg; but, though duly hanged in approbrium, it strangely refused to die. Why? That surely is a question that should exercise the *avant-garde*. Despite fifty years in which the ideological drama has been in secure possession of the critical field, why has its poor prostrate foe, though reviled and execrated, continued not only to live but even to flourish? Is it merely the notoriously poor taste of audiences? Or is it—please don't laugh too soon—because that theatre, the theatre that deals with people and stories instead of with ideas and theories, is immortal? Even as I write it, I realise that such a question would nowadays not even draw a laugh in response; just a polite snigger at my poor attempt at a witty paradox.

So complete, in fact, has been the Shavian-Ibsenite victory that in 1950 any defence of the theatre they defeated is considered to be no more than a naughty heretical joke. Daily, we playwrights are exhorted to adopt themes of urgent topicality, and not a voice is raised in our defence if we refuse. That refusal is universally and blandly taken to indicate that our minds are empty of ideas, and being so, are despicable. The Shavian standpoint again, but with that unfair and dishonest retreat from the Shavian logicality which I have deplored already. We recusants and heretics can no longer claim Shakespeare as our ally, for *Hamlet* is now loaded with social significance, while *Othello* has become a plea for racial equality, *Macbeth* a disquisition on absolutism, and *Lear*—well, *Lear* baffles them a bit, but as it has baffled the rest of the human race for over three hundred years, no great weakness in the argument is apparent. We are not even allowed to cite Congreve, Sheridan and Wilde, for it is now perfectly plain that their comedies were no more than a satirical comment on the society of their day—the comedy of manners, in fact, which is as superior, ideologically speaking, to the comedy of character and situation as is Mont Blanc to the Eiffel Tower (the simile Shaw used when comparing *Peer Gynt* to *Hamlet,* but that is by the way). Tchekov, happily spared the Shavian cat o'nine tails by writing too late, is, of course, a precursor of the Russian revolution, and the *Cherry Orchard* simply drips with contemporaneity. We really have no one to turn to at all, save Pinero who is still allowed us, but whose name is, anyway, only used as a term of reproach.

Where are we then, those of us who hold, as I do, that the whole cult of the play of ideas is itself a heresy and is founded on a misconception and a misreading? In the intellectual and critical soup, without a doubt, so shunned and scorned and abhorred that no one is ever likely to take us seriously enough even to enquire what we mean. But if anyone ever did, I think I should answer him thus: "The misconception on which your cult is founded is that ideology equals intellect. It doesn't. The misreading is of Ibsen, who was considerably less interested in his own ideas than were his followers, and considerably more interested in his own characters than were his critics."

Supposing I had thus captured the imaginary interlocutor's amused interest, I would shoot this question at him: "Why is *Ghosts* a masterpiece? Because of what it says about syphilis or because of what it says about Mrs. Alving?" And then, before he had time to think that one out, I should follow it with a designedly gabbled version of my theatrical creed.

"From Aeschylus to Tennessee Williams the only theatre that has ever mattered is the theatre of character and narrative." If I said that quickly enough it would fox him, I think, because he wouldn't like to be rude to one of those young, vital American dramatists who are so busy infusing new life into our old tired theatre, and it would certainly take him a second or two to think out exactly what ideology Aeschylus propounded—was it "count no man happy until he is dead," or was that just Sophocles? Anyway, while he is trying to remember I should press on and deliver my final blasphemy: "I don't think that ideas, *per se,* social, political or moral, have a very important place in the theatre.

They definitely take third place to character and narrative, anyway. You see, if the ideas are of contemporary significance they tend to divide the audience, and if they are not they tend to confuse it. No, old chap," I would conclude, my voice by this time rising a little nervously, as I watched the flush of anger mounting in my interlocutor's cheeks, "no, old chap. The trouble with the theatre to-day is not that so few writers refuse to look the facts of the present world in the face but that so many refuse to look at anything else."

And then, as I picked myself up from the floor, felt my swelling chin and poured myself a whisky with trembling hands, I would at least feel the warm virtuous glow of the man who at last has said his little say.

The Play of Ideas

Sean O'Casey

One cannot write about people without writing about things; for the food we eat, the clothes we wear, and the roofs that shelter us are all very near to us, and without them we perish. Even the atom bomb, so far away from us, is very close to us all. So we cannot keep ideas about things out of plays. We'd have to get ideas out of life before we could remove them from the drama. Indeed the very first glimmer of the conception for a play is an idea. There's hardly a thing written as a play, a novel, or a poem, that hasn't an idea under it, hovering over it, or in its very core. Life is constantly pummelling itself with ideas from morn till midnight.

No one can write about ideas without creating persons to express them; but it is one thing to have an idea in a head and quite another to place it in a play. It takes a mastermind to do that so that it will appeal to the imagination of an audience. Shaw and Ibsen are masters of this fancy. Shaw's plays are packed with punches for all kinds of reforms, yet there's hardly one of them that isn't glittering with the fanciful guile of a dramatist. Shaw and Ibsen are Israelites in whom there's a lot of guile, and grand guile too. And *Othello* (among other plays) is a melodrama; the acting editions showed us what they actually were, when all the poetry in them had been gutted out of them. Shaw's own play, *The Devil's Disciple,* is a melodrama, but one in which an intelligent being can sigh with safety. It is full of intelligent emotion—emotion lacking in such things as *Abie's Irish Rose, The Song of Bernadette,* and many plays dealing with a son's relationship with his mother or a husband's jealousy of his wife.

Mr. Rattigan seems to cherish the thought that such plays can create characters out of themselves; that relationship of mother with son, or the jealousy of a husband used as play themes will bring forth ready-born and fully matured characters into existence and into action without any tiring interference or help on the part of the dramatist; and, that, if the dramatist only chooses a suitable theme, the characters will flock, fully fruited on to the stage. They won't. It is just as hard to create a play with the theme of a mother and son relationship, or the theme of a jealous husband as it is to create one about the theme of a honeymoon or a holy well. And, anyway, what would these themes

Reproduced with kind permission of New Statesman & Society from *New Statesman and Nation* n.s. 39 (8 April 1950).

be but psychological discussions around the relationship of mother with son and a husband's jealousy of a wife? Again, Falstaff, probably the greatest character ever thrust upon a stage, had no relationship with a mother as far as I know, nor had he a wife to be jealous of.

It is exhilarating, in a perverse way, to hear it said that Ibsen's stealthy entry into the English theatre and Shaw's determined rush on to its stage killed the drama dead, though the dead drama refused to lie down. The fact is that these two dramatists brought a dead drama back to a serious and singing life again. The zeal for the theatre that had eaten them up gave them the courage and strength to drive, helter-skelter, the foolish, fustian plays that had cluttered the stage for so long, as can be seen from a glance or two at the plays mentioned in Shaw's two volumes of *Dramatic Opinions*—plays so prodigiously trivial that their names even are unknown to the younger souls of to-day. The previous playwrights had made a simpering whore of the drama, and it took Shaw and Ibsen—though they didn't make her a lady, thank God—to change her into a vigorous, dignified, and intelligent woman, able and ready to give an answer for the hope that was in her.

There is a lot to be said for the opinion that all, or most, of the older, greater works, if not loaded, are strongly tinted with social significance; that they comment on, and often condemn, the activity and manner of their time. In England alone, from Chaucer and Langland, up to Auden and T. S. Eliot, the life we lived, religious, civil, and political, and the life we live, have been examined and commented upon according to the period in which the life was lived and the works were written. The thinker, the playwright and the poet have shared in the struggle for the rights of man; and, if they didn't wield a sword, at least they carried a banner. They have helped to immortalise man's fight against intolerance, cod custom, ignorance, and fear.

Things change life as well as thought—the railway, the motor-car, the tractor, the harvest-combine, and even the proletarian bicycle. A new kind of life is with us, whether we like it or not. And a good deal of this life will flood into the theatre. The stalls that give rest to the bums hidden in satin and silk will soon be ghosts of the past; and the new life will demand new plays that deal with and interpret the life it lives. And here comes a pause. The plays written around the new life must be currents in the mainstream of drama, must be an offspring of the great tradition. When we decide, instead of playing at being kings or queens or cavaliers, to play at being proletarians, then let us play at being them, and not send them forth as lecturers in an academy hall, preachers in a pulpit, or speakers from a political platform, important as these activities can be. The dramatist must see poetry in the smoky hub-bub of a tavern, just as he may see it in the stately ceremonial of a cathedral, though he may realise that, while the life in a tavern is always real, that of the cathedral is often a sham.

Just now, the English proletarian is immersed up to his nose in the making out of football-coupons, a minor way of getting rich quick, a method condoned by the Government and applauded by the Roman Catholic hierarchy. But this won't last: already many millions of workers and peasants in other lands are pressing towards a fuller share of the necessaries of life, and are stretching out to grasp the higher things abounding above them. I look forward to the day with confidence when British workers will carry in their hip pockets a volume of Keats's poems or a Shakespeare play beside the packets of lunch attached to their belts.

Debate and Comedy

ALICK WEST

It is a common criticism, and a just one, though less just than it is common, that a Shaw play is like a debate. It becomes so because the dramatic conflict is not fought with naked weapons. In a way, it is a sham fight, for Shaw disarms his rebels. He never equips them with his own knowledge, and he imposes on the action the solution which his Fabianism demands. He degrades his rebels, as Sergius is degraded, in order to make easier the false realist's victory over them. Sergius's Byronism remains mostly in the stage directions; so does Morell's knowledge of Marx's *Capital;* so does Gloria's moral passion and the fervour of her belief in her mother's ideas; Tanner's scathing indictment of capitalism is banished from the play. What is dramatically most deeply stirring—the tension created in the final scene of *Arms and the Man* by the silent presence of Louka; the senseless waste of a life in *You Never Can Tell,* while the revellers dance; Morell, his socialism forgotten, kneeling to a sentimental prostitute as if she were the Virgin mother; the torturing defeat of the inarticulate rebel against capitalist injustice in that ironically named play *Captain Brassbound's Conversion;* the saint's realization of the futility of the saintliness which he yet clings to; Keegan listening to his fellow-countrymen laughing in hell—all this is muted. Nevertheless, the plays beneath the play are art, not debates. But they are like ghosts, that have not been allowed to enter a body.

For they would have rent the plays to pieces. There is a repressed revolutionary creative energy in Louka, in Gloria, in Brassbound, in the contrast between the saint's abstract idealism and Anderson charging at the head of the people's militia, in Keegan's biting satire on the blessings which English imperialism will bring to Ireland, in the fierce disgust at the socialist's abject surrender to Woman—an energy which makes one hate the self-complacent, comfortable, empty realism of the Bluntschlis, the Candidas, the Lady Cicely Waynfletes, the idiotic Broadbents. Yet these people are the victors, for Fabianism demands that they shall win. At the critical moment, therefore, Shaw stops his rebel fighting, and thereby annihilates his reality. Keegan ceases

Reprinted by permission of Lawrence & Wishart Ltd. from Alick West, *George Bernard Shaw: "A Good Man Fallen among Fabians"* (London: Lawrence & Wishart Ltd., 1950).

to be Keegan when he says he will vote for imperialism, and becomes an apology for Fabianism.

Shaw checks the dramatic conflict lest its intensity should make his position of compromise untenable; he desires safety, and he therefore arranges a harmless gentlemanly duel in which the false realist will always be sure of defeating the true rebel. The consequent loss of intensity in the dramatic conflict is the price Shaw paid for glozing over with Fabianism the conflict in society.

He halts and breaks the dramatic movement, and annihilates the dramatic tension, in order that his realist may win little victories. Because he is afraid of his defeat in the real conflict of the play, he turns the play into a debate, in which his realist may score points. Because he is afraid, he will do anything to get the reassurance of a laugh. When Marchbanks cries out "Horror! horror! horror!" and bows his head on his hands, Burgess breaks in with "What! Got the orrors, Mr. Morchbanks! Oh, thats bad, at your age. You must leave it off grajally." Caesar's address to the Sphinx ends with the words, "Have I read your riddle, Sphinx?" Whereupon, Cleopatra peeps out from the Sphinx's bosom and calls, "Old gentleman."

And one is glad of it; for the laughter relieves the embarrassment at Caesar's poetry.

Shaw's comedy is as contradictory as the plays themselves. Often it has this sane, clear, gay quality: as in *Arms and the Man,* where Raina's sentimental romanticism is outraged, not by Bluntschli's "realism," which is only the same sentimental romanticism in another form, but by the ravenousness with which he eats her last three chocolate creams and turns up the box in case there may be one more; or in *Captain Brassbound's Conversion,* when Sir Howard offers to return to Brassbound his mother's estate, and Lady Cicely remarks that as the property now costs £150 a year to keep up instead of bringing in anything, it would not be of much use to him. In *You Never Can Tell,* Dolly's high spirits are so infectious that one cannot stop reading. In the stage directions, there are still more invisible laughs and smiles, necessarily lost in a performance, and a note of good-tempered satire in the description of the characters, like that in Shaw's dramatic criticisms, which gives to them a reality they do not always keep when they begin to talk and act. Very good is the description of Finch M'Comas in *You Never Can Tell:* "He is about fifty, clean-shaven and close-cropped, with the corners of his mouth turned down purposely, as if he suspected them of wanting to turn up, and was determined not to let them have their way. He has large expansive ears, cod colored eyes, and a brow kept resolutely wide open, as if, again, he had resolved in his youth to be truthful, magnanimous, and incorruptible, but had never succeeded in making that habit of mind automatic and unconscious." And Shaw can make a room as living as a person, as in his description from the same play of Valentine's operating room with its wall paper "designed, with the taste of an undertaker, in festoons and urns; the carpet with its symmetrical plans of rich, cabbagy nosegays." Always in these introductory descriptions there is a friendliness towards the reader, a felicity of phrase (like Finch M'Comas's "large expansive ears" and those "rich, cabbagy nosegays"), and a sureness and directness of movement, which make one regret the novels Shaw did not write.

Much of Shaw's comedy, as he himself has said, uses the oldest stock themes of comedy—for example, in *Arms and the Man,* all the confusions and complications with Major Petkoff's coat which Raina lent to Bluntschli and his incurably romantic disposition prompted him to return in person, and with the photograph of herself which Raina had slipped into one of the pockets; or Valentine betting his landlord his six weeks' arrears of rent that he will pull out his tooth without his feeling it, and then gassing him; or Lady Cicely telling Brassbound's men to bath the Cockney Drinkwater, who is carried off howling and appears, at the end of the critical scene between Brassbound and Lady Cecily, with his mouse-coloured hair a flaming red. Old and simple it may be, but it is always a new variation; and in its effortless exuberance it does not only repeat the old themes, but is alive with their vitality. Shaw's most perfect, though not his most expressive, work is in his short comic interludes, like *How He Lied to Her Husband,* which has the movement of the gayest, lightest music, with irresistible runs and bursts of absurdity made reasonable.

There is a philosophy in the comedy which contradicts the plays' more explicit philosophy. Dramatically, Tanner's marriage to Ann is convincing, not because he is in the grip of the Life Force (which, without the scene in Hell, means not much more to the spectator, if he derives his knowledge only from the play, than it does to Ann, who says that it sounds like the Life Guards), but because he is a comic figure. He is the rebel who thinks himself a rebel, but is not; the clever man who understands nothing; and the more he works himself up, the more he misfires. With pleased anticipation, the audience watch the woman stalk her prey, knowing in advance that the spider, the bee, the marked down victim may career all across Europe in his thousand-pound car, but he will not escape. In his final speech, Tanner may proclaim the cosmic purpose of his marriage and his bold determination to be married in a registry office and sell all the wedding presents to pay for the distribution of *The Revolutionist's Handbook;* but he is let down once more.

> "ANN: (*looking at him with fond pride and caressing his arm*) . . . Go on talking.
> TANNER: Talking!
>   *Universal laughter.*"

The dramatic action makes Tanner and his Life Force equally comic.

But it also makes *The Revolutionist's Handbook* comic, as well as the Life Force; and when one remembers what was in *The Revolutionist's Handbook,* the laughter turns sour. For it serves the purpose, like Burgess's comic Cockney, of slurring over the class issue in the plays and facilitating an easy victory for the

Bluntschlis over Sergius. Consequently, there is a certain falseness in the "good fellowship" which Shaw said, in the introduction to his *Dramatic Opinions and Essays,* it was the function of comedy to create. His comedy also must serve his Fabianism; and therefore Shaw will not give full freedom to his comic vision, because he will not fully trust in the people. Just as the plays are haunted by voices which never speak out, so the popular comedy, not the Burgess class-collaboration comedy, never finds a voice or a character to say all that it means. What it does mean, is the opposite of that mysticism that places the energy of life outside people themselves; for the comedy springs entirely from the relations and the actions of the people themselves—both on the stage and in the audience, since the awakened pleasure of the audience contributes its momentum to the action. But Shaw, still holding to his Fabianism, suddenly becomes serious, and tells himself that power is not in the people, but in the individual and in the mystic principle by which the individual flatters himself he is possessed, in the realist and his Platonic-Bismarckian reality.

The saint remains outside the comedy. There is a continual disturbing, embarrassing change of key as the action moves between the plane of comedy and the plane of the saint. There are two different levels of life, the earth of laughing people, the heaven of solitary dreams. The earthly key is so distant from the heavenly that the comedy seems almost clowning, and Shaw almost a clown against his will. There is the same metaphysical separation of the mysticism from the comedy and of the saint from the clown as separates the Life Force from real action. The same distance separates also the saint from the audience: around the figure of Keegan is thrown a kind of glamour from another world; his holiness is not for the audience, living in the ordinary world and, unlike Keegan, at home in it; the play's message for them is that they must be practical realists and remember that rebellion is vulgar.

Technique, Symbol, and Theme in
Heartbreak House

FREDERICK P. W. McDOWELL

I

Heartbreak House, begun in 1913 and completed in 1916, is one of Bernard Shaw's most provocative plays and merits fuller aesthetic analysis than his critics have yet given it. Distinctive both for its architectonic firmness and its elusive symbolism, *Heartbreak House* is one of Shaw's major accomplishments as artist. It summarizes, furthermore, the themes and attitudes of his previous work, in particular the ideas broached in "The Revolutionist's Handbook" appended to *Man and Superman* (1903). It also holds in embryo Shaw's departures in doctrine and technique in the plays beginning with *The Apple Cart* (1929).

Existing criticism is either distrustful of the play or accepts it with reservations. To a post-Edwardian like Archibald Henderson, *Heartbreak House* seems obscure, fumbling, and confused. To the impressionist Stark Young—in a revised estimate in *Immortal Shadows* (1938)—the play is crude and contrived when compared with the plenitude of Chekhov. For these critics, it is too mechanically elaborated, too packed with paradox, too brilliant in its rhetoric to be quite human in its appeal. This same distrust appears in William Irvine's *The Universe of G.B.S.* (1949), to which I am indebted in defining the symbolism of the play's characters. Irvine feels that the work becomes amorphous in its last two acts and that its comic characters are inadequate to "symbolize a tragic significance." In *The Art of Bernard Shaw* (1936) Ben Gupta alleged that the play violates probability and presents its themes incompletely. Actually, a symbolic drama like *Heartbreak House* need only conform to the realities of the pattern superposed by the artist upon his material, and valuation of character and idea can be the more incisive for being implicit. In the criticism of the play, the balance has been restored by Edward Shanks in *Bernard Shaw* (1924), by Edmund Wilson in his essay on the later Bernard Shaw (*The Triple Thinkers,* 1938), and, above all, by Eric Bentley. His *Bernard Shaw: A Reconsideration* (1947) chooses to disregard the surface

Reprinted by permission of the Modern Language Association of America from *PMLA* 68 (June 1953).

inconsistencies of the play and to apprehend it as a vital and unique organism. E. Strauss in 1942 and Blanche Patch in 1950 both reported Shaw thought this play his greatest; and in the admittedly unequal contest between "Shakes" and "Shav" in Shaw's last skit in 1949, "Shav" confidently introduces a tableau sequence from *Heartbreak House* as a sample of his *Lear*.[1] It is, moreover, a work Shaw refused to explicate beyond the hints in his lucid Preface.

In Act I of *Heartbreak House,* several visitors come to an imposing country house in Sussex at the beginning of World War I, and proceed, together with the proprietor and his family, to unburden their hearts and minds. Three principal discussions are charted in a play which observes strictly "the unities" that Shaw had made use of immediately before in *Getting Married* (1908) and *Misalliance* (1909–10). Psychologically, Act I centers on Ellie Dunn's disillusionment with her romantic lover, Hector Hushabye, who had lied to her about his identity and his exploits. Ellie despises herself for having been duped by Hector, she accepts her disenchantment stoically, and she agrees with her friend, Hesione Hushabye, that "heartbreak" is "only life educating you." The denizens of Heartbreak House have all been similarly frustrated in their romantic and spiritual aspirations, and have had to adjust to an inexorable reality. Most of them, however, have lacked the courage for an adjustment radical enough to ensure salvation. Yet their bitter realism, strange and forceful to outsiders, will, in turn, "educate" them, if they are capable of learning from experience. In Heartbreak House, Ellie thus passes beyond a false romantic exaltation to a more reasoned idealism which will no longer so calmly disregard the facts of experience.

The Second Act is another discussion after the visitors to Heartbreak House have had dinner and have become accustomed to its strangely ambiguous milieu—a mixture of the evasively artificial and the genuinely real. In this act, Mangan, the capitalist, is exposed, whom Ellie had at first been willing to marry on the rebound from Hector. The elderly and grotesque Captain Shotover, who has learned most in Heartbreak House and who is now one of those "so sufficient to themselves that they are only happy when they are stripped of everything, even of hope,"[2] convinces her that such a marriage would be self-betrayal. The introduction of a burglar for farcical effect in this act is a structural blemish since it both displaces focus from Boss Mangan and has nothing to do with the idea of "heartbreak."

The Third Act, on the lawn outside the house later in the evening, features still another discussion. It becomes increasingly frenetic as the characters feel a doom settling upon them which materializes at last in an enemy bombing raid, the only sequence in the play which leads to much overt action. In this act Ellie Dunn is disillusioned by Shotover, whose wisdom she finds to be, in large part, alcoholic. This disillusionment, however, Ellie can cope with. As a result of the insight and tolerance gained from heartbreak and experience, she can now accommodate the illusion to the reality, and can penetrate to the vein of spiritual basalt underneath the Captain's changeableness. Although this play chronicles Ellie Dunn's adjustment to life, she is only incidentally its center, for Captain Shotover and his family have actually more to do with producing its uncanny effect. Wishing to present a cross section of upper and middle class England during the early war years, Shaw introduced a number of major characters, all of whom are basic to his purpose. These characters eagerly discuss abstractions which have more than a speculative interest for them and give us, incidentally, the involutions of Shaw's own thought.

II

Its subtitle, "A Fantasia in the Russian Manner on English Themes," suggests Shaw's method in writing the play and also the extravaganzas on politics, which begin with *The Apple Cart* (1929). To a greater degree than previously, Shaw in *Heartbreak House* used characters as abstractions; in contrapuntal fashion, in fitful entrances and exits, the characters possess the vitality of recurring musical motifs. In Chekhov's dramas people who are also types drift onto the stage, say what is on their minds, indulge in discussion if so inclined, and, in capricious, erratic fashion, drift off again. Frequently they are so preoccupied that they make no attempt to comprehend other people or a total situation. Dialogue then becomes fragmented and discontinuous when characters only express themselves and make no effort to communicate with others. Weaving disconnectedly in and out of its scenes and concentrating so completely upon himself, Captain Shotover, for instance, reveals how eccentric he is, and intensifies the simmering tensions of the play. A dynamic method, this use of the disjunctive, unpredictable entrance and exit produces a greater sense of conflict among the characters than had been possible in Shaw's pre-Chekhovian disquisitory plays like *Getting Married* and *Misalliance,* upon which *Heartbreak House* was in part modelled. In *Heartbreak House,* there is more of an illusion of overt action than in these previous discussion plays, though there is, in actuality, little. The extravaganzas which follow *Heartbreak House* reveal its influence in their Chekhovian foreshortening or exaggeration of character and incident, but none of them uses its shifting technique so extensively. By virtue of its freer construction and larger imaginative lines, the fabric of *Heartbreak House* is fuller, more complexly woven, and more imposing. This carefully modulated looseness, together with its rhetorical virtuosity and its sardonic grotesquerie, unmistakably makes of *Heartbreak House* a "fantasia," and removes it further from the realist's realm than similarly foreshortened and exaggerated plays like *The Apple Cart* (1929) and *The Simpleton of the Unexpected Isles* (1934). In *Heartbreak House* a high potential of creative force operates: Shaw thereby gains credibility for a stylized imaginative world, whose relation to mundane reality is only tangential. Accordingly, characters are free to act without conforming to a rigid logic of motive. Given the bold outlines of this world, its intermittently loose accretion of substance does not mean a dissipation of intensity. In short, Shaw evoked in *Heartbreak House* an atmosphere whose flickering lights could encompass both the everyday and the domain of the spirit in its solitude.

This Chekhovian counterpoint of the perpetually dissolving scene is fused with the dialectical discussion of ideas, the principal method of earlier plays like *Captain Brassbound's Conversion, Major Barbara,* and the Hell sequence of *Man and Superman.* Just prior to the composition of *Heartbreak House,* dialectical ingenuity had been carried to its *reductio* in *Getting Married* (1908).[3] In this work, characters in shifting groups discuss ideas and do nothing else; there is no action at all if we disregard an offstage marriage, the entrance of the Lord Mayor's lady, Mrs. George, and her subsequent trance. Interactions between a personality and the ideas impinging upon it provide dramatic tensions if they do not provide the forthright dramatic scenes of *The Doctor's Dilemma, Candida,* and *Pygmalion:* action, if no longer manifest, is felt to subsist in the explosive effects of challenging ideas upon contrasting temperaments. In its discussions between tightly-joined groups of characters, *Getting Married* is symmetrically composed of a number of box-like units. Similarly constructed discussions become a chief device in *Heartbreak House* and the political extravaganzas which follow it. Though these later plays, as we have seen, are all somewhat Chekhovian in their contrapuntal use of the symbolic character and though they all reveal the influence of *Heartbreak House,* they are more significant as dialectical *tours de force* in the typically Shavian manner. If it more nearly approximates "the Russian manner" than these plays, like them *Heartbreak House* is also distinguished for its dialectical adroitness, and illustrates Shaw's life-long belief that "it is in the conflict of opinion that we win knowledge and wisdom."[4]

Without its solid basis in social polemic ever being obscured, *Heartbreak House* simultaneously achieves the quality of dream. In Shaw's play, however, overtones of nightmare creep in as cataclysm approaches, and supplant the tranquil note of Chekhovian fantasy. This is the result of Shaw's having pictured a hollow society for the Hell he deemed it to be, instead of merely having another Father Keegan declaiming that this life is Hell, "a place where the fool flourishes and the good and wise are hated and persecuted."[5] Like the Hell of *Man and Superman,* nothing is real in the Hell of *Heartbreak House,* as long as people persist in wearing their usual masks. Because its roots are in social actuality, the Hell of Heartbreak House is far more terrifying and macabre than the brittler, more serene nether world of quiet dream featured in *Man and Superman.* The murky brilliance of *Heartbreak House,* its continuing energy, and its emotional stridencies, often approaching the hysterical, separate the play in mood from Chekhov and bring it closer to Dostoevski or to the Tolstoy of *The Power of Darkness.* To argue either that Shaw is inferior to Chekhov or that Chekhov's influence upon Shaw was negligible is beside the point. The subtitle of the play establishes the fact that its technique is Russian (and specifically Chekhovian), but its themes English or Shavian. If the themes are thus Shavian, so is the tone generated by them. Shaw's characters, too, are his own and establish the authentic Shavian mood. As in Chekhov, symbolic purport of a character does not obscure his existence as a human being, but the coincidence of the two in Shaw is tighter. Shaw's characters are thus a degree closer to the allegorical, and are less tentative, less creatures of whim, and less passive.

Although Shaw's characters are more impersonal than Chekhov's, still in *Heartbreak House* and in most of the discussion plays thereafter the links between individual and abstraction are tenuous enough to ensure his vitality. To contrast with the static figures of allegory, Shaw's characters in these later plays are receptive to experience and assimilate it eagerly; from it they seek to extend their own ideas rather than to impose them upon it. Being capable of development, they thirst for a moment of revelation and the rebirth of spirit it leads to. Like the Tanner of *Man and Superman,* they feel that "the birth . . . of moral passion" is a transcendent experience. In many of Shaw's earlier plays, one or more characters are "educated" by a "superior" person less given to false illusions—Brassbound and Hallam are disabused by Lady Cecily Waynflete, or Anthony Anderson and his wife are instructed by Dick Dudgeon. The self-knowledge achieved is efficacious, spiritual change results. *Heartbreak House* and the plays after it are also "conversion" plays, but follow the lead established in Shaw's middle period by *Major Barbara, John Bull's Other Island,* and *Androcles and the Lion.* In these plays self-knowledge has become more acutely self-conscious, and results from a character's own sensitivity to disheartening circumstance rather than from the influence over him of a superior individual. Drama in the relatively plotless plays which follow this middle period is conceived more pointedly still as a spiritual awakening—witness the Patient's rejection of ignoble ease once she is aware of it in *Too True to Be Good* (1932), the education of Sir Arthur Chavender to political reality by retirement to a Welsh sanatorium in *On the Rocks* (1933), and the dedication of Pra and Prola to a purposive future in *The Simpleton of the Unexpected Isles* (1934).

If the characters in these later plays are sometimes one-dimensional—as with Boss Mangan in *Heartbreak House*—and are grotesques in the manner of Dickens, they more often have greater complexity. Merely "flat" characters would be incapable of the continued development Shaw posits for his main figures. Even grotesques like Captain Shotover and Lady Ariadne Utterword possess unexpected depths below their surface peculiarities. At his best, Shaw has been able not only to fuse abstractions with personality, but to give it psychological density as well. Part of this richness of impression produced by the stylized characters of *Heartbreak House* results from the extensions of meaning they acquire when Shaw makes of them recognizable literary types or associates them with myth and legend. It is significant, too, that, except for Ellie Dunn, all the characters in the play are at least middle-aged, and have, to offset their present esoteric propensities, an authenticity conferred by manifold realistic experience in the past. The wealth of suggestion associated with the loosely symbolical, and absent from the tightly allegorical, informs the majority of Shaw's characters in this play. Shaw, in fact, recognized the danger of the allegorical oversimplification of character from the days of *The Perfect Wagnerite* (1898). In practice, he managed to avoid this danger in most of his later work: "an allegory is never quite consistent except when it is written by someone without dramatic faculty, in which case it is unreadable. There is only one way of dramatizing an idea; and that is by putting on the stage a human being possessed by that idea, yet none the less a human being with all the human impulses which make him akin and interesting to us."[6]

III

In the play, symbolic characters move about within the confines of an elusive and complex symbol of social England and, by extension, of pre-World War I Europe, Heartbreak House itself: says Shaw, "It is cultured, leisured Europe before the war" (p. ix). The accoutrements of the manor are all symbol. The main drawing-room, in the form of a ship, indicates England's maritime supremacy and her colonial enterprise. A drawing-board and vise therein are symbols of a like supremacy in the crafts and industry; a teak table, and an observatory and flagstaff outside, connote her role as leader of an empire. To Lady Utterword, coming back to Heartbreak House after many years, it possesses "the same disorder in ideas, in talk, in feeling" which had driven her from it. It is, as Ellie Dunn claims, an "agonizing house," a "house without foundations," in short, the house erected by aristocrats on the shifting sands of their own indifference. The barbarian aristocrats, like the Philistine middle class, have become skilled in acquiring money and in exploiting men, yet they do it with a difference. The world of Heartbreak House, artificial and hollow as it is, is preferable to the more energetic but completely amoral world on the outside, to the fiercely competitive and inhumane world of business. If the House represents an England adrift without standards, it also encloses within it the drifting soul, and becomes a symbol of that soul. In its residual integrity, the soul will not tolerate impostors like an unrepentant Mangan. Life in Heartbreak House, hypocritical as it sometimes is, has yet within itself the probity essential to salvation, as Hector Hushabye indicates to Randall, Lady Utterword's ineffectual lover: "In this house we know all the poses: our game is to find out the man under the pose" (p. 93). Heartbreak House is at once a symbol of a moribund aristocracy or a moribund England—as such it is a veritable Hell on earth—and a symbol of the enlightenment and rebirth of which it is capable—as such it holds within it the promise of Heaven on earth. Rebirth is at present possible for the individual Englishman in Heartbreak House; but Shaw is insistent that war-time England as a nation has not yet broken through convention to knowledge of its possibilities, simply because most individual Englishmen are apathetic.

Nurse Guinness, who is the shrewd but uneducated Briton and the chief servant in Heartbreak House, tells Ellie Dunn that "this house is full of surprises for them that don't know our ways" (p. 4). The biggest surprise of all is the proprietor himself, Captain Shotover. He is the gruff, irascible, unpredictable squire of literature, who, true to type, produces frustration when he tries to be kind to Ellie Dunn and whose captious behavior perplexes all outsiders. If like the aristocracy he is out of touch with social reality, he, like the elusive genius of England he also represents, is in touch with a spiritual reality which will ensure his ultimate salvation and that of his class. Once its members are forcibly awakened, they will become responsible leaders and redeem a now calloused England. Since Shotover possesses long-range vision and since his instincts make him uneasy about the present order, he is entitled to be England's critic in spite of his blindness to imminent reality, or his false illusions about it. The trouble is that the spirituality of which Shotover and England are capable has never been applied to her pressing social problems. Shotover has done glorious deeds in the past and is now frustrated by his incapacity. He is inadequate to the oppressive present which he can only evade through rum. Only when he is drunk can he escape the dreams which torture him when he is sober, the dreams or the idealism or the life-giving illusions which he now tries to repudiate, which have guided him so well in the past, which he must return to if he is to keep the ship of souls, Heartbreak House, from foundering "on the rocks."

To maintain order on a ship with desperadoes for crew, Captain Shotover had been forced to sell his soul in Zanzibar to the Devil and had purportedly married a "black witch." We find in the Captain overtones not only of the latent superman, but of the world-weary Faust as well. The outlines of the legend are thrown into high relief by the Captain's grotesquerie: he is both Faust and his parody, a great soul and its caricature. Tense, whimsical, mercurial, iconoclastic, the Captain is less perceptibly concerned with his own soul than is Faust. When the Captain does focus upon the Eternal, the process, if heartfelt and sincere, is faintly ludicrous: the incongruity between his intermittently farcial behavior and his serious cogitations will not leave our minds. The Faust-like thirst, by an apparent madman, for wisdom and knowledge, amounts, at times, to patent absurdity, an absurdity far richer in its possibilities, however, than static conventionality.

The symbolism underlying this Zanzibar episode is richly ambiguous; besides a condemnation of England for her failure in colonial leadership, a less pejorative interpretation asserts itself. The Captain finds that a knowledge of evil provides a deepened insight and a preliminary to salvation: it enables him to be "redeemed" by his negress wife in Jamaica some time later. To know the workings of God, the ramifications of the Life Force, one must be in part the Devil's disciple. One must know the suffering caused by evil, in Shaw's view a misplaced spiritual energy or an aborted self-fulfillment; and he must also realize that much of what the world considers good is but hardened convention, is, in actuality, the most insidious sort of evil because it masquerades as good. As Bishop Bridgenorth puts it in *Getting Married*, "If we are going to discuss ethical questions, we must begin by giving the devil fair play . . . England never does . . . And the consequence is that we overreach ourselves; and that the devil gets the better of us after all. Perhaps thats what most of us intend him to do."[7]

Despite his present waverings and evasions, despite downward revisions entailed by experience and disillusion, despite his failure to attain a definitive balance between the real and the ideal, the Captain's hard core of idealism entitles him to be a spiritual judge, as England herself, despite her shortcomings, must hold others to the ideals she sometimes inexcusably disregards. If it lets him disregard the immediate present, this vein of imperishable illusion causes Shotover to aspire to fuller and deeper knowledge, to "the seventh degree of concentration," a disembodied mental state which anticipates the "whirlpool in pure force" desired by the ancients in *Back to Methuselah*. Through this seventh degree of concentration, he hopes to discover a psychic ray, which will destroy all those who prey upon the human race and too openly flout, therefore, his remaining idealism. To find his psychic ray, the Captain continually experiments with dynamite in the garden outside his house. This dynamite is a complex symbol, at once representing the destructiveness and chaos—the death wish—at the heart of modern civilization; the nemesis which dogs the heels of modern man; in the Captain's experimenting with it, the need to live dangerously; and, in its explosive proximity to the stolid barony of Heartbreak House, the violence and absurdity of modern life.

The Captain's daughter, Hesione Hushabye, is an incarnation of feminine energy; her first name recalls the less aggressive femininity of the Hesione of mythology, whose husband, Telamon, is the sort of hero that Hector Hushabye ought to have been. One of the "mystical progeny" of Captain Shotover and the witch of Zanzibar, she is *la femme fatale*, the absorbing woman who calmly, even eagerly, wreaks destruction upon a prostrate lover and who accepts the annihilation of his personality as her just due. She is a further refinement upon the acquisitive, passionate women of Shaw's early plays, especially as that type had developed into the sexually possessive Ann Whitefield of *Man and Superman*. Ellie Dunn, successively her friend and antagonist, recognizes Hesione's malevolent influence, and can accuse her of obliterating her husband Hector's identity, while Hector himself says of the Captain's daughters: "There is some damnable quality in them that destroys men's moral sense, and carries them beyond honor and dishonor" (p. 38). A deep and inexhaustible vitality aligns her at times with the earth-force, the "Hertha" of Germanic mythology, or with the *élan vital* of creative evolution. She becomes, in fact, a more disembodied incarnation of the Life Force than her prototype, Ann Whitefield, had been.

Of "statuesque contour," Hesione has a formidable spirit of enterprise, which sweeps away all opposition and which ought to be more constructively employed than in taming a husband. If in comparison with her sister, Lady Utterword, she represents the British home-bred female, like the more intelligent women of this class she finds domestic horizons too constricting. Kindly but officiously she seeks, therefore, to manage the personal life of her friend, Ellie Dunn. Hesione's restricted life has also interfered with her intellectual development, so that she has little conception of ultimate issues. Why Ellie Dunn reads Shakespeare or why Mazzini Dunn should have selflessly devoted his life to liberal politics is incomprehensible to her. These deep-lying concerns are beyond the grasp of a purely instinctive, untrained femininity. With her restlessness she unites an engaging candor which enables her to admit upon Ellie's questioning that her beautiful hair is partly false, to reject the pretentiousness of her sister, and to countenance extra-marital love for her husband, if it would allow him to regain the exaltation he had once known with her.

If Captain Shotover is the archetype of the sage disguised as madman, Hector Hushabye, Hesione's husband, is the archetype of the hero disguised as fool, a latter-day Parsifal. At the beginning, his energies are creative, but they have been watered down by Hesione's aggressive maternalism: he is "married right up to the hilt." Half longing for the affection he despises and which undermines him, he is the half-willing victim of a mother-fixation. The name Hushabye indicates in Hesione's case the outpouring of possessive passion; in her husband's case, its mute reception. His first name, Hector, points to a sleeping heroism which awakens in crisis, when the burglar intrudes in the second act, and then when the planes come over at the end of the play. The Captain, as the spirit of England, brings out the best in Hector, who symbolizes the present undirected heroism of her young men.

How difficult it is in modern life for primitive energies to express themselves constructively is seen in Hector's thwarted romanticism. A modern Othello in imaginative power, he relates his purely fictitious exploits to any Desdemona who will incline her ear, whereas he never mentions his real acts of daring and heroism. His ruin has been his intriguing moustache, irresistible to women; equally irresistible are the Arabian costumes his wife insists he wear instead of evening clothes. Hector thus squanders on sexual will-of-the-wisps the energy of a spacious soul, not at home in the modern world. Frustrated heroism becomes infantile maundering, or else romantic bluster, when, with an imagined adversary, he goes through a pantomime sword-play. In spite of his strong instincts and his recurring strength of vision, he is defeated by a society not yet ready for the radical altruism potentially his.

Captain Shotover's other daughter is Lady Ariadne Utterword, as artificial, as voluble, as punctilious as her name would signify, yet not without some of the winsome appeal of the deserted Ariadne of mythology. Vital and feminine, she yet has some of the grand manner about her, too, especially in the scenes she stages from time to time. She is English hypocrisy at home and abroad, and yet not so gratuitously foolish, says Shaw, as she at first seems. She is respectability incarnate, and dreads the need to think independently; like Tartuffe or her prototype, Fielding's Lady Booby, she has no aversion to hiding behind convention when it suits her purpose. Exuding more powerfully than Hesione "the strange fascination of the daughters of that supernatural old man," Lady Ariadne as vampire invites Hector to be her lover so long as he is discreet: "I am a woman of the world, Hector; and I can assure you that if you will only take the trouble always to do the perfectly correct thing, and to say the perfectly correct thing, you can do just as you like" (p. 38).

Her hypocrisy has a wider significance, for it embodies what Shaw later expressed about social England: "Bourgeois morality is largely a system of making cheap virtue a cloak for disastrous vices."[8] Through her as through the capitalist, Mangan, Shaw condemns middle and upper class England as one "huge conspiracy and hypocrisy."[9] Both would agree with one of Mangan's prototypes, the Sir George Crofts of *Mrs. Warren's Profession,* that "the world isnt such a bad place as the croakers make out. As long as you dont fly openly in the face of society, society doesnt ask any inconvenient questions; and it makes precious short work of the cads who do. There are no secrets better kept than the secrets everybody guesses."[10] As wife to a governor of a crown colony, her love of power and of exaggerated deference have been satisfied abroad. Her pride, her overbearing nature, and her love of caste are repudiated by her father, who—as honorable England—throughout the play refuses to recognize her. Better the disorder and chaos of Heartbreak House than the desiccated sense of propriety that Lady Utterword would impose upon it. She can only understand a prescriptive morality; she has "goodness" rather than "virtue," to reverse Shaw's observation upon Julius Caesar.

In Lady Utterword are united a horror of the unalloyed truth and a cold heart. Though she has come home for her health to Heartbreak House, no one can cure her of self-induced heartlessness. Alone of the people in Heartbreak House, she cannot learn from experience since she alone has no heart to break—even Boss Mangan is more emotionally responsive than she. Some gleam of salvation appears possible for her, however; she at least regrets her lack of heart, although at the end she resists the change she feels the house is working upon her: "It wants to break my heart too. But it shan't" (p. 112). Here is the "change of heart" motif which appears in all the later Shaw and which he had previously stressed in "The Revolutionist's Handbook" of *Man and Superman,* the contention "that man will return to his idols and cupidities, in spite of all 'movements' and all revolutions, until his nature is changed."[11] If England is to survive as leader of an empire, if she is to set her own house in order at home, she can no longer muddle through under unregenerate laissez-faire, but must continually supplement, in Ruskinian fashion, the arid political economy of tradition with irrationalist insights to make from it "vital economy." Thus Ariadne wishes sporadically for the regeneration, the

Forsterian sympathy and understanding heart, from which she would recoil were it to come. Imperialistic pride is reinforced by pride of caste at home when, at the end of the play, Lady Utterword refuses to take shelter in an air-raid cellar because the servants are there. Like England's fumbling attempts at political reform, Lady Utterword's self-lacerations produce no lasting effect. A momentary humility fades away when she can accuse Ellie Dunn of her own besetting deficiency, an overwhelming conceit. Like Lady Utterword, political England will also go on its unthinking way until hauled up short by disaster. At present it is blind to the workings of divine Grace which must precede reform and which alone can sustain it. The play is thus more radical than any doctrinaire advocacy of socialism could have made it: it treats symbolically the more fundamental question of the foundations for an enduring liberalism.

The first of the three visitors to arrive at Heartbreak House and to be disconcerted by the candor there is Ellie Dunn. She possesses the youth, beauty, and novelty which Captain Shotover says are needed in this House to revitalize it. She is, accordingly, English youth and womanhood at its best—by extension England at its best—with her resourcefulness, her resilience, and her intelligence. So consistently is her name linked with Shakespeare's that some of the virginal strength of his heroines gathers about her. Like Barbara Undershaft and Lavinia, whom she resembles, Ellie does not lose her illusions, but she has had to revise them radically; heartbreak, if shattering, is at least "the beginning of peace." It is thus proper that at the end of the play she should become Captain Shotover's "white wife," that she should give her "broken heart" and "strong sound soul to its natural Captain, my spiritual husband and second father" (p. 109).

Ellie's father, Mazzini Dunn, is a man of resourcefulness and character, whose first name betokens his liberalist idealism. In fact, he hearkens so closely to the ideal that he becomes an easy prey to anyone unscrupulous enough to exploit him and his brains. His principles are beyond reproach, yet he lacks the vigor and the realism to objectify them in action. A curious narrowness of vision, too, is implied in his inability to comprehend his daughter's romantic cravings early in the play and her psychological difficulties, then and later. In short, his idealism is too self-contained to be effective, and his life-illusion too abstract and programmatic. The point of the satire upon Mendoza and his brigands in *Man and Superman* is once again made here, that a doctrinaire liberalism is often unrealistic, if not socially dangerous. Mazzini and, to a degree, Hector Hushabye and Captain Shotover represent the futility of an active idealism without a discriminating political intelligence. If Ariadne's lack of heart is appalling, almost as alarming is Mazzini's unrealism. Like the aristocrats, he trusts too implicitly to drift; his past disillusionments prevent him from being prepared for the emergencies that are soon bound to come. That Mazzini's idealism is vulnerable is implied in the way he quails before Hesione's plain speaking: he will not be the "happier" for it, he says.

Mazzini is, however, an admirable character, witness his respect for culture as symbolized in an unqualified love for Shakespeare and the quixotic fervor of his convictions. His troubles are those any saint would experience in the alien world of capitalism; and the way he is mercilessly utilized by the worthless Mangan poses the perennial Shavian question: "Does society deserve its potential saviors?" His is a short-range saintly impracticality balanced by a long-range sureness of vision. In this respect, he looks forward to Saint Joan and back to Father Keegan of *John Bull's Other Island,* and represents perhaps what Father Keegan might have been had he come under the heel of Broadbent.

The butt of the play and its principal object of satire is Boss Mangan. Though he is respected in the city, he complains he is looked upon as a fool in Heartbreak House. He is the court fool, or the Vice in the morality plays, but the victim of the farcical and the slapstick rather than the victimizer; he is a Falstaff without the joviality, the cause that wit is in other men, if lacking it himself. He has succeeded because he has no moral inhibition, because he is more unscrupulous than any of the other characters. Through superior cunning and resort to the law of the jungle in business, Mangan has lent Mazzini just enough money to float his enterprises but not enough to remain solvent. Mangan closes in at the kill and buys them up; as Shaw described this process in *The Intelligent Woman's Guide to Socialism and Capitalism* (1928), "the money is made by coming in on the third reconstruction."[12] Under capitalism, Shaw maintains, the spoils belong to the victor who has had no part in producing them.

Mangan has also usurped Hector Hushabye's role of leader; his self-righteous, aggressive social Darwinism is more immediately effective, too, than the wisdom of Shotover. With respect to humanistic values, Mangan's mind is sterile; he "takes no risk in ideas" and confines his thinking to a saving of sixpence at all costs. Mangan is ruthless at several removes, as the interlocking directorates and holding companies of modern finance appeared to the socialists. That Mangan only seems formidable is revealed by how easily Ellie Dunn hypnotizes him in the second act and by how completely he loses control when, as the result of his sojourn in Heartbreak House, he is unmasked. He objects to this stripping away of pretense, because he has so much to hide, so little to show that is positive, and so little in the way of moral reserves. The illusion he lives by—that sheer brutality is the only sort of power—is false, yet he stubbornly refuses to recognize that fact. Hector in disgust says that Mangan is not even a great swindler, but only an empty façade of a man.

If spiritually Mangan does not exist, professionally he has also become a shadowy figure. The captain of industry, even if he is ruthless in his methods, no longer has tangible control over his holdings. With some truth, Mangan can say that his is "a dog's life" and that he doesn't own anything. Hollow as he is, Mangan from another point of view is all too solidly real. Through English lethargy, he has become a power in the government, operating silently but with deadly intent behind the scenes, as the immovable road-block to the constructive energies of others. Like Undershaft and Lazarus, Mangan *is* the government of his country; if Mangan has Undershaft's cunning, however, he does not have his social intelligence. He is rather a caricature of the amoral capitalist in Shaw's previous plays, a Sir George Crofts, a Hector Malone Senior, a Broadbent bereft of their modicum of dignity. Mangan is made monstrous by Shaw's hatred for what he represents, and is to Shotover one of "these hogs to whom the universe is nothing but a machine for greasing their bristles and filling their snouts" (p. 42).

The rich and suggestive texture of the play makes credible a character who never appears, a Hastings Utterword, the "numskull" colonial official, "governor of all the crown colonies in succession." In his lack of feeling he is more consistent than his wife, "heartless" Lady Ariadne, who is subject at least to fits of introspective realism and frequent amorous transports. If unnatural pride dams up the springs of Ariadne's humanity, the springs with Hastings have all but dried up, so that Ariadne herself can say of him, "Catch anyone breaking Hastings' heart!" (p. 114). Distinguished by his ability "to work sixteen hours a day at the dullest detail," he soon forges ahead; his stolidity, says Lady Utterword, will yet win out over the naïve idealism of Mazzini and the one-dimensional cunning of Mangan. Unfeeling stolidity becomes a more formidable danger, in Shaw's eyes, than forthright felony, since it assumes so readily the guise of an august benevolence and is, therefore, not easily known for the sham that it is. As the evil genius in the British character which most needs repudiation, the specter of Hastings' personality flutters over the scene. It is significant that Hastings never gets to Heartbreak House. Whereas catastrophe will entail a change of heart—only abortive it is true in Ariadne's case—for the other characters, Hastings, most in need of inner light, is furthest from experiencing it. Hastings forces us to realize how formidable, yet how inescapable, is the spiritual revolution required to countermand "this half-century of the drift to the abyss" (p. xviii).

IV

With these characters to give intellectual consistency to them, Shaw works out certain themes and conveys certain truths. Foremost is the truth that there is no final truth, that truth is tentative, relative, unfolding itself in time, like the Life Force which embodies it. Truth is not fixed or constricted; inflexible and water-tight categories represent but partial views; rigidly absolute distinctions and standards are false distinctions and standards. In Shaw's view, as expressed in the late play *Buoyant Billions* (1947), most people think uncritically in terms of "either soot or whitewash." More supple of mind, Hesione Hushabye in *Heartbreak House* comments with understanding upon her erring husband to Ellie Dunn: "People don't have their virtues and vices in sets: they have them anyhow: all mixed" (p. 27). All the characters in *Heartbreak House* are a mixture of the strong and the weak; admirable qualities are hardly to be separated from the reprehensible. In this play, Shaw is interested in the multiple facets of personality, in the same way he claimed to be in *Everybody's Political What's What* (1944): "It is generally admitted that even good men have their weaknesses: what is less recognized is that rascals have their points of honor."[13] Despicable as he is, even Mangan has a vigor and enterprise lacking in his effete antagonists, recalling in this respect the Lopahin of *The Cherry Orchard*. That even his qualities are necessary to a reconstructed England is implied early in the play when Captain Shotover, representing elder England, claims that both Mazzini Dunn, the political idealist, and Mangan, the energetic capitalist, are needed for work in his garden—though Shotover soon dismisses Mangan as "not able-bodied." *Heartbreak House* itself is a composite fabric of ideas and attitudes advocated by these "mixed" characters as Shaw's mouthpieces. The truth being thus provisional and the fusion of partial views, Shaw adopts paradox as basic. Sensitive to opposing forces in a given situation, Shaw stresses a Coleridgean or Nietzschean polarity, the dynamic principle that truth is a resolution of conflicting opposites rather than an initial accommodation to preconceived categories.

The borderline relationship between sanity and madness, between truth and absurdity, is the chief paradox of the play, as it had been of others like *John Bull's Other Island*. Hesione Hushabye's observation early in the play upon her father's idiosyncrasies sets its psychological tone, "He is as mad as a hatter, you know, but quite harmless and extremely clever" (p. 14). If less violent and incoherent, the Captain has the anarchic largeness of line and the nervous intensity of Dostoevski's underground man; at least they both hate bitterly the "straightforward" man of action. The purport of this work is that the apparently mad are in reality the sane: the most sensible individuals are Captain Shotover, carrying about with him his sticks of dynamite, coming out with startling statements, and struggling to achieve the seventh degree of concentration; Hector Hushabye, the ineffectual marital "lap-dog"; and Mazzini Dunn, the impassioned but quixotic liberal. Conversely, the all-too-sane person like Mangan has no real strength in a crisis, and the "respectable" and socially domineering Lady Utterword has no final grasp on reality. Neither one possesses a perceptive imagination, and its concomitant, self-criticism. One striking feature of this play is the way it chronicles the transition in Hector Hushabye and Shotover from apparent incapacity or insanity to an undeniable competence or wisdom. The Captain's wisdom, for instance, is definitely established at the end of the second act when his burglar antagonist, Billy Dunn, pays tribute to his marvelous powers of perception. Fools become prophets, saviors, healing powers in a society going on the rocks because it is so timorously sane, while its capitalist tin-gods or its slaves to hypocrisy are its real fools. The opposite to the normally accepted view is often the truth. Ellie Dunn, for example, rejects the widespread fallacy that sex attraction is the prime requisite for marriage, and allies herself spiritually with the Captain instead of seeking once again the romantic ecstasies she had known briefly with Hector. If reality consists of a dynamic mosaic of conflicting forces, any valid philosophy of life must therefore reconcile its discordancies: this fusion of opposites, of the ideal with the pragmatic, of the illusion with the reality, of youthful dream and aged wisdom, is intimated in the union between Ellie Dunn and the Captain.

Far along in the play, Lady Utterword says of Heartbreak House that all it lacks is horses, and, without meaning to do so directly, she exposes the weakness of this country-house society: it consists of two sorts, she says, the equestrian, and the neurotic. Both these sets—the extrovert inhabitants of Horseback Hall with their quest of stolid pleasure and the introvert inhabitants of Heartbreak House with their self-centered neuroticism—have squandered their spiritual patrimony. This class has put culture and power into "separate compartments," exploiting a genteel culture to buttress a hollow respectability, while rejecting the rightful uses of power; it has kept its Karl Marx and its Henry George and its William Morris and its John Ruskin on the library shelf. It has defied the will of God instead of working to make it prevail; it has scorned the social passion for doing good as it has all the other life-giving passions. In varying degree, moral earnestness survives in Hector Hushabye, Mazzini Dunn, and Captain Shotover as a harsh indignation against the indifferentism of present-day England. It is difficult for even this saving but discouraged remnant to keep its eye on reality; it is much easier to glance away from it, as Captain Shotover does through the opiate of rum. The aristocracy, Mazzini Dunn says, "are very charming people, most advanced, unprejudiced, frank, humane, unconventional, democratic, free-thinking, and everything that is delightful to thoughtful people" (p. 114). He is even at ease with them in his pajamas—where else could he feel that way? And yet these people will not think beyond their immediate needs; they apparently do not know "how suddenly a civilization which has long ceased to think (or in the old phrase to watch and pray) can fall to pieces when the vulgar belief in its hypocrisies and impostures, can no longer hold out against its failure and scandals."[14] In the powerful close to the first act, this charming but disastrous irresponsibility is pointed up. Hesione Hushabye needs money to run the house; she turns to her father, Captain Shotover, the eccentric inventor, and asks him for it. Why is he so behindhand with his latest death-dealing invention, "something that will murder half Europe at one bang"? Doesn't he know that they can't live on nothing? Better to live on the proceeds of death and keep up the gaiety of the Hall, to fiddle while Europe burns, than to exist more modestly. A short, sweet, swift, gay life is best even if it ends by tempting fate.

Captain Shotover as England's critic is disgusted with the pointless lives his daughters and their men are leading, and with the utilitarian ethic of the younger generation—though in his own failure to bring his ideals to bear fruitfully upon modern life he had also shirked his responsibilities. Now, having examined present-day England and seen what it is, he no longer feels he can evade them; he is almost overwhelmed by how corrupt and rotten society has by now become. In a poetic passage which once more elaborates a concept broached in *Man and Superman,* "to be in hell is to drift: to be in heaven is to steer," Shotover repudiates the course of drift which is now England's and which is bound to result in wreck:

CAPTAIN SHOTOVER: At sea nothing happens to the sea. Nothing happens to the sky. The sun comes up from the east and goes down to the west. The moon grows from a sickle to an arc lamp, and comes later and later until she is lost in the light as other things are lost in the darkness. After the typhoon, the flying-fish glitter in the sunshine like birds. It's amazing how they get along, all things considered. Nothing happens, except something not worth mentioning.

ELLIE: What is that, O Captain, O my captain?

CAPTAIN SHOTOVER: [*savagely*] Nothing but the smash of the drunken skipper's ship on the rocks, the splintering of her rotten timbers, the tearing of her rusty plates, the drowning of the crew like rats in a trap. (p. 116)

England's drifting has been the more ruinous since she has neatly provided herself with a rationale for all her evasions: a strict determinism, which has taken "mind from the universe" and has ended in "the banishment of conscience from human affairs" (p. xvii).

The chief sins of modern society are, as we have seen, hypocrisy and an adherence to, or at least toleration of, capitalist values. These devils are now so entrenched that their violent exorcising is necessary. The time is past when theorizing and a half-hearted liberalism will suffice; more than gradualist reform is needed to awaken an indifferent England, oblivious still to spiritual realities. Unlike the Don Juan of *Man and Superman,* the artist-philosopher of *Heartbreak House,* Captain Shotover, is no longer at ease in his Platonic heaven of contemplation. Neither has England heeded the warnings of those who, like the Captain and Mazzini Dunn, have had some idea where she is heading. Only a catastrophe can now lead to regeneration, a catastrophe symbolic of the violence Shaw now began to feel necessary to effect social change, a violence implicit in Tanner's "The Revolutionist's Handbook" (1903), as it had been latent in even the mild dynamic of the Fabians. All that will save England, the Captain asserts, is that clear thinking and that decisive action she now seems to have lost. Hector Hushabye also feels things can't last as they are: "We sit here talking, and leave everything to Mangan and to chance and to the devil. Think of the powers of destruction that Mangan and his mutual admiration gang wield! It's madness: it's like giving a torpedo to a badly brought up child to play at earthquakes with" (p. 115). Hector had said previously when a distant drumming had been heard in the sky—Shaw's adaptation of the harplike twanging in *The Cherry Orchard*—that it was no railroad train but "Heaven's threatening growl of disgust at us useless futile creatures. I tell you, one of two things must happen. Either out of that darkness some new creation will come to supplant us as we have supplanted the animals, or the heavens will fall in thunder and destroy us" (p. 100). Thus is combined the theme of nemesis and of creative evolution, Euripides is given a Bergsonian tinge.

Shaw has, in effect, domesticated into the English social scene the *Götterdämmerung* of Wagner. In a 1922 Preface to *The Perfect Wagnerite,* Shaw admitted the applicability of its theme—the forcible supplanting of the established order before spiritual renewal may begin—to the Western Europe of World War I. In the Preface to *Heartbreak House,* Shaw had stated that "nature's long credits" can be exhausted through "reckless overdrafts"; then it is all up save for the catastrophe we have willed. In the last act of the play, the rumbling in the sky grows louder, Ellie and Hesione believe it to be Beethoven, Hector recklessly turns up the lights and raises the blinds to invoke the calamity he hopes will be a scourge. With resolution, the late irresponsibles await their doom, "a melancholy accomplishment" at best, this dying, Shaw says, since their lives have been futile. Yet this courage counts greatly in their favor and will abruptly propel them toward a more purposive future, should they escape the extremity now threatening them. Impending ruin causes them at last to feel the force of Don Juan's declaration in *Man and Superman* that "it is not death that matters but the fear of death. It is not killing and dying that degrades us, but base living, and accepting the wages and profits of degradation" (p. 110). With pride, Shotover can say at the end of the play: "The judgment has come. Courage will not save you; but it will show that your souls are still live" (p. 120). Those who turn their backs to the challenge are destroyed: Boss Mangan and the burglar, Billy Dunn, who both have mulcted society, are appropriately blown up with the dynamite of Captain Shotover. Even the weakest of the Heartbreak House inhabitants, Randall the Rotter, the ineffectual lover of Lady Utterword, whose only accomplishment is flute-playing, has felt renewal from his defiance of Fate. After the raid he and his flute make contact, and to the sprightly notes of "Keep the Home Fires Burning," the curtain goes down.

In the ever-shifting conspectus of the play, its final tragic chords are aptly resolved in the farcical. Even a tragic catharsis must not be taken too seriously, Shaw would imply—or perhaps modern life cannot educe the wholly tragic, since we have lost a religious basis for art and life. The absurd will out in even the profoundest spectacle. More onerous than any mere Götterdämmerung, Shaw hazards, would be a lethargic acceptance of a benumbing fate, an all too likely contingency were we to lose the thread of the absurd, the critical objectivity of the comic spirit as a preliminary to decisive action.

The key to the later Shaw is in *Heartbreak House,* the passing beyond self-knowledge to positive action, action, however, deriving from resources deep within. Shaw recognizes now the heroic element in Nietzschean striving and would insist that the will must actively direct these dynamic forces within. Accordingly, the men who give in without struggle to the "demon daughters" of Captain Shotover and allow themselves to be propelled "beyond honor and dishonor," who drift with their emotions, only confound self-realization with self-enjoyment. In *Heartbreak House,* a worthy self-realization entails a Puritan voluntarism, wherewith to render vision effective. The Captain therefore can say that the "man with the thorn in the flesh," not with the pretty woman, does the most with his life: happiness in itself is not a good, because "happy" people are only half alive. The Captain and Hector sporadically inveigh against women because they entangle men and make them forget everything but love: Hector asks, "Is there any slavery on earth viler than this slavery of men to women?" (p. 97) and the Captain will join Boss Mangan should he ever find "the land where there is happiness and where there are no women" (p. 72).

For the regeneration of society, the spiritually disembodied superman is no longer enough. *Heartbreak House* elaborates the famous paradox in "The Epistle Dedicatory" to *Man and Superman,* that a constructive self-realization implies an eventual renunciation of self: "This is the true joy of life, the being used for a purpose recognized by yourself as a mighty one; the being thoroughly worn out before you are thrown on the scrap heap; the being a force of Nature instead of a feverish selfish little clod of ailments and grievances complaining that the world will not devote itself to making you happy. And also the only real tragedy in life is the being used by personally minded men for purposes which you recognize to be base" (p. xxxi). The so-called religious plays which follow *Man and Superman—John Bull's Other Island, Androcles and the Lion, Back to Methuselah,* and *Saint Joan*—explore the nature of this "purpose" as it bears upon personal psychology; *Major Barbara* and *Heartbreak House* assert that absorption in such a purpose is not enough if it blunts our social perceptions, a point of view Shaw remained loyal to in the plays which follow *The Apple Cart* (1929). In *Heartbreak House,* Captain Shotover contrasts his youth—or, symbolically, England in her prime—with the inanition of present-day England (1916), whose people do not have the courage to realize their potentialities:

> I see my daughters and their men living foolish lives of romance and sentiment and snobbery. I see you, the younger generation, turning from their romance and sentiment and snobbery to money and comfort and hard common sense. I was ten times happier on the bridge in the typhoon, or frozen into Arctic ice for months in darkness, than you or they have ever been. You are looking for a rich husband. At your age I looked for hardship, danger, horror, and death, that I might feel the life in me more intensely. I did not let the fear of death govern my life; and my reward was, I had my life. You are going to let the fear of poverty govern your life; and your reward will be that you will eat, but you will not live. (p. 87)

The post–World War I Shaw who adds a practical program to this Nietzschean base is implied in what follows this passage in the play. Captain Shotover regrets his inability to act: he feels descend upon him the vegetative happiness that he has always dreaded, "the happiness that comes as life goes, the happiness of yielding and dreaming instead of resisting and doing, the sweetness of the fruit that is going rotten" (p. 89). Young England has not his excuse of aged debility for its failure to make good the truth it tries to evade. Randall, the idler, and Mangan, the boss, flourish because we do not use our inherently greater strength to subdue them, while they make mock of us, Hector asserts, because they dare do more than we: "There is enmity between our seed and their seed. They know it and act on it, strangling our souls. They believe in themselves. When we believe in ourselves, we shall kill them" (p. 42). And, of course, the Captain's denunciation of drift, and his emphasis upon knowledge of "navigation" accord with Shaw's enlarged conception of the heroic as leading to purposive action. The question now is not so much, "What is wrong with us?" as "What are we going to do about it?" In the closing stage direction to *Too True to Be Good* (1932), Shaw recognizes the vitality to be derived from the Pentecostal Flame, which will impart its secrets to those choice souls attuned to it; yet Shaw votes for the heroine of the play who has also had the strength to act, to reject her hypochondriac inheritance and her former supine life.

Heartbreak House looks forward to *The Apple Cart* (1929) and the other plays which follow it in the admission that in some contingencies violence can be condoned, and is preferable to inaction: the inhabitants of Heartbreak House have deliberately chosen at the end of the play the holocaust they could with prudence evade. In *The Apple Cart,* the need for urgent action to avoid the stranglehold of the cartel, Breakages Limited, is stressed; in *On the Rocks* (1933), both Sir Arthur Chavender and Hipney feel a dictatorship better than indifferent democracy, because at least dictators do something; and in *The Simpleton of the Unexpected Isles* (1934), the criterion used by the avenging angel to determine whether a person shall live or disappear is social usefulness.

If a superb wit, an abundance of comic invention, a wealth of irony and of paradox, and a sure eye for personal idiosyncrasy mark all of Shaw's plays, certain of them like *Major Barbara, Man and Superman, Saint Joan,* and *Heartbreak House* are more spacious, and reveal an intenser clarity and greater emotional fervor. If Shaw's vision is more crystalline in these plays, it is also more complex, for in them an enquiring and speculative mind explores with dialectical precision the ethical and philosophical questions put to it by modern life. In spite of their definiteness of ideology, these major plays of Shaw produce an artistic effect of indefiniteness. They are exploratory rather than dogmatic, elusive rather than conclusive. Shaw in them is preoccupied with his subject to the point of obsession; he worries over it, and he defines it tentatively only after an exhausting effort of mind. To try therefore to epitomize the "meaning" of these plays is as fruitless as to try to extract the essence in paraphrasable form of a play of Ibsen's or Chekhov's or Strindberg's. In each case, the work as a total aesthetic experience resists such summary treatment. In Shaw's greatest plays are those symbolic intonations, those spiritual resonances, that indefiniteness of suggestion we associate with greatness in literature and which we do not usually associate with a temperament so drily rational as Shaw's sometimes seems to be. Because it has this larger than life quality and this inexhaustibility more unmistakably than any of his other works, *Heartbreak House* is a play which reveals Shaw at his most impressive.

Notes

1. E. Strauss, *Bernard Shaw, Art and Socialism* (London), p. 76; Blanche Patch, *Thirty Years with G.B.S.* (New York), p. 53; "Shakes versus Shav," *Buoyant Billions, Farfetched Fables & Shakes versus Shaw* (New York, 1951), p. 137.

2. *Heartbreak House, Great Catherine, and Playlets of the War* (New York: Brentano's, 1919), p. 90. Subsequent references to *Heartbreak House* and its Preface will be by page number incorporated into text of article.

3. *Misalliance* (1909–10), a similar play, is less incisive in its dialectic and relies heavily upon the farcical.

4. Preface to *Misalliance*, in *Misalliance, The Dark Lady of the Sonnets, and Fanny's First Play* (New York: Brentano's, 1914), p. lvi.

5. *John Bull's Other Island*, in *John Bull's Other Island and Major Barbara* (New York: Brentano's, 1907), p. 97.

6. *The Perfect Wagnerite* (New York: Brentano's, 1912), p. 30.

7. *The Doctor's Dilemma, Getting Married and The Shewing-up Blanco Posnet* (New York: Brentano's, 1911), p. 233.

8. H. C. Duffin, "Bernard Shaw and a Critic," *Cornhill Mag.*, Jan. 1924. Quoted in Eric Bentley, *Bernard Shaw: A Reconsideration* (Norfolk, Conn., 1947), p. 77.

9. "The Impossibilities of Anarchism," 1893. Quoted in Bentley, p. 89.

10. *Plays: Pleasant and Unpleasant: I, Unpleasant* (New York: Brentano's 1905), p. 221.

11. *Man and Superman: A Comedy and a Philosophy* (New York: Brentano's, 1912), p. 206.

12. New York: Brentano's, p. 238.

13. Dodd, Mead & Co., p. 191.

14. "The Revolutionist's Handbook," *Man and Superman*, p. 217.

Adam and Eve:
Evolving Archetypes
in *Back to Methuselah*

Daniel J. Leary and Richard Foster

Margaret Schauch suggests that "Shaw was affected . . . by the researches and speculations . . . of . . . Sir James Frazer and his peers. . . ." She notes that "Two recurrent symbolic figures stand out in Shaw's work. They are the clear-headed and unsentimental . . . Hero . . . and the Mother-Goddess, presented either as a human or an openly allegorical figure."[1] Shaw's Adam and Eve are just such symbolic figures of the essential male and the essential female. Indeed, much that T. S. Eliot suggests about Milton's Adam and Eve is applicable to Shaw's treatment of these same characters. Eliot writes: "In *Paradise Lost* Milton was not called upon for any of that understanding which comes from an affectionate observation of men and women. But such an interest in human beings was not required—indeed its absence was a necessary condition—for the creation of his figures of Adam and Eve. . . . They are the original *Man and Woman,* not types, but prototypes."[2] Initially they act as a standard to measure deviations from the ideal norm throughout the play, but eventually one sees that man can and must go beyond even this norm. Fragmentation of these matter-bound ideal specimens begins almost immediately with the introduction of the "adventurer" Cain and his luxury-loving, highly ornamented wife, Lua. To keep a relatively full perspective of man's nature, one must consider man as Adam-Cain and woman as Eve-Lua.

Adam and Eve and the significance of their fragmentation and modification in *Back to Methuselah* can, perhaps, best be understood by relating them to Jack Tanner and Ann Whitefield of *Man and Superman.* In that earlier drama it becomes evident that the purpose of the male is the creative quest for higher expression of mind, while the purpose of the female is to assure the continuance of the race. Since woman is the vehicle of a more direct inheritance from life, since she is biologically primary and man biologically secondary, woman succeeds in ninety-nine cases out of a hundred in reducing man's intellectual creativity by turning him back to his specifically biological function—the

From *The Shaw Review* 4 (May 1961): 12–23, 25. © 1961 by the Pennsylvania State University. Reproduced by permission of the Pennsylvania State University Press.

function for which, according to Shaw, she invented him—which means turning him from adventurer or visionary, first, into the worshipper of herself—hence romance—and secondly, when the hook of family maintenance has been swallowed with the bait of sexual attraction, into a bread-winner for herself and her children. And thus, Tanner, the philosopher of Creative Evolution, is ironically made the sacrifice of his philosophy; for it is really Creative Evolution—the Life-Force—that has triumphed through Ann's superlative sexual prowess: at the close, Tanner is about to father the Superman or his ancestor. *Man and Superman* opens with a funeral and, like *Don Giovanni,* closes with an invitation which is really a summons to death.

But Tanner's personal "tragedy" need not be re-enacted endlessly. It seems to have been Shaw's belief that since sex is unnecessary for the primordial, self-splitting amoeba, sex is a man-willed device that is not permanently necessary, at all. And in *Back to Methuselah,* which he proffered as his second major contribution to the iconography of Creative Evolution, Shaw dramatizes against the evolutionary rise of mind the corresponding decline of sex as a social and biological tension between fragmentary opposites. This decline may be read as a progressive equalization of the sexes toward full intellectual identity; man, the agency of creative thought, is gradually freed from sensual and sentimental enslavement to woman; and woman, the guardian of the race's physical health and continuity, is gradually freed for more and more intellectual activity.

Shaw, moreover, gives full expression to his Manichean tendencies in *Back to Methuselah* by suggesting, through evolutionary modifications in his characters, not only the decline of sex, but also the elimination of matter with its corollaries, limited time and death. The rise and decline of matter and sex in this series of plays can be seen as a carefully graduated curve. In "In the Beginning," Shaw presents a Lilith who is not the Talmudic first wife of Adam, but rather the Creative Will, the Elan Vital, fragmenting itself into male and female, into Adam and Eve, in an evolutionary experiment. At first Adam and Eve are not fully committed to matter, but once they do make such a decision and accept sex, the dimensions of matter, and death, they become quite human. Next Shaw presents detailed portraits of ineffectual politicians, as well as a very human father and daughter. Soon, the play introduces characters such as Napoleon and the "Elderly Gentleman" who seem to promise, in varying degrees, a return to the original archetypes with, however, evolutionary modifications. In the last sections of the play, characters are identified as Youth, Maiden, Oracle, Love, Authoritative Nymph, but these embodied abstractions are eventually displaced by the completely detached, almost sexless, and totally impersonal He-Ancient and She-Ancient. At the close of the play evolution has come full circle, for images of Adam and Eve return to the stage but seem to be reabsorbed into the spirit of Lilith.

The entire garden scene, of course, is an attempt to develop a new religious myth out of the Old Testament story. In general, the placing of Adam and Eve in the Garden before the will had been partly deadened by the weight of precedent provided an excellent basis for Shaw's ideas about Creative Evolution. According to Shaw, since Adam and Eve were without any accumulated heritage, they had to advance with rapid strides, and as their intellect was not fully developed, the Will which produces evolution without being subject to it was more active than it needs to be now. Shaw dramatically realizes this accelerated process by having a deer fall dead and immediately begin "changing into little white worms."[3] This accelerated evolution is repeated at the end of this cycle when "Condensed Recapitulation" makes it possible for human beings to be born—as were Adam and Eve—full grown and to become Elders in four years. There is also something of William Blake—perhaps even of John Milton—in Shaw's creatively evolutionary concept of the "fall" in the Garden, for he seems to believe that having an innocent intellect and an immortal body was not enough. Man loses the Garden through a knowledge of good and evil, through sex, but in the struggle to return he gains a great deal more in augmented self-knowledge and intensified awareness.

All is dependent on man. Thus we have the following pivotal passage:

EVE: To desire, to imagine, to will, to create. . . .

SERPENT: In one word, to conceive. That is the word that means both the beginning in imagination and the end in creation (p. 10).

This exchange, with its mention of four spiritual capacities and their identification with man's self-creation, has application to each of the five plays of this series. These four capacities of desiring, imagining, willing and creating are not merely "per accidens" reflexes like the jealousy, hate, fear and love which the Serpent identifies for Adam and Eve as they advance from innocence to knowledge; rather, they are essential human characteristics and are representative of Life-Force or Lilith working through and eventually beyond matter to attain new levels of self-awareness. The first play presents man's early discovery that something was wrong with his desire for a limited span of life and his growing desire for a return to longer life. "The Gospel of the Brothers Barnabas," Play II, reveals man imaginatively working out his desire into theory. Play III, "The Thing Happens," presents a limited realization of the theory through the wills of a few. Plays IV and V present two aspects of this future creation: "The Tragedy of an Elderly Gentleman" reveals the crushing discouragement of a shortlived human being before this ideal of the future; and the last play projects us "As Far As Thought Can Reach" to see where this possible creation might evolve.

In the first act of this Shavian myth the way is deftly prepared for the Serpent's message. Adam is first seen in the Garden between the dead deer on the ground and the Serpent coiled in the Tree of Knowledge—between death and Life. Adam first cries out despairingly, "But we [too] shall cease to be. . . . I will not have it. It must not be, I tell you" (p. 5). However, the accelerated Evolutionary Will working within him insists that change is more necessary than security. Thus, almost immediately, he retracts this statement and explains to Eve that, "I want to shed myself as a snake sheds its skin. I am tired of myself. And yet I must endure myself, not for a day or for many days but for ever" (p. 5). Eve comments: "It is strange that I should hear voices from all sides and you only from within" (p. 5). She hears the literal word but Adam, not yet burdened with sex duties, hears the spirit, the inner voice that insists he be more than he is. Eve with her greater drive toward the preservation of life agrees with Adam in his first desire, but not in his second. She says:

EVE: No: I do not think about myself: what is the use? I am what I am: nothing can
        alter that. I think about you (p. 5).

Notice that these comments deal not only with longevity, the cardinal tenet of Shaw's new religion, but also establish, at their fundamental level, the distinct roles of male and female, both biological and cultural. Adam acts; he is the potential warrior, statesman, capitalist, artist, thinker, the potential builder of civilizations, the essential and elemental male as doer. Eve, on the other hand, keeps; she cares for the father, for the child, for the dwelling; she is the custodian of the seed, the keeper of the enabling sexual mystery.

Lilith is the Life-Force that walks in the garden in the cool of the evening, and the serpent seems to be her voice. Consequently, the Serpent is a complex figure reflecting characteristics of both sexes. As a phallic symbol, he represents the voice of our first parents' will, of their sex desire; as a creature that shuffles off his mortal coil he represents birth and death; as a Blakean "dragon" figure, he can be seen as the necessary revolution before the "Higher Innocence"; and as the Serpent in the Shavian Garden, his action makes it clear that if there is any apparent evil in the Garden, it is an accidental by-product of the Life-Force's creative experiments and not an eternal mark on man's degraded soul.

It is the Serpent that tells Adam and Eve they are limited only by their own vision, that instead of asking "Why?," they should ask "Why not?" (p. 7). They are the result of a fragmented Lilith and, in terms of this religion of evolutionary pantheism, they are a deity and can make something out of nothing, can make their desires come true.

The subtle Serpent, the voice of the Creative Will, tempts man and woman to explore the possibilities of sex, matter and time.

THE SERPENT: Man is deeper in his thought than I am. The woman knows that there
                is no such thing as nothing; the man knows that there is no such thing
                as tomorrow (p. 14).

Eve reacts to the Serpent's praise by succumbing to the temptations of sex and matter. Eve's insistence that there must be "something" leads her to accept the sole task of populating and caring for the physical world—her assumption of this Astarte role gradually reduces the play's various Adams to son-lovers searching for an ideal woman to take care of them. Indeed, Adam's reduction starts when he wills to accept the possibility that there may be no tomorrow for him. This is a serious temptation, for it leads to procrastination, a weakness that will eventually force man to reverse his decision and once again seek immortality. This tendency toward irresponsibility is given dramatic objectification by Cain's laugh which becomes his identifying trait, as well as by various male politicians later in the pentateuch who shrug off their duties with dismissive laughter.

The acceptance of sex and death in the garden, at worst is a "felix culpa," for the growing complexity of our primogenitors' lives is in fact the Life-Force in operation attempting through trial and error to arrive at the best means to use life. This growing complexity can be observed in the changing tone and vocabulary of the dialogue. At first the interchanges are simple:

EVE: Yes: that must not be. But it might be.

ADAM: No, I tell you it must not be. I know that it must not be.

EVE: We both know it. How do we know it? (p. 5).

Soon, however, after this kindergarten phase, in which the Serpent teaches them the meaning of the words, kill, death, love, fear, jealousy and hope, Adam reflects his movement from "The Songs of Innocence" to "The Songs of Experience," in the growing complexity of his utterance:

ADAM: I was troubled with the burden of eternal being; but I was not confused in my mind. If I did not know that I loved Eve, at least I did not know that she might cease to love me, and come to love some other Adam and desire my death (p. 16).

In this new and complex life, Adam and Eve instinctively seek for security and vow to be "Wife and Husband" (p. 18), the inverted order of the phrase suggesting that Adam's reduction has already started, that his sense of exploration has been over-shadowed by Eve's instinct for survival.

Act II opens some three hundred years later, at a time when there are many new Adams and Eves and fragmentation is well advanced. Adam has assured his role of a provider for his family, and when Eve talks of manna he grumbles, "Go on with your spinning; and do not sit there idle while I am straining my muscles for you" (p. 34). The Garden of Eden has been transformed from a kindergarten into a "kitchen garden," into which comes not the Serpent, but Cain, bringing not the temptation of sex but of violence.

On one level Cain and his wife, Lua, represent the illusion lovers, the people who in "Don Juan in Hell" preferred the pleasures of Hell to the truth of

Heaven. Yet, carnal blusterer that he is, Cain imagines possibilities greater than himself, and can boast to Eve: "I do not know what I want, except that I want to be something higher and nobler than this stupid old digger whom Lilith made to help you to bring me into the world and whom you despise now that he has served your turn" (p. 30). Eve, the careful mother, accuses Cain of being, not Superman, but "Anti-man," and she sees his intuition of the life of the mind as the bully play-boy's dream of selfishness and idleness. But Cain, the slayer who compensates for Abel's blood by endangering his own life as he sheds the blood of others, has nevertheless a true instinct "which tells me that death plays its part in life" (pp. 32–33). As an active, undomesticated male extension of Adam's death wish, Cain, like the more sophisticated and philosophized munitions king, Undershaft, is the agency by which the ground is cleared for the evolutionary production of higher forms of life.

Eve, as a creature of hope, rejects the patient acceptance of Adam and the ruthless impatience of Cain. She dreams of the "Life-Bringers," those who "never want to die, because they are always creating either things or wisdom" (p. 32). The possibility of total destruction through the Cains of the future stirs Mother Eve to put her faith in "Enoch, who walks on the hills, and hears the Voice continually, and has given up his will to do the will of the Voice, and has some of the Voice's greatness" (p. 32). The character of Enoch represents an important foreshadowing of the concluding play's Ancients, since, according to "Genesis," he was the father of Methuselah and was himself translated to heaven while still alive.

The second play of the series, "The Gospel of the Brothers Barnabas," introduces the second stage of man's struggle to better himself. Part I ended with Eve's desire that Enoch might have more time to develop, and in "The Gospel" that desire is given imaginative form through a scientific theory. In a fuller and more unifying sense, Part I is the scriptural text and Part II is the sermon, the application, the exegesis of that text. Anyone who failed to notice how Shaw had injected new biological significance into the old legends and religious symbols of Western culture could not help understanding after listening to the new Gospel.

The entire section is built up of the struggle between two forces: the politicians, Lubin and Burge, representing the practical and materialistic view toward this religion, and the brothers, Franklyn and Conrad Barnabas, representing the visionary and spiritual view. It soon becomes clear that no merger is possible between matter and spirit for the forces operate on entirely different levels: the politicians are completely irresponsible; the Barnabas Brothers are completely dedicated.

In the preface Shaw wonders "whether the human animal, as he exists at present, is capable of solving the social problems raised by his own aggregation, or, as he calls it, his civilization" (p. xiv). Burge and Lubin give ample reason for worry: they have not, as Shaw pictures them, advanced very far beyond the masculine capacities of Adam and Cain. Burge is most like that "old vegetable"

Adam. His stupidity has limited his rudimentary conscience, but not his brute ability to hold England together. But Adam did not need brains simply to hoe the garden, any more than Burge needs them to maintain the simple requirements of the "status quo." And like Adam, Burge has a good solid wife to keep him at it: "I want to cultivate my garden," he says wearily to Franklyn Barnabas, "I am not interested in politics. . . . I haven't a scrap of ambition. I went into politics because my wife shoved me into them, bless her!" (p. 49). As dangerous as Burge is, he is a simple digger, a limited plodder. Lubin, however, is intelligent and ruthless, and reminds one of Cain, having both his impulsiveness and his amorality. "You have no continuity," Burge says to him; "and a man without continuity can have neither conscience nor honor from one day to another" (p. 71). Lubin's lack of conscience and lack of a responsible historical sense combine with his playboy's capacity—again like Cain's—for trivial romantic dalliance. His flirtation with Savvy has a certain charm; but in terms of the play's values, it must be found, in a man pushing seventy, a sign of virtual adolescence. Unlike Shotover in his relationship with Ellie Dunn, Lubin is not a Superman attempting, at least figuratively, to revitalize his energies through the stimulation of sex; he is only a cynical politician wooing the new generation's vote. Seen as a single force, Lubin-Burge merge into a complex, relatively intelligent Adam, presenting on the one hand a choric Horatian intelligence vegetating in a state of amused detachment from life, on the other hand, a sexually agitated and irresponsibly adolescent Cain. If, at last, civilization has evolved the concept of the statesman, it is clear that man has become far too involved in matter to fulfill adequately the demands of that role.

The Brothers Barnabas, like the Serpent, are the voice of new possibilities. Conrad, the scientist, and Franklyn, the theologian, have combined to produce a new "metabiological gospel" which proposes that though man now dies in intellectual adolescence, he can will to live longer and so attain wisdom and intellectual adulthood and implement it, through longer life, in action. Shaw emphasizes the importance of this new partnership:

FRANKLYN: Unless this withered thing religion, and this dry thing science, have come alive in our hands, alive and intensely interesting, we may just as well go out and dig the garden until it is time to dig our graves (pp. 43–44).

That is to say, either Creative Evolution has a meaning or we are no more advanced than the Philistine, Adam. But Shaw links the brothers and their gospel to the very highest aspirations of man. Indeed, he suggests that Franklyn, by combining the will of religion with the intellect of science, is the spiritual father of the newly evolving Methuselah, when he has him say: "I felt it to be my vocation to walk with God, like Enoch" (p. 39).

Savvy is the physical daughter of Franklyn Barnabas, but she is not fated to live beyond the "normal" span of man's life. She reflects in too many ways the conservative qualities of the old Eve; for she is a woman neither committed to the practical stupidities of Cain and Adam as seen in Lubin and Burge, nor capable of understanding, though sympathetic to, the contemplative projects of Abel and Enoch as seen in the Brothers Barnabas. Imaginatively, Savvy rejects both extremes and continues to cling to the old compromise between body and soul.

Savvy's very name suggests the savage new generation's upper class society whose total lack of responsibility results in inability to cooperate with the Life Force. The self-centered morality of Savvy, as the closed morality of Lubin-Burge, constitutes a matter-orientated society whose only hope for development, perhaps for survival, rests in a spiritual conviction that life means something beyond matter, sex and time, that life must be lived responsibly. Consequently, Shaw draws a new, matter-detached Eve from the poverty-stricken working classes, not only to show that the Will can suddenly take effect anywhere on any social strata, but also to imply that the millennium will only occur when poverty and classes have been abolished, when the social conscience is free of artificial material considerations. The young clergyman, Haslam, the male figure singled out for longevity, also is free of material considerations and appears as a simple, frank and vital soul.

Part III, "The Thing Happens," is a transitional period during which the first examples of the longlived appear. Shaw's world picture of A.D. 2170 presents the "whites" as embodying man's irresponsible stupidity, while the "colored" races represent all earthly knowledge. Shaw, however, explains that the "colored" races simply reach maturity faster than the innately superior "whites." Having willed to live long enough to reach this necessary maturity, Haslam, who once had seemed "boyish" and had been over-shadowed by the physical vitality of Savvy, now has become the superannuated Archbishop and the parlormaid has become the perennial Domestic Minister, Mrs. Lutestring. As longlivers they are about to revive the slipping white race by re-enacting at a higher level the original creative union of Adam and Eve. Certain of their sexual qualifications are important as signs both of sexual continuity and of evolutionary progress. Mrs. Lutestring, utterly revolted by Burge-Lubin's childish liveliness, "never was very fond of children . . ." (p. 121). The Domestic Minister, with her ideal of dispassionate efficiency in human affairs, is clearly quite different from Eve, the instinctively domestic and universally life-protective Mother principle. We must interpret this as a sign of evolutionary progress, as we must the utter passionlessness of the Lutestring-Haslam union. Adam and Eve, we presume, in both youth and middle age were bound by love—as were Haslam and Savvy, but now the Archbishop and the Domestic Minister, both well along in their third century, are bound only by an intellectual awareness of their social duty. Procreation is not self-indulgence; it is a matter of will. It is noteworthy that the one sexual continuity, and a typically Shavian one, between Adam and Eve and the longlivers, is that the female is the instigator of consummation: "Have you time to come home with me and discuss the matter?" Mrs. Lutestring inquires. "With pleasure," the gallant Archbishop acquiesces (p. 127).

At the same time continuing fragmentation of the archetypes can be seen in Shaw's depiction of the various leaders of the future. There is the Accountant-General, Barnabas, the scientist descendant of the capable if dull Conrad of the "Gospel." His rejection of all but statistical truth labels him as the Adam of science, a clod and a plodder, dissociated from the imaginative freedom of Enoch's and Franklyn's vision. He is also Cain-like in his primitive instinct to annihilate the longlivers, to annihilate life itself. "What reason can you give for killing a snake?" he cries in justification; "Nature tells you to do it" (p. 128).

The President, Burge-Lubin, combines the stupidity of his illustrious forebearers with none of their modium of intelligence. He has the trivially adolescent sexual preoccupation of Lubin without Lubin's imaginative intelligence: "Oh, these sex episodes!" he shudders, after unsuccessfully "propositioning" the modern Lua, the negress Minister of Health: "Why can I not resist them?" (p. 100). And he has Burge's stupidity and affable bluster without either the moral asset of Burge's crude conscience or the practical asset of his solid Wife-Mother. Together Burge-Lubin and Barnabas—the combination of cheap politics and narrow-minded science—are placed in admirable dramatic contrast to the scientific religion Shaw envisioned in Part II and which is fulfilled in Part IV.

Part IV, "Tragedy of an Elderly Gentleman," takes place in the year 3000, a time when Mrs. Lutestring's worst suspicions have apparently proven themselves in the events of the years between A.D. 2170 and 3000: the shortliving white race, mixing with the colored races in an instinctive attempt to replenish its physical and intellectual vitality, has actually deserted its traditional homeland and become absorbed into the alien life and blood of the Middle East, thus symbolically regressing to its source.

The principal dramatic tension is achieved by juxtaposing an elderly gentleman representing the shortlived minority with Zoo, a young female longliver. Their Bergsonian difficulties in communication present yet another type of regression to source, for the human race would appear to be returning to the original innocence of Adam and Eve, though on a higher level. The old terms taught by the Serpent are forgotten and are as useless to Zoo as matter will seem to the Ancients in Play V. The conflict between the two characters is particularly significant in terms of the sexual evolution it seems to reflect. Zoo looks like a "dowdy and serious" Savvy, who looked like Eve; and Zoo has an official mother-nurse relationship to "Daddy" since shortlivers, however old and wise, suffer terrible attacks of discouragement in the Ireland of the longlivers. "You have many of the ways and weaknesses of a baby," she says to him. "No doubt that is why I feel called on to mother you. You certainly are a very silly little Daddy" (p. 152). The old man, proud descendant of the early English heroes, Bulge and Bluebin—Burge and Lubin, of course—becomes annoyed at these offenses to his dignity, and tries at one point to impress upon

Zoo the superiority of his sex, age, and material possessions. This arrogance arouses in Zoo the instinct to kill her charge whom she suddenly sees as an "evil child"; one must presume this to be, as an expression of the Life-Force, a good instinct of the superior life forms to obliterate—as Cain instinctively slew animals and inferior men—the crippled and inadequate forms. In Zoo, we have come a long way from Mother Eve, to whom all life was indiscriminately dear. Though Zoo resists her murderous instinct, the traumatic event changes her politics, and she becomes a "liberal" dedicated to the principle of exterminating the world's shortlivers. As Zoo points out, "a good garden needs weeding . . ." (p. 172). This change in Zoo, and the elderly gentleman's gradual conversion, through "discouragement," to the clearsighted realism of the longlivers, are prophetic of the end of present day civilization. The old man, who combines the best qualities of Burge and Lubin, is the last and finest flower of the shortlivers. In the end it is inevitable that he should say to the oracle, "I cannot live among people to whom nothing is real. . . . I implore to be allowed to stay" (pp. 201–202). But it is equally inevitable that this crippled, elderly baby should crumple at the touch of the Oracle, who is his new, highly dispassionate, wholly objective, and potently intense supermother.

The adventurer-destroyer facet of man's personality is also rejected in this play. "The Man of Destiny," Napoleon—the full name is "Cain Adamson Charles Napoleon"—meets or rather intrudes upon the Oracle and wants to know "How am I to satisfy my genius by fighting until I die?" The Oracle had but one solution for this Nietzschean Superman, and it was that he should die immediately. However, in contrast to the Elderly Gentleman, who dies nobly, Napoleon, this narrow, pompous "war-god" who sought personal glory, is—like the much more amiable Commander in "Don Juan in Hell"—turned into a living statue, transfixed and impotent, to contemplate, perhaps for eternity, the statue of Falstaff, the saint of sensible cowardice.

There is a hint in this section that the immortality looked forward to goes beyond the concept of personal deathlessness. These plays are, after all, myths calculated to encourage us to live more fully, more responsibly. Man must learn to think of his life, not in the materialistic sense of a few years, but in the Bergsonian sense of mankind's duration. Shaw wanted to present a religion that would encourage men to behave like gentlemen, and in the Shavian vocabulary "gentleman" has a very central meaning. Shaw tells us that "the real gentleman says . . . I hope and I shall strive to give to my country . . . more than it has given to me; so that when I die my country shall be richer for my life. . . . What the country needs, and should seek through its social deduction, its social sense, and religious feeling, is to create gentlemen and when you create them, all things shall be added unto you."[4] The Elderly Gentleman finally comes to realize that his life is important only as a fulfillment of something greater; and the most poignant aspect of this "tragedy" is that Shaw apparently identifies himself with the Elderly Gentleman and unflinchingly admits that his own class with its charm, its eloquence, its art, its Bernard

Shaws, must be removed even as Heartbreak House must be blown up, to make room for a classless society even more fully dedicated to the idea of mankind's development.

At the close of *Man and Superman* another gentleman, Jack Tanner, is invited to the feast that will be his death, but there is the cheerful promise that a Superman will develop through his sacrifice. The Elderly Gentleman's death gives no such hope for man. The opening scene presented the old man with his back to the land looking out to the sea. Caught between one world that is dead and another that is yet to be born, he is psychologically ready to have his ideals stripped away. Thus he claimed that "blood is thicker than water," but by the end of the play he leaves his family in disgust. He talked of "Bulge and Bluebin and their majestic spirit" but abruptly loses all faith in politics. He had respect for orthodox faiths but at the close sees the mummery of the Oracle's ceremony. His civilized and gentlemanly manners collapse under the strain of reality to a point where Zoo finds it almost necessary to destroy him. He defended the value of his short life but finally prefers to die than go on living it. His disenchantment reaches its nadir in his contemplation of the Envoy, his son-in-law, who represents the complete disintegration of the political state under the selfish, uncontrolled, cowardly, lying, even drunken, rule of unthinking politicians who are all related at least in law to Lubin and Burge. In this world of senseless bloodshed and political lies he finds himself to be a gentleman without a cause. The Oracle—called "The Pythoness" and situated in a fountain where "serpents curl . . . in the vapor" (p. 197)—like the Serpent in the Garden, is the voice of the Life-Force and once again has prepared the world for a new and vital experiment: the old Eve has disappeared, the Cain figure has been destroyed, and Part IV ends with the death of the old Adam.

Having explored his "dark night of the soul" Shaw returns to take us in Part V, "As Far As Thought Can Reach," into the year A.D. 31, 920, where a group of young people is discovered, significantly enough, in a garden, dabbling in the arts, fulfilling their leisure and their intelligence. There are no vestiges of the shortlivers remaining. There are, moreover, no more simple producers, no more heroes, no more statesmen. The last representative of unfettered scientism disappeared centuries ago with the maniacal Barnabas, and even Pygmalion, the harmless scientist of this play, who is checked and qualified by the imagination in his dependence on Martellus, is doomed, in the evolutionary scheme of things, to extinction.

The evolutionary movement of this series of plays, the discarding of sex, time and matter, has reached its logical end. As one of the Ancients explains to the younger longlivers, man now lives long enough to put away the things of a child, and man's "body is the last doll to be discarded" (p. 251). The pattern of this series of plays has been the movement from desire, to imagination, to will, to creation. In Part IV man made himself into a more responsible human being by accepting and acting in terms of a long life. Now, in Part V man seeks immortal responsibility by becoming pure spirit. Sex, science, politics, war, art and all the other concepts so engrossing to the Elderly Gentleman are put away as dolls fit only for children.

On stage it was not enough to have the Ancients talking about the shaping and creating of vortexes. Shaw sought for an objective and dramatic way of presenting this new non-material creation in the process of happening, and to do this he hit upon the theory of Condensed Recapitulation. Soon after the play's opening, one of the She-Ancients arrives among the children to break open the egg in which a full grown girl is ready to be delivered. This egg, from which the teen-age Newly Born emerges after a few taps of the She-Ancient's wand, appears to be a community project and responsibility. The She-Ancient's antiseptic role as mother in this "delivery" is significant, for it totally dispenses with the services of a nurse, even one like Zoo, who could have had more or less human relations with the child. Mother Eve is no longer necessary. In the Ancients, Creative Evolution has at last arrived at man as Seer and thinker, and subordinate human capacities and talents have been sloughed off along the way. In them there is apparently neither sexual activity nor biologically significant sexual difference.

The youths, however, are not yet done with sex and art. Shaw associates art with sentimentality, romantic love, and the body. Ecrasia, who seems to be related to Spenser's Acrasia and the decadent Bowre of Bliss—related, too, to the earlier Lua—is the simultaneous priestess of both sex and art. The defection of The Maiden from sex and Martellus from art has the same significance as Don Juan's spurning the devil's temptations in the hell sequence of *Man and Superman*. The spirit of Ecrasia's reign must have an end; it will either grow up or be destroyed by Pygmalion.

Shaw links this dissatisfaction with art and matter to his belief that man must transcend sex. He presents the artist Martellus as one who, having grown dissatisfied with fleshly beauty as the object of his art and having turned to portraying Ancients, only to give that up in turn because he could not make them "live," has turned at last to Pygmalion, the scientist, in his artist's quest to make a living thing. They produce two human puppets, Ozymandias and Cleopatra. These automata, whose names suggest the futility of masculine power and feminine wiles, are portrayed as creatures who have no original impulses, who are slaves of internal reflexes, and thus are related to Adam and Eve. They also reflect Cain and Lua in that they are selfish, vain, and totally lacking in self control, dedication and a sense of responsibility. All the emotions taught to Adam and Eve by the Serpent are found in these creatures: jealousy, love, hate, fear, desire to kill, and all of them are seen to be motor reflexes. Like savages and children, they resent injuries and seek to requite them by inflicting immediate suffering on those who make them suffer; they are, therefore, revengeful. They are sensitive and readily take offense; having taken it, they sulk until they are appeased by flattery or apologies. They are, in short, human beings, and in their brief moments on the stage, they "recapitulate" most of the mistakes made by the plays' various Adams and Eves. Their behavior after killing Pygmalion is rather like that of the biblical Adam and Eve after the fall. When the He-Ancient appears they are terrified and wildly accuse each other of the crime. To the end of their lives they are victims of the illusion that they are important. In their destruction by fire, man's body is symbolically disposed of, and the time of the spirit's apocalypse in Shaw's cyclical epic has finally arrived.

The Ancients have come to the very same position of choice as did Adam and Eve in the first play. Adam and Eve were also afraid of accidental death but they found an answer in matter. The Ancients seek for the answer by losing matter.

THE HE-ANCIENT: I am the eternal life, the perpetual resurrection; but (*striking his body*), this structure, this organism, this make-shift, can be made by a boy in a laboratory. . . . Sooner or later, its destruction is certain (p. 250).

Indeed, in the "Sixth and Last Fable" of *Farfetched Fables* (1948), written when Shaw was ninety-one, it seems as though the Ancients succeeded in their effort to disengage themselves from matter. The teacher in this fable explains to his students that "the Disembodied Races still exist as Thought Vortexes, are penetrating our thick skulls in their continual pursuit of knowledge and power, since they need our hands and brains as tools in that pursuit."[5] At the close of this fable the Angel Raphael descends upon the group as an "embodied thought" and explains his presence by saying, "If the body can become a vortex, the vortex can also become a body."[6] Apparently the need for a dialectic between matter and spirit has reasserted itself and a new cyclical action has begun.[7]

At the very end of "As Far As Thought Can Reach" Eve surveys her progeny, and as a mother baffled at what has happened but proud of her "clever" children, pronounces that "all's well." Adam, on the other hand, thinks it is "foolishness" to have carried this evolution thing so far. Cain vanishes with a characteristic romantic flourish by quoting one of his descendants: "Out, out, brief candle!" And finally Lilith, summing up the entire Pentateuch, can say:

LILITH: . . . after passing a million goals they press on to the goal of redemption from the flesh, to the vortex freed from matter, to the whirlpool in pure intelligence that, when the world began, was a whirlpool in pure force. . . . I am Lilith: I . . . compelled my enemy Matter, to obey a living soul. . . . Of life only is there no end; and though unbuilt, and though its vast domain is as yet unbearably desert, my seed shall one day fill it and master its matter to its uttermost confines (pp. 261–262).

Shaw closed his Metabiological Pentateuch in a garden and with a heightened vision, with an apocalypse and resurrection that like the Bible presented again a paradise, but one that was non-material. The first four plays of the series ended with a death or a discouragement that proved to be but one aspect of the regression-progression pattern of the "Rebirth Archetype." Adam's loss of vision and Cain's death-wish gave birth to Eve's desire to go beyond sex, Lubin and Burge's stupid materialism force the Barnabas imagination beyond matter, the Elderly Gentleman's despair which rejects Cain, Lubin and Burge is but the birth trauma of a will to go beyond time, and in the final play, the last of the human illusions, Ozymandias and Cleopatra, are destroyed by the Ancients who go beyond art, nature, science, and even religion, in their self-creation. Thus Shaw has his He-Ancient say:

THE HE-ANCIENT: . . . I . . . ceased to walk over the mountains with my friends, and walked alone; for I found that I had creative power over myself but none over my friends. And then I ceased to walk on the mountains; for I saw the mountains were dead (p. 251).

The He-Ancient is the fulfillment of Enoch, who walked on the mountains with God. But this Enoch of the future needs no mountains, and has discovered that he is his own God.

Notes

1.   Margaret Schauch, "Symbolic Figures in G. B. Shaw," *Science & Society,* XXI (Summer, 1957), pp. 201–211. Arthur H. Nethercot, in his *Men and Supermen* (Cambridge, 1954), pp. 103–104, has also briefly dealt with Eve in *Back to Methuselah* as the "Mother Woman."

2.   T. S. Eliot, "Milton II," *On Poetry and Poets* (New York, 1957), p. 177.

3.   *Back to Methuselah: A Metabiological Pentateuch* (London, 1930), p. 6.

4.   *The Socialism of Bernard Shaw,* ed. James Fuchs (New York, 1926), p. 82.

5.   *Buoyant Billions, Farfetched Fables, & Shakes Versus Shav* (London, 1950), p. 127.

6.   *Ibid.,* p. 130.

7.   Of course this same characteristic of continuity, so deeply rooted in Shaw's philosophy, is to be found in the structures of most of his plays. One has only to think of *Caesar and Cleopatra, Saint Joan or Major Barbara* for confirmation of Shaw's statement to Paul Green: "My plays are interludes, as it were, between two greater realities. And the meaning of them lies in what follows them. The beginning of one of my plays takes place exactly where an unwritten play ended. And the ending of my written play concludes where another play begins." Paul Green, *Dramatic Heritage* (New York, 1953, pp. 125–126).

The Avant-Garde Shaw:
Too True to Be Good
and Its Predecessors

STANLEY WEINTRAUB

I never burlesque anything; on the contrary; it is my business to find some order and meaning in the apparently insane farce of life as it happens higgledy-piggledy off the stage.

—Bernard Shaw, Preface to *Major Barbara* (1906)

In the first years of the present century, Shaw produced one play in which—off stage—a squealing pig is transported, with enormous difficulty, in a motor car, and another play in which the second act opens with the stage filled by a motor car under which appear the legs of a mechanic. They may have been the earliest theatrical uses to which the new technology had been put.

A few years after that, in the infancy of the airplane, Shaw followed *John Bull's Other Island* and *Man and Superman* with a play about an armaments manufacturer—Major Barbara Undershaft's father—who, only two years after the Wright brothers flew their motorized box kite, constructs "aerial battleships." Several plays later, in *Misalliance,* Shaw would write in an airplane crash just off stage, from which emerges the theater's first woman pilot. A decade beyond, in *Back to Methuselah* (1921), Shaw amused himself if not his audience by anticipating television, and even phonevision, in a farcical scene. Yet he never fancied himself a theatrical H. G. Wells, and indeed has long been considered a playwright of ideas who put his new wine in old, Victorian, theatrical bottles. He even fostered the notion, telling producer John Vedrenne that the comic music-hall turns he wrote for his characters were the jam which made the pill (of the message) go down and telling critic William Archer that he was a "rather old fashioned stage manager."

The motor car in *Man and Superman,* Shaw confided, had been suggested to him by actor Robert Loraine, who was soon to become addicted to fast cars and airplanes. If so, Shaw was nevertheless quick to adopt the radical notion. One of

From *The Unexpected Shaw: Biographical Approaches to G.B.S. and His Work* (New York: Frederick Ungar, 1982); first printed in *Shaw Seminar Papers* (Toronto: Copp Clark, 1966). © Stanley Weintraub.

the last Victorians—he died in 1950—he was also avant-garde in the uses to which he put the stage and the techniques he foresaw which would revolutionize the staging of plays.

The only contribution that Shaw made to the modern drama, H. L. Mencken once scoffed, was to state the obvious in terms of the scandalous. Yet in theory as well as in practice, Shaw was an advanced playwright often a generation ahead of his contemporaries. As far back as 1896, for example, Shaw, commenting as a working drama critic, rather than playwright, suggested that "any play performed on a platform amidst the audience gets closer home to its hearers than when it is presented as a picture framed by a proscenium. Also, that we are less conscious of the artificiality of the stage when a few well-understood conventions, adroitly handled, are substituted for attempts at an impossible scenic verisimilitude. All the old-fashioned tale-of-adventure plays, with their frequent changes of scene, and all the new problem plays, with their intense intimacies, should be done in this way."[1]

Today we might consider Shaw's remarks as an anticipation of theater-in-the-round techniques. And his plays, when performed on the arena stage for which he never wrote, exhibit a high level of adaptability to the "new" method. What he thought the playhouse should look like is still largely an ideal. As he wrote in 1926, the "sort of theatre" his newer plays needed was one which had to "combine" the optics and acoustics of a first-rate lecture theater and a first-rate circus.

After his first decade as a dramatist Shaw had already outgrown Ibsenite realism—something which *Don Juan in Hell* makes sufficiently obvious. Soon he was objecting that to have props and settings "as real as in your drawing room at home" was actually unconvincing: "In fact, the more scenery you have the less illusion you produce." The charm of the earlier theater, even the theater of David Garrick, he thought, was "its makebelieve. It has that charm still, not only for the amateurs, who are happiest when they are most unnatural and impossible and absurd, but for audiences as well." Anticipating the way his own *Don Juan in Hell* would be performed after his death, he observed in 1900, before *Don Juan* was even written, "I saw Browning's 'Luria' performed in the lecture theatre of University College, London, with a pair of curtains for scenery and the performers in ordinary evening dress. It produced a hundred times more illusion," he thought, than a real-scenery, open-air performance of *As You Like It* which he had just seen. "A play that cannot do better without scenery than with hired trappings is not worth . . . attention."[2]

Those of Shaw's plays written in the Neanderthal era of films even anticipated the possibilities of that medium. A Shaw critic once observed that the treatment of the stage directions in *Caesar and Cleopatra*

> anticipates the technique of the movies with uncanny accuracy. It will be remembered that the play was written in 1898. The . . . film production in

which Claude Rains and Vivien Leigh appeared followed precisely the 1898 stage direction:

The moonlight wanes: the horizon again shows black against the sky, broken only by the fantastic silhouette of the Sphinx. The sky itself vanishes in darkness, from which there is no relief until the gleam of a distant torch falls on great Egyptian pillars supporting the roof of a majestic corridor. At the further end of the corridor a Nubian slave appears carrying a torch. Caesar, still led by Cleopatra, follows him. They come down the corridor, Caesar peering keenly about at the strange architecture and the pillar shadows, between which, as the passing torch makes them hurry noiselessly backwards, figures of men with wings and hawks' heads, and vast black marble cats, seem to flit in and out of ambush. Further along, the wall turns a corner and makes a transept in which Caesar sees, on his right, a throne, and behind the throne, a door.[3]

In 1898, of course, this could be done only with words, for readers.

Strangely enough, much of Shaw's modernism consists of his adapting to the modern stage, and his bringing back to life, theatrical conventions which had been discarded when naturalism and realism took hold in the theater. In order to make ideas behave dramatically, for example, he wanted his characters to be able to step out of their roles now and then to become bigger than life. Thus he made use of the prenaturalistic stage convention that characters may have written into their roles an artificial amount of self-consciousness. The device not only permitted the use of the ironic wit Shaw loved but made possible a clarity of expression in dialogue unavailable to a doctrinaire realist. Thus, of his characters in *Saint Joan*, Shaw wrote that "it is the business of the stage to make the figures more intelligible to themselves than they would be in real life; for by no other means can they be made intelligible to the audience. . . . All I claim is that by this inevitable sacrifice of verisimilitude . . . the things I represent these three exponents of drama [in *Joan*] as saying are the things they actually would have said if they had known what they were really doing."

Shaw was never, he insisted, "a representation[al]ist or realist." Rather, he said, he "was always in the classic tradition, recognizing that stage characters must be endowed by the author with a conscious self-knowledge and power of expression, and . . . a freedom of inhibitions, which in real life would make them monsters. . . . It is the power to do this that differentiates me (or Shakespear) from a gramophone and a camera. The representational part of the business is mere costume and scenery; and I would not give tuppence for any play that could not be acted in curtains and togas as effectively as in elaborately built stage drawing rooms and first-rate modern tailoring."[4]

Shavian characterization permitted non-realistic eloquence in places in the dialogue where it becomes necessary. This was justifiable not only on the grounds of psychological validity but because of its consistency with the self-consciousness of the role. Ibsen and others modified downward the level of dramatic language, Ibsen even commenting in a letter that writing "the genuine, plain language spoken in real life" was a "very much more difficult art" than writing poetic or pseudo-poetic lines for a character to speak. "My desire," Ibsen added, "was to depict human beings, and therefore I would not make them speak the language of the gods." Realist writers who attempted to represent life as it was accepted at first the limits of normal expression. If they were concerned with surface emotions, these limitations presented no difficulty; conversational resources for the discussion of meals or money or other basic needs remained adequate. But a dramatist could not express the whole range of human experience while committed to the language of probable conversation. To overcome this limitation, Shaw employed the player whose speech had a vitality beyond what would be normal for his role, using ordinary conversational speech throughout the play but shifting into intensified rhetoric (possibly poetic prose, or even verse) at the points of crisis. The technique is psychologically valid, for at times of crisis or peaks of emotion we all reach for another and more metaphorical level of language (at its lowest, that of the formerly unprintable variety). In some of the earlier plays the rhetorical heightening is formal, as in Caesar's apostrophe to the Sphinx, or the great impassioned speeches of Don Juan and the Devil. In some later plays the technique is still traditional. Joan, for example, has a great outburst which narrowly literal critics condemn as out of keeping with Joan's earthy, peasant intellect—her passionate, biblical-cadenced renunciation of her recantation.

In some of the earlier plays there is a foreshadowing of a nonrealistic Shavian technique to come, particularly in "mad" Father Keegan's chat with the grasshopper (*John Bull's Other Island*) and the Mayoress's great speech from the depth of a trance (*Getting Married*). In the later plays there is sometimes "a sudden shift to a patterned, semi-poetic, ritualistic speech [which] indicates a passionate intensity of perception or revelation which transcends the ordinary levels of the play." We see it in the darkness at the close of the first act of *Heartbreak House,* in the operatic trio of Captain Shotover, Hector, and Hesione. We see it in the quintet of Adam, Eve, Cain, and Serpent and Lilith as they vanish one by one to end the last scene of *Back to Methuselah.* We see it in the chanting praise, and agonized rejection, of Joan in the epilogue to *Saint Joan.* We see it again in such allegorical and extravagant plays of the 1930s as *Too True to Be Good* and *The Simpleton of the Unexpected Isles.* Scenes and speeches such as these do not escape from a commitment to reality—they provide for Shaw and later dramatists who use this device opportunities for creating a reality of ideas and emotions which goes beyond a commitment to external details.

A logical step beyond is Shaw's player who is both actor and character in the same person—the self-conscious character, or actor directly aware of his audience. This was a Shavian anti-illusionary device used as early as the turn of the century in "Don Juan in Hell" yet still considered in current playwrights the epitome of modernity. Shaw had combined two of the most primitive, yet most basic, elements of the self-conscious theater in his work; the platform of the philosopher and the stage of the clown. Perhaps he was only as avant-garde as Aristophanes. "Theatre technique," Shaw observed, "begins with the circus clown and ringmaster and the Greek tribune, which is a glorified development of the pitch from which the poet of the market place declaims his verses. . . ." He might have added that Shavian theater techniques include the amusement park's distorting mirrors held up to human nature, the old-fashioned yet timeless routines of burlesque and the music hall, and the exhortations of what Shaw called "the roofless pavement orator." In post-Shavian refinements these are the techniques of *Waiting for Godot,* Ionesco's *The Chairs,* or Genet's *The Balcony* and the techniques, too, of Bertolt Brecht. By destroying stage illusion and by inhibiting the possibilities of empathic identification between audience and characters, the playwright, theoretically at least, creates a distance which forces the spectator to look at the action on stage in a detached and critical spirit: what Brecht called, years later, his "alienation effect." The playful shifting in and out of illusion enlivens not only the later works, however. We see it in the earlier comedies as well, as when the amoral artist Louis Dubedat in *The Doctor's Dilemma* confides that he is a disciple of Bernard Shaw or when the critics who attend the premiere of *Fanny's First Play* (a play within the frame of the critics' dialogue) declare that while the play is too good to really be by Fanny O'Dowda, one had to eliminate Shaw from the possibilities. "I've repeatedly proved that Shaw is physiologically incapable of the note of passion," says one. The others also eliminate Shaw:

VAUGHAN: Well, at all events, you cant deny that the characters in this play are quite distinguishable from one another. That proves it's not by Shaw, because all Shaw's characters are himself: mere puppets stuck up to spout Shaw. It's only the actors that make them seem different.

BANNAL: There can be no doubt of that: everybody knows it. But Shaw doesnt write his plays as plays. All he wants to do is to insult everybody all round and set us talking about him.

TROTTER: [*wearily*] And naturally, here we are all talking about him. For heaven's sake, let us change the subject.

The audience, then, is given little opportunity to absorb itself imaginatively into the play, for the playwright jests directly with his audience. Again, Shaw in *Misalliance,* realizing that his audience knows very well indeed that he is the author of *Man and Superman,* has his book-mad character John Tarleton, who is constantly advising people to read this and that, observe: "Still, you know, the superman may come. The superman's an idea. I believe in ideas. Read Whatshisname."

No one in a Shaw audience could possibly mistake the reference, and each one is thus taken out of the play and into the playwright's confidence. Similarly, when Private Meek in *Too True to Be Good* turns out to be messenger, translator, intelligence officer, and almost every other military specialist wrapped up in one, we find this out through cross-talk reminiscent of traditional music-hall sketches, and the absurdity reinforces the nonrealism while making the obvious point that the system and the setting are equally absurd. It does not surprise us that the sergeant is a disciple of John Bunyan, only that the zany Private Meek is not another self-confessed disciple of Bernard Shaw.

"To call Shaw's plays forerunners of the theatre of the absurd," says one of the better Shaw critics, "would be indeed farfetched."[5] Yet eighteen pages later the critic writes, quite accurately, "In *Too True to Be Good*, more than in any of his other plays, Shaw dramatizes the absurdity of the human condition." Among the numerous irrational and absurd speeches and happenings pointed to is that of the Doctor and the Microbe, with the latter insisting that he did not give the Patient measles but rather that she gave it to him; the following lines are quoted:

> THE DOCTOR: The microbe of measles has never been discovered. If there is a microbe it cannot be measles: it must be parameasles.
>
> THE MONSTER: Great Heavens! what are parameasles?
>
> THE DOCTOR: Something so like measles that nobody can see any difference.

"Irrational dialogue," says the critic, forgetting his earlier words, "suggests an irrational universe," and he observes in a footnote that "This particular dialogue, anticipating dialogue in absurdist plays, differs little from the lecture on Spanish and neo-Spanish in Ionesco's *The Lesson*." Yet a much earlier play, a one-act farce produced in July 1905, *Passion, Poison and Petrifaction,* anticipates Ionesco's *The Bald Soprano* (with its "English clock" striking "seventeen English strokes") by nearly half a century. It begins with the bedroom clock striking sixteen:

> THE LADY: How much did the clock strike, Phyllis?
>
> PHYLLIS: Sixteen, my lady.
>
> THE LADY: That means eleven o'clock, does it not?
>
> PHYLLIS: Eleven at night, my lady. In the morning it means half-past two; so if you hear it strike sixteen during your slumbers, do not rise.

In this play, as in others by Shaw, it is not that the stage is all the world but rather that all the world is the stage:

> PHYLLIS: Will your ladyship not undress?
>
> THE LADY: Not tonight, Phyllis. [*Glancing through where the fourth wall is missing*] Not under the circumstances.

Later someone is poisoned, and an antidote is suggested "if an antidote would not be too much of anticlimax." Adolphus, the victim, declares, "Anticlimax be blowed! Do you think I am going to die to please the critics?

Out with your antidote. Quick!" And Adolphus then eats the plaster ceiling for the lime in it.

Shaw, who in the subtitle calls this farce a "tragedy," is thinking along the lines of the later Ionesco, who spoke of "the tragedy of language." Throughout the play the dialogue is no more real than the action, for the dialogue communicates the absurdity of the society Shaw shows in his distorting mirror. There is a thunderstorm, and maid and mistress anticipate the worst:

LADY MAGNESIA: In case we should never again meet in this world, let us take a last farewell.

PHYLLIS: [*embracing her with tears*] My poor murdered angel mistress!

LADY MAGNESIA: In case we should meet again, call me at half-past eleven.

It is difficult to keep in mind that this was written in 1905, in the comfortable years of Edward VII. But Shaw's sense of the absurd would keep surfacing until it became the dominant mood of his plays in the 1930s, where the duologues in one of his playlets of the period, *Village Wooing,* are between "A" and "Z" and where the conversation has the most vitality it anticipates the playwrights of a later generation in using clichés in cross-talk as an assault on human reason.

Z: Excuse me. Could you tell me the time?

A: [*curtly*] Eleven.

Z: My watch makes it half past ten.

A: The clocks were put on half an hour last night. We are going east.

Z: I always think it adds to the interest of a voyage having to put on your watch.

A: I am glad you are so easily interested [*he resumes his writing pointedly*].

Z: I never cared much for geography. Where are we now?

A: We are on the Red Sea.

Z: But it's blue.

A: What did you expect it to be?

Z: Well, I didnt know what color the sea might be in these parts. I always thought the Red Sea would be red.

A: Well, it isnt.

Z: And isnt the Black Sea black?

A: It is precisely the color of the sea at Margate.

Z: [*eagerly*] Oh, I am so glad you know Margate. Theres no place like it in the season, is there?

A: I dont know: I have never been there.

Z: [*disappointed*] Oh, you ought to go. You could write a book about it.

A: [*shudders, sighs, and pretends to write very hard!*] [*A pause.*]

Z: I wonder why they call it the Red Sea.

A: Because their fathers did. Why do you call America America?

Z: Well, because it is America. What else would you call it?

When Noel Coward would write such uncommunicative absurdities in *Private Lives,* it would be considered ultrasmart; when Pinter would put together such talk in *The Caretaker* and other plays in the postwar theater, critics would talk of his breaking new ground. But *Village Wooing* was the play Shaw wrote after *Too True to Be Good,* in the very early 1930s.

As an aside, it is worth mentioning another anticipation of midcentury playwrights, this one from *Heartbreak House:*

RANDALL: Really, Hushabye, I think a man may be allowed to be a gentleman without being accused of posing.

HECTOR: It is a pose like any other. In this house we know all the poses: our game is to find out the man under the pose. . . .

RANDALL: Some of the games in this house are damned annoying, let me tell you.

HECTOR: Yes, I've been their victim for years. I used to writhe under them at first, but I became accustomed to them. At least I learned to play them.

RANDALL: If it's all the same to you, I'd rather you didn't play them on me. . . .

More than a generation later, Edward Albee would pick this up in having his characters talk about game playing in *Who's Afraid of Virginia Woolf?,* and Pinter and Osborne in England would do much the same thing.

Even the ancient world was a stage for Shaw, who begins *Caesar and Cleopatra* with an old-fashioned, prenaturalistic prologue. Spoken by the Egyptian god Ra, it is a lecture which makes the audience well aware that it *is* an audience and that the play is a play:

(. . . *He surveys the modern audience with great contempt; and finally speaks the following words to them.*) Peace! Be silent and hearken to me, ye quaint little islanders. . . . I ask you not for worship but for silence. Let not your men speak, or your women cough; for I am come to draw you back over the graves of sixty generations. . . . Are ye impatient with me? Do you crave for a story of an unchaste woman? Hath the name of Cleopatra tempted ye hither? . . .

In similar spirit, after the improbable incidents of the first act of Shaw's *Too True to Be Good,* the act ends with the announcement by one of the cast: "The play is now virtually over; but the characters will discuss it at great length for two acts more. The exit doors are all in order. Goodnight." The play ends with the impassioned but interminable oration of a young man which goes on while the other characters exit, leaving him to preach in solitude; at last he is enveloped in fog and darkness. In the opening words of Shaw's last stage direction, *"The audience disperses. . . ."* It has become part of the play. We will return to this scene.

After his first few plays satisfied his commitment to Ibsen, Shaw was always "ready to stop the overt action for a good discussion or good lecture, or even step out of the proscenium frame to harangue the audience in behalf of a relevant philosophy or sociology which is beyond, if not indeed antithetical to, the illusion achieved by plodding realists and the designers who provide scenic realism."

Since the 1890s this had been Shaw's principle as well as his practice. His early plays as well as the concluding chapters of *The Quintessence of Ibsenism* show that he rapidly outgrew the confines of realism, and if Shaw's later plays belong at all "to the genre of realism it is by virtue of their engagement to reality, chiefly by comprising a conflict of ideas, principles, ways of thinking, and ways of living. For the sake of reality, Shaw was always prepared to violate realistic structure and verisimilitude, to turn somersaults of the most farcical or fantastic kind, and to be arbitrary with his plot or discard plot altogether."[6]

A playwright who often directed and cast his own plays, Shaw was as much interested in the problems of staging as he was in the intellectual and emotional climate he was writing into his plays. Because they became for him aspects of the same problem, he experimented not only with new theoretical wine in familiar bottles, and finely aged wine in new and unfamiliar bottles, but with the indivisibility of technique and theme. The result was often a play which by orthodox, contemporary standards only baffled orthodox contemporary critics. Max Beerbohm in 1903 was convinced that *Man and Superman,* particularly the "Don Juan in Hell" interlude, was a "peculiar article" and "of course, not a play at all." Paradoxically, Max added, "It is 'as good as a play'—infinitely better, to my peculiar taste, than any play I have ever read or seen enacted. But a play it is not."[7] Within two years Max had recanted, admitting that the failure had been his own—his own narrowness of theatrical imagination.

Sometimes the complaints about Shaw's playcrafting were really expressions of frustration at not finding a conventional plot and predictable characters moving within it. When Shaw was ninety-four he observed that this was an old story: "Now it is quite true that my plays are all talk, just as Raphael's pictures are all paint, Michael Angelo's statues all marble, Beethoven's symphonies all noise."[8]

In 1908, when a fictitious interviewer from the *Daily Telegraph* had prodded G.B.S. for "some notion of the plot" of *Getting Married,* which proved to be one of Shaw's most talky dramas, the author, with jesting truthfulness, responded:

MR. SHAW: The play has no plot. Surely nobody expects a play by me to have a plot. I am a dramatic poet, not a plot-monger.

INTERVIEWER: But at least there is a story.

MR. SHAW: Not at all. If you look at any of the old editions of our classical plays, you will see that the description of the play is not called a plot or story but an argument—an argument lasting three hours, and carried on with unflagging cerebration by twelve people and a beadle.[9]

Unprepared by conventional drama for this genre of theater, a later critic wrote of *The Apple Cart:* "Here is the final exaggeration of all of Shaw's tendencies as a dramatist. Action has totally disappeared and all the characters sit on chairs, hour in and hour out. And in the place of human emotion is the brain of Shaw, bulging larger and larger, filling the stage, hard and brilliant, glittering like a jewel."[10]

The cerebral fantasies and dramatic debates—Shavian plays of passionate ideas—were to come to life in a variety of symbolic or naturalistic settings. When Shaw's plays after World War I were inaugurated by *Heartbreak House,* one unsung Shaw commentator noted that Shaw's "was a grave message: it would issue gravely if it were not for the instinct for absurdity which has never deserted him." But it caused his public, unready for this approach to drama, to desert him when *Heartbreak House* was first staged in 1920. It played to nearly empty houses, and even a return look arranged for the London reviewers failed to convince any of them that they had been wrong the first time. After sixty-three performances it had to close. No one could make head or tail of it, Shaw explained. "The house is not Heartbreak House at first: the fly walks into the parlour with the happiest anticipations, and is kept amused until it gets fixed there as by a spell. Then the heartbreak begins, and gets worse until the house breaks out through the windows, and becomes all England with all England's heart broken. In vain do the tortured spectators beg for the house without the heartbreak, or to be at least allowed to go home. They are held ruthlessly on the rack until the limit of human endurance is reached after three hours of torment. . . ." In description Shaw made the play sound more like *The Ghost Sonata* of Strindberg than a play by G.B.S.—but what he had written was a play of a nature almost unique to himself at the time: "serious farce," almost a contradiction in terms.[11] Like some of the later plays of Strindberg, it had the disconnected quality of a dream.

It is just possible, in fact, that the play is largely the dream of Ellie Dunn, who falls asleep in the Hushabye (Heartbreak) House before the play is two pages old. Similarly, a later Shavian play in which the *Heartbreak House* techniques and themes are extended, *Too True to Be Good,* may also be largely the dream fantasy of a woman, ill and delirious, who fantasizes her recovery and escape from her sickbed. Shaw doesn't even make a distinction between sleeping and waking consciousness; the Patient insists in Act III as she had in Act I that what happens is contained in her dream. If she belongs to both fantasy and reality, however, do the other characters also?

A number of twentieth-century critics have pointed out that although medieval and renaissance drama sometimes used the device of a dream, it is only modern drama that uses dream structure and dream imagery significantly. Here again Shaw's contribution is significant. One of the earliest twentieth-century plays to combine both approaches was Shaw's *Man and Superman,* which combines what is apparently a conventional play with a dream vision in which grand, representative figures of myth parallel characters in the play. Martin Esslin, in *The Theatre of the Absurd,* suggests that "the first to put on the stage a dream world in the spirit of modern psychological thinking was August Strindberg. The three parts of *To Damascus* (1898–1904), *A Dream Play* (1902), and *The Ghost Sonata* (1907) are masterly transcriptions of dreams and obsessions, and direct sources of the theatre of the Absurd." Strindberg himself wrote of his aims in his introductory note to *A Dream Play:* "In this dream play . . . the author has sought to reproduce the disconnected but apparently logical form of a dream. Anything can happen; everything is possible and probable. Time and space do not exist. On a slight groundwork of reality, imagination spins and weaves new patterns made up of memories, experiences, unfettered fancies, absurdities, and improvisations. The characters are split, double and multiply; they evaporate, crystallize, scatter and converge. But a single consciousness holds sway over them all—that of the dreamer. . . ."

Concurrently, and differently, Shaw was using the concept of the dream vision, uninfluenced by Strindberg. The concepts with which they were working were part of the then-current intellectual climate, and each, according to his nature, had put these ideas into his playwriting. Shaw, in the "Don Juan in Hell" episode in *Man and Superman,* had projected into his art a momentary vision of bodiless intelligences who manifest themselves by willing ghostly forms and engage in a Shavio-Mozartian quartet without time, space, or dimension. Here is Shaw's own description of his aims, from the program notes for the 1907 production at the Royal Court Theatre:

The scene, an abysmal void, represents hell; and the persons of the drama speak of hell, heaven and earth as if they were separate localities, like "the heavens above, the earth beneath, and the waters under the earth." It must be remembered that such localizations are purely figurative, like our fashion of calling a treble voice "high" and a bass voice "low." Modern theology conceives heaven and hell, not as places, but as states of the soul; and by the soul it means, not an organ like the liver, but the divine element common to all life, which causes us "to do the will of God" in addition to looking after our individual interests, and to honor one another solely for our divine activities and not at all for our selfish activities.

Hell is popularly conceived not only as a place, but as a place of cruelty and punishment, and heaven as a paradise of idle pleasure. These legends are discarded by the higher theology, which holds that this world, or any other, may be made a hell by a society in a state of damnation: that is, a society so lacking in the higher orders of energy that it is given wholly to the pursuit of immediate individual pleasure, and cannot even conceive the passion of the divine will. Also that any world can be made a heaven by a society of persons in whom that passion is the master passion—a "communion of saints" in fact.

In the scene presented to-day hell is this state of damnation. . . .

Continuing to use elements of dream and of myth, Shaw often combined the two, as in *Androcles and the Lion, Pygmalion, Back to Methuselah,* and *Saint Joan.* One critic remarked that Shaw "would have furiously protested against our ascribing to him any such notion as that life is a dream. But when we look at some of his finest works this is what they say. Take such a masterpiece as *Pygmalion,* for example. Here we have the complete transformation of a vulgar, dirty and illiterate girl into a dazzling lady, brought about by cleansing her, dressing her, and altering her diction. The play is incidentally a Cinderella story.[12]

The critic might have added that Shaw, in a realistic setting, had utilized the myths of both Pygmalion and Cinderella and, as dreams do, inverted elements of them. *Saint Joan,* too, uses a figure about which an entire mythos has grown up. Shaw presents her story as a realistic chronicle and then concludes with a dream fantasy apparently no less real than the earlier reality yet one which wrenches the audience, moved by Joan's death, back into a more objective frame of mind, its humor leaving the audience nonetheless "guilty creatures sitting at a play." An alert audience, watching the epilogue, would realize that the appearance of the clerical gentleman from the Vatican, in 1920 costume, breaks the illusion of the dream, just as when the "Dream in Hell" interlude in *Man and Superman* closes, we have the following lines in the transitional scene:

MENDOZA: Did you dream?

TANNER: Damnably. Did you?

MENDOZA: Yes. I forget what. You were in it.

TANNER: So were you. Amazing.

Shattering illusions, even the stage illusion of the dream, was always basic to Shaw's techniques, as it was to his themes. But one final illusion remains to be shattered—the very absurdity of the conclusion of *Too True to Be Good,* in which Aubrey Bagot, the burglar turned preacher, exhorts the audience in a speech of conspicuous absurdity as (in Shaw's stage directions) the lights go on in the auditorium, the audience begins to disperse, and the curtain goes down on the still-preaching protagonist. Shaw wrote to the producer, H. K. Ayliff, while the play was in rehearsal, to confide that he was both theatrically stupid and inconsiderate to the actor to leave the speech at the curtain incomplete and depend upon a backstage technician to drop it at the right instant. Since any delay whatever would ruin the effect, Shaw promised to send Cedric Hardwicke, the Aubrey Bagot of the production, a peroration which could close the play even if the curtain failed utterly to descend. Then, to Hardwicke, he offered

> apologies for the indelicacy of leaving you with an uncompleted thought, and the blunder of placing you at the mercy of the curtain dropper, who is always late. I enclose a complete peroration which will see you through even if the stage hands do a lightning strike and the curtain does not come down at all. If and when it does fall, go on at full pitch for a word or so after it touches the ground. Then turn your back to it and walk up stage and off through the centre opening, preaching away *fortissimo* all the time to the end. They will hear you in front *after the fall of the curtain*—which is essential—and hear your voice away into silence quite naturally. I have attached a typed copy which will fit into your book. Paste it in. . . .[13]

Shaw did not tell Hardwicke (who was to speak the lines), as he told Ayliff,[14] that the words, although indistinct to the audience, should give the impression of meaning something. They didn't, he confessed, but they would serve their purpose.

The eloquent final lines, then, were the ultimate absurdity. If Aubrey Bagot's reactions were to a world he conceived as absurd, Shaw had, for the wrong reasons, kept him in character to the end. Yet the very absurdity of the finale was itself absurd. The lines were written only to gain time to get the curtain down.

Notes

1. *Our Theatres in the Nineties,* II, 84. As a futurist Bernard Shaw was no H. G. Wells, yet it is interesting to note that Shaw seems to have anticipated other playwrights in practice as well as in theory. A long list of stage "firsts" can be assigned to Shavian drama. The first automobile on stage appears in *Man and Superman* (1903), and the first airplane makes its entrance (via an off-stage crash) in *Misalliance* seven years later—along with the first aviatrix. The first Zeppelin appears in *Heartbreak House* (1917), and the first robot in *Back to Methuselah* (1920), where one also conducts telephone conversations via a television screen.

2. "On the University Dramatic Society," a G.B.S. lecture published in the *University College of Wales Magazine,* XXII (January 1900), 167–68.

3. Homer Woodbridge, *G. B. Shaw: Creative Artist* (Carbondale, Ill., 1963), p. 52.

4. Shaw in a letter to Alexander Bakshy, June 12, 1927. In *The Theatre Unbound,* by Cecil Palmer. Reprinted in E. J. West, ed., *Shaw on Theatre* (New York, 1958), p. 185.

5. Bernard F. Dukore, *Bernard Shaw, Playwright* (Columbia, Mo., 1973), p. 218.

6. John Gassner, "Bernard Shaw and the Making of the Modern Mind," *Dramatic Soundings* (New York, 1968), p. 635.

7. Max Beerbohm in the *Saturday Review*. Reprinted in his *Around Theatres* (New York, 1954), pp. 268–72.

8. Shaw, "The Play of Ideas," *New Statesman,* May 6, 1950. Reprinted in West, op. cit., p. 290.

9.   Reprinted in the *Bodley Head Bernard Shaw* (London, 1971), III, 667–68. This was a Shavian self-interview.

10.   Francis R. Bellamy, review of *The Apple Cart, Outlook,* March 12, 1930, p. 429.

11.   A curious anticipation of the term occurs in Shaw's draft press release for the first production of *The Doctor's Dilemma* in 1907. The play "will probably be called a *farce macabre,*" he prophesied, adding, "The death scene is an unprecedented mixture of fanciful poetry and pathos with ludicrous realism and biting irony" (Berg Collection, New York Public Library).

12.   Lionel Abel, *Metatheatre: A New View of Dramatic Form* (New York, 1963), p. 106.

13.   Undated but described as written the day after the play opened at Malvern in 1932. Quoted in Cedric Hardwicke, *A Victorian in Orbit* (New York, 1961), pp. 183–84.

14.   Shaw to H. K. Ayliff, tls, August 8, 1932. Hofstra University Library.

Shaw's Superman:
A Re-examination

CARL H. MILLS

W hen he proposed his theory of creative evolution in *Man and Superman,* in the preface to *Back to Methuselah,* and in *Back to Methuselah* itself, George Bernard Shaw had two long-range goals in mind: the development of superior human intelligence and the eugenic breeding of a super-race of "supermen." Nowhere in any of his works, however, did Shaw give anything like a precise description of his superman. In *Man and Superman,* the play in which he distilled all of his mature social, political, and evolutionary thought, the superman is incorporated into the character of Don Juan, who is considerably "upstaged" by his modern descendant, Jack Tanner. Indeed, the play is more familiar to audiences without its third act and Don Juan's superhuman performance in the Dialogue in Hell scene. Not only does Tanner overshadow the Don Juan–Superman of the third act—he also acknowledges the play's exclusion of an explicit description of the Shavian superman: he says in "The Revolutionist's Handbook" that the cry for the superman has always been silenced by demands for a description of him and by accusations that those who desire the breeding of a superman do not know exactly what they want. "The proof of the Superman," Tanner explains, "will be in the living; we shall find out how to produce him by the old method of trial and error, and not by waiting for a completely convincing prescription of his ingredients."[1]

Shaw's idea of a superman and of a super-race has frequently been misinterpreted and maligned, innocently and deliberately. The postscript to *Man and Superman* describes the kind of misinterpretation of the Shavian superman that has occurred for over sixty-five years: "not all of my reviewers have understood me: . . . many of them offer, as samples of the Shavian philosophy, the likest article from their own stock. Others are victims of association of ideas: they call me Pessimist because my remarks wound their self-complacency, and Renegade because I would have my mob all Caesars instead of Toms, Dicks, and Harrys. Worst of all, I have been accused of preaching a Final Ethical Superman: no other, in fact, than our old friend the

From *The Shaw Review* 13 (May 1970); 48–58. © 1970 by the Pennsylvania State University. Reproduced by permission of the Pennsylvania State University Press.

Just Man Made Perfect! This misunderstanding is so galling that I lay down my pen without another word."[2] Shaw soon had to take pen in hand again, to correct misinterpretations of the superman, and to attack his critics. He indicates in the preface to *Major Barbara* that there had been a more vicious kind of misinterpretation, one that still holds sway: "it is assumed that Nietzsche gained his European reputation for a senseless glorification of selfish bullying as a rule of life, just as it is assumed, on the strength of the single word Superman (übermensch) borrowed by me from Nietzsche, that I look for the salvation of society to the despotism of a single Napoleonic Superman, in spite of my careful demonstration of the folly of that outworn infatuation."[3] It must have seemed ironic indeed for Shaw to find that when his critics attacked the Shavian superman they often focused on the "Nietzschean" word *"übermensch"*: writing to his German translator in 1906, he says "Man & Superman will have the same title all over the world. Mensch und Übermensch is precisely right. . . . Mensch and Übermensch affirms its essentially philosophic quality and *dignity*."[4]

During the eighty-five-year history of Shaw's notion of a superman there have been two persistently false impressions of the superman: one is based on deliberate misinterpretation of Nietzsche's phrase "big blond beast" and on Shaw's approval, with explicit reservations, of Mussolini, Hitler, and Stalin. Shaw's reservations have been conveniently overlooked by those who disapprove of everything Shavian. Another false impression is based on romanticism, expressed through comic-strip supermen (and television supermen) who are paragons of strength, military prowess, and virtue (or vice). Neither false impression is remotely like Shaw's superman—one is deliberately distorted reality; the other is naively distorted illusion.

Some of the distortions of the Shavian superman can be set right by looking at the degree to which Shaw's nineteenth-century contemporaries influenced his vision of the superman. Those influences vary; some have been overemphasized and some overlooked. It is those exaggerations and omissions that contribute significantly to the misunderstanding and criticism of Shaw's superman.

Thomas Carlyle's philosophy of hero-worship is only lightly reflected in Shaw's vision of the superman, but it has generally been given more credit than is due to it. Shaw's superman and Carlyle's hero are similar in only a few ways; critics of Shaw's superman have, however, drawn an analogy between the two and have also attributed superman-worship to Shaw, thereby condemning Shaw and his superman for the same reasons that they condemn Carlyle's short-sighted hero-worship and Carlyle's hero.

Although Shaw expressed his admiration for Nietzsche by writing "I want the Germans to know me as a philosopher, as an English (or Irish) Nietzsche (only ten times cleverer), and not as a mere carpenter of farces,"[5] Nietzsche's concept of the superman did not influence Shaw as much as Shaw's critics have suggested. It was Nietzsche's prose style, with its forcefulness and Carlylean eccentricities, first read by Shaw in translation, that influenced him more than Nietzsche's *"übermensch."* In 1896 Shaw writes: "the only excuse for reading them [Nietzsche's epigrams] is that before long you must be prepared either to talk about Nietzsche or else retire from society, especially from aristocratically minded society (not the same thing, by the way, as aristocratic society) since Nietzsche is the champion of privilege, of power, and of inequality."[6] The exaggeration of Nietzsche's influence on Shaw's superman concept is responsible for much of the criticism that is still heaped upon Shaw; *i.e.,* Caesar's "indifferent" burning of the library at Alexandria in *Caesar and Cleopatra* is imputed to an arrogant and brutal Shavian superman, and Shaw's temporary and reserved approval of European dictators in the early 1930's is called "Aryanism" and Fascism.

How much did Nietzsche influence Shaw? and how similar are their supermen? Shaw spelled out the major likeness: "Nietzsche's criticism of morality and idealism is essentially that demonstrated as at the bottom of Ibsen's plays. . . . So far I am on common ground with Nietzsche. But not for a moment will I suffer anyone to compare me to him as a critic. Never was there a deafer, blinder, socially and politically inepter academician."[7] Other than this, there are few similarities.[8] Nietzsche said that man would be to the superman as the ape is to man, "a laughing-stock, a thing of shame." Shaw often used a similar analogy to compare man to the superman. In his favorite comparison, contemporary man is to the Australian bushman as the future superman will be to Julius Caesar. All of Shaw's supermen, because of their Puritanical devotion to the spirit of the life force, want to be free from the tyranny of their passions. They constantly attack Hedonism and Epicureanism. Because he believed that to secure the freedom to do the superman's work the pleasure instincts must be subdued, Nietzsche, too, continually attacked Hedonism and Epicureanism. Nineteenth-century evangelical morality, according to Nietzsche and Shaw, had two harmful effects: it either wasted the life force by being used as an excuse for Hedonism, or it turned against the instincts of life and condemned them, whether they were secret or outspoken and impudent. Finally, John Tanner may be indebted to Nietzsche for the maxims for revolutionists in "The Revolutionist's Handbook," as has often been suggested, but there is much more of Blake in those maxims—and of Shelley, too—than there is of Nietzsche.

Even though there are a few affinities, the supermen of Shaw and Nietzsche are not nearly as similar as critics have made them. Nietzsche's superman is closer to Carlyle's hero than he is to Shaw's superman. The major difference between the supermen of Shaw and Nietzsche stems from Nietzsche's despair over modern civilization and his consequent search for salvation through a few select supermen. Shaw was careful to point out, as I have indicated, that Nietzsche was the "champion of privilege, of power, and of inequality." Nietzsche was, like Shaw, anti-Darwin, but with this difference: he felt that the struggle for existence is asserted rather than proved and that the species do not evolve towards perfection; "the weak always prevail over the strong," he writes, "because they are the majority, and because they are also more crafty. Darwin forgot the intellect (—that is English!); the weak have more intellect."[9] Shaw was a creative evolutionist and humanitarian socialist; Nietzsche was neither—he was completely contemptuous of the social equality for which Shaw worked all his life: " 'Equality,' as a certain definite process of making everybody uniform, which only finds its expression in the theory of equal rights, is essentially bound up with a declining culture. . . . Our socialists are decadents."[10] Perhaps Shaw's own analysis of Nietzsche's views on socialism and evolution highlights best the wide differences between the two men and their supermen: "to him [Nietzsche] Modern Democracy, Pauline Christianity, Socialism, and so on are deliberate plots hatched by malignant philosophers to frustrate the evolution of the human race and mass the stupidity and brute force of the many weak against the beneficial tyranny of the few strong. This is not even a point of view: it is an absolutely fictitious hypothesis."[11]

We must look to the works of Ibsen and Wagner for the most significant literary influences on Shaw's concept of the superman. It was Ibsen's philosophy rather than his dramatic technique, however, that interested Shaw the most. The interest was first expressed in "The Quintessence of Ibsenism" and later throughout *Our Theatres in the Nineties.* In the preface to the first edition of "The Quintessence of Ibsenism" Shaw writes: "it is not a critical essay on the poetic beauties of Ibsen, but simply an exposition of Ibsenism."[12] Shaw's exposition is actually an argument for viewing Ibsen's plays, particularly *Brand, Peer Gynt,* and *Emperor and Galilean,* as predictions by Ibsen that the world-will will attempt to create a superman.

In *Brand* Ibsen described a noble and heroic priest who attempts to teach men that God is young and powerful and that God demands heroic effort from man. Ibsen and Shaw strongly disapproved of Brand's making God an idol to whom he sacrifices himself and those he loves. "Ibsenism," as Shaw calls it, has two outstanding characteristics that are paramount in Shaw's concept of the superman: the superman's heroic energy and his willingness to serve what inspires him rather than sacrifice himself to it. But Peer Gynt is "everybody's hero," writes Shaw; "he has the same effect on the imagination that Hamlet, Faust, and Mozart's Don Juan have had."[13] Peer Gynt avoids Brand's error by establishing as his ideal the realization of himself through utter satisfaction of his own will; he feels that he has been something merely by having been himself. Both Shaw and Ibsen felt, however, that there is one step further that must be taken by a "superman": to be one's self is to slay one's self and to follow out in everything, guided by insight, the world-will. In Shaw's philosophy that will is the life force; in Ibsen's philosophy it is the will of God.

In both philosophies the truly worthwhile mode of existence is to be used up in the service of the guiding force rather than to sacrifice one's self to it without first having done everything possible to further its intention.

Shaw called *Emperor and Galilean* "a play about the superman" and a play in which Ibsen tried to describe how the world-will operates. Maximus the mystic advised Julian to create a synthesis of Christianity and paganism in the "God-Emperor" who will then make an evolutionary leap and swallow up both the emperor and the Galilean. Julian fails, however; "it was something for Julian to have seen that the power which he found stronger than his individual will was itself will, but inasmuch as he conceived it, not as the whole of which his will was but a part, but as a rival will, he was not the man to found the third empire."[14] The clue to Julian's failure is given to us by the Devil in *Man and Superman,* who is "everybody's hero" and who serves only his own will and the individual wills of his followers: he says "beware of the pursuit of the superman—it leads to an indiscriminate contempt for the Human."[15] To the Devil "human" means the passions and their gratification; he has contempt for any superhuman attempts to control them. His will is a rival will to the life force. Julian was also guilty of that contempt in *Emperor and Galilean;* consequently, he suffered "the punishment of the fool who pursues the better before he has secured the good."[16] Shaw's superman does not make the mistakes that Brand, Peer Gynt, or Julian make. Shaw began where Ibsen left off, learned Ibsen's lessons, and formed a notion of a superman that excludes those weaknesses and yet includes all of the worthwhile characteristics of Brand, Peer Gynt, and the Emperor Julian.

It is the revolutionary Wagner of the years spent in exile after the German Revolution of 1848 whom Shaw admired and whose ideas he discussed in "The Perfect Wagnerite." In the preface to the first edition of "The Perfect Wagnerite" Shaw points out that his ideas were quite similar to Wagner's and that he formulated them much as Wagner did: they both learned more about music in their youth than anything else and then participated in "the revolutionary school." As with Ibsen, Shaw was attracted primarily by Wagner's ideas; his interest in the operas was secondary.

"The Perfect Wagnerite" is no more a Shavian discussion of Wagner's music than "The Quintessence of Ibsenism" is a discussion of Ibsen's poetry; it is an argument for viewing *"Der Ring des Nibelungen"* as Wagner's prediction that the life force will attempt to create an order of heroes, or supermen, who will replace the highest order of men, or gods. According to Shaw's analysis, the god Wotan unites with the vital woman, Erda, and after trial and error, creates the superman-hero Siegfried. The ultimate fruit of the union is not the hero, but true will, or the image of woman, similar to Goethe's eternal feminine image that draws man onward and upward and that significantly influenced Shaw's theory of creative evolution. True will is called Brunhilde, and Wotan tells Erda in "Siegfried" what Brunhilde's purpose shall be:

> Die du mir gebar'st
> Brunhilde,
> Sie weckt hold sich der Held:
> Wachend wirkt
> Dein wissendes Kind
> Erlosende Weltanthat.[17]

Siegfried is, in essence, "a totally unmoral person, a born anarchist, the ideal of Bakoonin, an anticipation of the 'overman' of Nietzsche;"[18] he is, like the heroes of Carlyle and Ibsen, also the legitimate successor to the old god Wotan.

Wagner's hero-savior and Shaw's superman are much more similar than has generally been indicated, although the ideas of the two writers on some other subjects are quite dissimilar. There is much in Wagner's works that is un-Shavian: Wagner's theory of redemption through suffering, his notion of transfiguration through death, and his idea of the desirability of negating the will are all contrary to Shaw's philosophy. Wagner became a pessimist, a nationalist, and an amorist, who "Lohengrinized"; these were all abhorrent to Shaw.

If Shaw's concept of the superman is a synthesis of ideas suggested to him by Carlyle, Nietzsche, Ibsen, and Wagner, he owes to Carlyle the idea of the hero's superior leadership, even though he and Carlyle admired different great men; he owes to Nietzsche the idea of the hero's iconoclasm and free spirit, even though he and Nietzsche disagreed about the catholicism of man's future superhumanity; he owes to Ibsen the idea of the hero's inspiration from within himself and from the life force, even though he and Ibsen disagreed about the ability of the life force, through creative evolution, eventually to achieve a universal super-race of god-emperors; and he owes to Wagner the paramount idea of the hero's social consciousness and political dedication, even though he and Wagner disagreed about the methods of accomplishing social reforms. Shaw's superman is just that: "Shaw's Superman"; he is a refinement of and improvement of Carlyle's hero, Nietzsche's overman, Ibsen's God-Emperor, and Wagner's hero-savior, all brought up to date and conforming to the theory of creative evolution formulated by Lamarck, Butler, and Shaw.

In addition to the description of Shaw's superman that I have been composing here based on Shaw's acknowledged influences on his vision of the superman, it is possible to glean from *Man and Superman* and from Shaw's other works a more complete description of the Shavian superman than the vague hints about him given us through John Tanner. One ingredient for the superman that Shaw constantly insisted on is a superior mind unencumbered by conventional morality; but he always denied that a superior mind is the result of a superior body, and had several of his characters say or demonstrate that life has not measured the success of its attempts at improvement by beauty or the bodily perfection of the results. Shaw's supermen are seldom physically handsome; but they are people with superior and unreasonable minds—unreasonable because, as Shaw frequently suggested, the superman will often reject society's conventional attitudes toward sex, marriage, and morality, especially if those attitudes stand in the way of man's political, social, or evolutionary progress toward the breeding of an improved race. Society is often attracted by the superhuman rebel and champions him, but unfortunately, society champions only the rebel's inherent iconoclasm, not his sincere desire for human progress: "the world has always delighted in the man who is delivered from conscience; he has always drawn large crowds."[19] When the rebellion and iconoclasm of the superman become dangers to the conventions of society, however, he is no longer championed: "if a great man could make us understand him, we should hang him."[20]

The superman who appears before any significant and enduring evolutionary progress has been achieved, whether he be a moralist, founder of a religion, poet, or philosopher, will seem to be a madman whose conscience does not correspond to that of the majority. Shaw explains the relationship between the "interim" superman, who he thought would have to be unconventional, *per se*, and the majority of society, in "The Sanity of Art":

> The superman will certainly come like a thief in the night, and be shot accordingly. . . . On the other hand, we cannot ask the Superman simply to add a higher set of virtues to current respectable morals; for he is undoubtedly going to empty a good deal of respectable morality out . . . and replace it by new and strange customs, shedding old obligations and accepting new and heavier ones. Every step of his progress must horrify conventional people; and if it were possible for even the most superior man to march ahead all the time, every pioneer of the march toward the Superman would be crucified.[21]

It will often be necessary for the superman to support popular political views against his better judgment. In his assertion of the political need for the superman, Shaw says that the politician who holds popular convictions with prodigious energy is the man for the mob, while the more frail sceptic, who is cautiously working for long-range progress, has no chance, "unless he happens by accident to have the specific artistic talents of the mountebank as well, in which case it is as a mountebank that he catches votes."[22] Here again, the superman will be championed because of his dazzling chicanery, not necessarily because of his sincere desire for political progress. The superman will only become politically unpopular when he displays outwardly a sincere political altruism.

Along with a superior mind, genius is another outstanding characteristic of the Shavian superman. Shaw defined that genius as an unusual amount of intellectual capacity and artistic ability that the superman uses to serve mankind in all possible ways. The life force chooses the superman to aid evolutionary progress by increasing man's intellectual consciousness: our minds,

Shaw believed, are nothing but knowledge of ourselves, and the superman who adds to such knowledge creates new mind as surely as any woman creates new men. Because of his compelling desire to create and to increase man's intellectual consciousness, the genius-superman sometimes can be ruthless and unscrupulous. Since marriage began, Shaw reminds us, the great artist or genius has been known as a bad spouse or as a likely candidate for the description— Marchbanks in *Candida,* Dick Dudgeon in *The Devil's Disciple,* Lady Cicely Waynflete in *Captain Brassbound's Conversion,* Cusins in *Major Barbara,* and John Tanner in *Man and Superman* are all unfit for marriage. For Shaw the important part of the greatness of the genius lies in his willingness to squander even himself if necessary.

Shaw's critics have been fond of calling him a "Schopenhaurist," basing that label on one idea from Schopenhauer's reputation, his pessimism.[23] The "pessimism" of Schopenhauer, implicit in his works or reputed, Shaw flatly rejected. What attracted Shaw to Schopenhauer's works was Shaw's conviction that *The World as Will and Idea* "is the metaphysical complement to Lamarck's natural history, as it demonstrates that the driving force behind Evolution is a will-to-live, and to live, as Christ said long before, more abundantly."[24] Beyond this all-important general influence of Schopenhauer on Shaw, several other characteristics of the Shavian superman-genius were undoubtedly suggested to Shaw by Schopenhauer's essay on genius. In the essay Schopenhauer described the genius, his relationship to society, and the services he performs for evolutionary progress. According to Schopenhauer, a genius has a double intellect, one for himself and the service of his will and the other for the world, of which he becomes the mirror because of his purely objective attitude toward it. The work of art, poetry, or philosophy produced by the genius is simply the result of his contemplative attitude. Not only does the genius have a double intellect; he also leads a double life, one that is common to all mankind and the other that is purely of the intellect. In his intellectual pursuits the genius devotes himself to the constant increase, rectification, and extension of real, systematic knowledge and insight. At the same time the genius remains untouched by his own fate so long as it does not disturb him in his work. The second life of the genius, his intellectual life, is his chief mode of existence; his personal life, common to all mankind, is something subordinate, serving only to advance ends higher than itself.[25] Several of Shaw's major characters who have these "superhuman" traits lead (or try to lead) such a double life: Don Juan in "Don Giovanni Explains," Jack Tanner and Don Juan in *Man and Superman,* Caesar in *Caesar and Cleopatra,* Saint Joan, and Andrew Undershaft in *Major Barbara.*

In addition to his dual intellect and dual existence, Schopenhauer called the genius a *lucida intervella* of the whole human race: a genius is a man in whose mind the world is presented as an object in a mirror but with a degree more of clarity and greater distinction of outline than is attained by ordinary people. It is from the genius that mankind may look for most instruction, because the deepest insight into the most important matters is to be acquired by close study of things as a whole. Shaw's supermen are likely to be philosopher-statesmen, social prophets, or saviors of society, says Edmund Wilson, men who may often be unpopular, "acting in the right of their own superiority and giving people what they know to be good for them."[26] Genius is thus defined by Schopenhauer and dramatized by Shaw as an eminently clear consciousness of things in general and, therefore, also of that which is opposed to them: one's own self. The best expression of this selfishness of the superman-genius is spoken by Shaw's Don Juan in the third act of *Man and Superman:* "I tell you that as long as I can conceive something better than myself I cannot be easy unless I am striving to bring it into existence or clearing the way for it. That is the law of my life. That is the working within me of Life's incessant aspiration to higher organization, wider, deeper, intenser self-consciousness, and clearer self-understanding."[27]

There is one further characteristic of the Shavian superman that was suggested to Shaw by Schopenhauer's essay on genius. The genius is not only selfless, like Shaw's superman, or set aside from society like Nietzsche's superman, but he is also unique as an artist-philosopher. The genius will not only produce thoughts and works that could never have come from others, but as knowledge and thought form a mode of activity natural and easy to him, as they do for Shaw's Don Giovanni and Don Juan, he will also delight in them at all times and so apprehend all things more quickly. He will take a direct and lively pleasure in every increase of knowledge, in the purely intellectual life of humanity, with its effort to increase knowledge by means of the sciences and its desire to perfect the arts.[28]

Shaw's superman works for human progress and betterment as Schopenhauer's genius does because he has a rather peculiar kind of instinct, which Shaw renamed the life force, that drives him to give permanent form to what he sees and feels without being conscious of any further motive. It seemed to Schopenhauer that in the case of the genius the will to live, which is the spirit of the human species, is conscious of having by some rare chance and for a brief period attained a greater clarity of vision and is trying to secure it, or at least the outcome of it, for the whole species to which the individual genius belongs in his inmost being.

Shaw's superman, then, is nature's "philosopher pilot," who helps man achieve both the immediate and the long-range goals of evolution because he is a creative evolutionist and because the life force, which drives him relentlessly, demands that evolution be progressive, universal, and creative. "Shaw's supermen are not an elite served by a mass of 'herdmen,'" says Julian Kaye, "but all mankind bred and educated up to the level of the great men of the past."[29] John Gassner and Archibald Henderson also tell us that Shaw's superman is a creative evolutionist who serves all mankind: "Don Juan's vision of the Superman is a vision of an improved species of man who would give Shaw the better society for which he agitated as a socialist," Gassner says.[30]

Henderson calls the matured form of Shaw's superman "the ethical man," convinced of the bankruptcy of education and progress as practiced and understood, inspired with faith in the inner-will of the world, and resolved to develop the power to live more abundantly for all men.[31]

Until more of that abundance is available to all of mankind, Shaw's superman will, with his genuine altruism and universal humanitarianism, continue to be a selfless, objective iconoclast, whose guiding instinct will be the life force of creative evolution and whose purpose in life will be to expose wrongs, attack shams, and destroy retrogressive conventionality through ridicule.

Notes

1. Bernard Shaw, *Man and Superman*, Ayot St. Lawrence ed. (New York, 1930), p. 178. All references to Shaw's works are from this edition except where noted.

2. *Ibid.*, p. xl.

3. Bernard Shaw, *Major Barbara*, p. 211.

4. MS letter to Siegfried Trebitsch, 19 July 1906. (My italics.) Used with the permission of the Public Trustee and The Society of Authors, London, and the Henry W. and Albert A. Berg Collection, New York Public Library. All letters to Trebitsch cited are here.

5. MS letter to Siegfried Trebitsch, 26 Dec. 1902.

6. Bernard Shaw, *Our Theatres in the Nineties* (New York, 1931), II, 94.

7. *Loc. cit.*

8. See also Carl Levine, "Social Criticism of Shaw and Nietzsche," *The Shaw Review*, X (January 1967), 9–17. In the article Professor Levine discusses some similar objects of satire in the social criticism of Shaw and Nietzsche; *i.e.,* hypocrisy, religion, democracy, socialism, and marriage. The criticism of these by Shaw and Nietzsche, Professor Levine points out, stemmed primarily from an implicit faith in the future of mankind—a practical faith in Shaw and a more visionary one in Nietzsche. Except for giving a brief and general description of the difference between Shaw's Superman and Nietzsche's, Professor Levine does not discuss the Superman figure in any great detail.

9. Nietzsche, "Skirmishes in a War with the Age," *Twilight of the Idols,* in *The Complete Works of Friedrich Nietzsche,* tr. Thomas Common, ed. Oscar Levy (New York, 1964), XVI, 71. All references to Nietzsche's works are from this edition.

10. *Ibid.*, pp. 95–96.

11. *Our Theatres in the Nineties*, II, 95.

12. Bernard Shaw, "The Quintessence of Ibsenism," *Major Critical Essays* (New York, 1931), p. 14.

13. *Our Theatres in the Nineties*, II, 260.

14. "The Quintessence of Ibsenism," p. 62.

15. *Man and Superman*, p. 134.

16. *Ibid.*, p. 133.

17. Richard Wagner, "Siegfried," tr. Stewart Robb, in *A Treasury of Opera Librettos*, ed. David Legerman (Garden City, New York, 1962), p. 962.

18. Bernard Shaw, "The Perfect Wagnerite," *Major Critical Essays*, p. 212.

19. *Ibid.*, p. 225.

20. *Man and Superman*, p. 223.

21. Bernard Shaw, "The Sanity of Art," *Major Critical Essays*, p. 300.

22. *Man and Superman*, p. 191.

23. Bernard Shaw, *Collected Letters 1874–1897*, ed. Dan H. Laurence (New York, 1965), p. 317.

24. Bernard Shaw, *Prefaces by Bernard Shaw* (London: Constable and Co. Ltd., 1934), p. 492.

25. Arthur Schopenhauer, "On Genius," *The World as Will and Idea*, tr. R. B. Haldane and I. Kemp (London, 1948), III, 138 *et passim*.

26. Edmund Wilson, "Bernard Shaw at Eighty," *George Bernard Shaw: A Critical Survey*, ed. Louis Kronenberger (New York, 1953), p. 130.

27. *Man and Superman*, p. 127.

28. Schopenhauer, "On Genius," *loc. cit.*

29. Julian Kaye, *Bernard Shaw and the Nineteenth-Century Tradition* (Norman, Oklahoma, 1958), p. 107.

30. John Gassner, "Bernard Shaw and the Puritan in Hell," *The Theatre in Our Times* (New York, 1954), p. 159.

31. Archibald Henderson, *George Bernard Shaw* (New York, 1956), p. 597.

The New Woman and the New Comedy

BARBARA BELLOW WATSON

W hen Shaw thinks about women, something remarkable happens. He makes no assumptions. It would be wonderful enough to make no assumptions about what women are fitted for, what their place in society should be. The real wonder is to begin thinking about women without assuming that there is any mystery at all. Shaw does so and instead of wearing himself out trying to solve a mystery that does not exist, sets to work observing the life around him. Experience indicates that if man is not mysterious, woman is not mysterious either. If woman is an enigma, isn't man? "I always assumed that a woman was a person exactly like myself, and that is how the trick is done."[1]

The trick is Shaw's creation of a long list of interesting characters who happen to be females, and that contribution alone should make him a patron saint of the women's movement. Beginning nearly a hundred years ago with the independent and intelligent women in his novels, and continuing through his last plays, Shaw turned out a distinctive product, the Shavian woman—the quintessence of the New Woman. But the full significance of this Shavian woman emerges only as an element in a larger pattern in which the woman as character and the woman as theme are largely interchangeable. And in changing the treatment of women, in placing women as subjects at the center of the dramatic structure, Shaw changed radically the structure of comedy itself. The Shavian comedy of ideas is full of ideas on all kinds of subjects, but the revolutionary aspect of its comic structure is tied most essentially to its ideas on women.

If conflict is at the center of drama, the enduring themes of drama in our culture have been conflicts between the needs or conscience of the individual and the requirements of social institutions, political, religious or sexual. In comedy the pattern has been even more specific. A funny thing happens on the way to the wedding. There is conflict between the sexual wishes of the powerless young and the restrictive rulings of the unreasonable old. It is understood that there is only one happy solution for such a conflict. When lovers marry, comedies can end. In Greek, Renaissance and Restoration comedy, and in the sentimental plays that mark the decline of the comic spirit after the Restoration,

From *Fabian Feminist: Bernard Shaw and Woman,* edited by Rodelle Weintraub (University Park and London: The Pennsylvania State University Press, 1977), 114–29. © 1977 by The Pennsylvania State University. Reproduced by permission of the publisher.

this pattern manifests itself in various ways, but remains essentially an expression of the social values of a relatively stable society. In some sense, Shakespeare may indeed be our contemporary. In another, our age, beginning in the eighteenth century, is no more like Renaissance England than it is like ancient Greece, and since comedy is so specific to the values of a particular culture, Shakespeare is less our contemporary in the comedies than in the tragedies and histories. It is probably significant that comedy fell into a long coma during just the period when this fundamental change in social expectations was beginning. Social stability, the reliable repetition of the patterns of life, could no longer be counted on. And once a new consciousness had been shaped by the conditions of modern life, it was no longer possible to construct any comedy with real vitality upon the old pattern. In Shavian comedy the pattern has shifted radically. Instead of the conflict between the individual with state and church, specifically in comedy the conflict between the lover and the laws and mores of marriage, Shavian drama deals preeminently with the conflict between the individual woman's humanity and the rigidity of the sex role assigned to her. This shift in subject matter represents also a profound shift in the structure of the comedy, reflecting an essentially changed society.

The revolutionary structure of Shaw's comedy is not, of course, an isolated phenomenon. The new drama of Ibsen, Strindberg and Chekhov is one in which the woman is not only more important but important in a quite different way. Woman has changed from being primarily an element in the plot to being primarily an element in the thought of the play. Her part in the action becomes less a matter of circumstance, less external, and more a matter of her own personality and volition, more internal and psychological. Literature in general during this whole period (beginning before the French Revolution with the rise of the romantic consciousness) shifts its center of gravity from exterior to interior events, reflecting the individualism, the egalitarianism, and the psychological preoccupations of the time, and it is not surprising that the man of action should begin to be replaced at center stage by the woman of awareness. The man of sensibility is there also, but it is obvious that the possibility of having a woman as hero increases when the heroism is inner. The young man adventuring his way to success never disappears in fact or fiction, but his story begins to convey less to both men and women than that of the woman who cannot adventure against the world but does struggle, lighting up in the hopelessness of her attempt the whole landscape of the struggle that each one is puzzling out alone. Since every woman has, in addition to personal conflicts of her own, the universal conflict of the individual female with the expectations of a sex role that is made to fit everyone and no one, the woman's struggle for self-realization has a special weight. This is not yet the Shavian woman, the "woman of action," but it is the same atmosphere that will produce her at a later stage. Even outside the realm of literature, public debate on "the Woman Question" has more than a hundred years of tragicomic history. Here too, though the outer conflicts with the world of men and laws have been monstrous and ludicrous enough, the inner conflicts have been the distinctive mark of this particular liberation. The cant concerning women has been institutionalized into a prison and internalized so thoroughly that every outward conflict exacerbates an inner war, the war of the born self against the assigned self. Melodramatic, tragic, pathetic in other fictions, this war undergoes a transformation in Shavian comedy, where it becomes funny, triumphant and profound.

In this new kind of comedy the revolutionary nature of the new era is given its artistic expression. If the traditional pattern of conflict is between the spontaneous desires of the young and the stiff resistance of the old, with the marriage of young lovers as the goal and the triumph, the relation of this theme to traditional society is easy to see. The desired conclusion is simply wedding, a reciprocal process by which society accedes to lovers and they to society. At this point the young ones begin to become old ones; the very triumph by which they have forced society to accept and legitimize their union integrates them into the structure of legal and social institutions. The young lover, once wedded, becomes a shareholder in the status quo, an old father in the bud. There could be no more perfect expression of traditional society than this ending that implies an eternal recurrence of the same patterns generation after generation. There is always a Polonius to remind us that in his time he suffered much for love and to prove that this makes no difference to his deeds. The order of society, in this view, is tantamount to an order of nature. That is where Shaw breaks off from the tradition, and that is where the unromantic woman, the individualized woman of his plays, becomes by her very existence a revolutionary theme. Shaw sees society, and even nature, as capable of genuine evolution, of an escape from recurrence, and his comedy reflects that view in its very structure. Both the nature of the conflict and the nature of its resolution differ in Shaw from the traditional comic pattern, even when the events of the plot seem most conventional.

Both thought and character in the Shavian drama proclaim the possibility of radical change, for they defy law itself, not just some abuse of the law. They defy custom itself, not just some perversion of custom. They are, in fact, essentially criminal, in the sense R. P. Blackmur, in his discussion of *Madame Bovary,* suggests that beauty and vitality are essentially criminal in their disturbance of conformist social being. Shaw's heroines and the vital geniuses among his heroes are criminals of the triumphant genus revolutionary. All subscribe to Andrew Undershaft's motto, "Unashamed," and all, unlike the tragic nonconformists of nineteenth-century fiction, Emma Bovary, Tess, Anna Karenina, know how to emerge as winners in the battle of life. Their secret is simple: it is total subversion. Instead of being punished for breaking one law while keeping others, they succeed by overturning the whole code. Criminality, in Shaw, is an intellectual thing. The illusions that harm you are the illusions you believe, and our laws are a codification of our illusions.

In comedy the most complete rejection of tradition is a play that ends with its leading characters *not* getting married and treats this ending as a rapturous fulfillment. There is one whole category of Shavian courtships in which the woman escapes from marriage and from the tyranny of love with the same swoon of relief that drops other women into a lover's arms. In *Captain Brassbound's Conversion,* Lady Cicely, a gifted moralist and tactician, finds herself almost mesmerized into marriage in the last minutes of the action but, reprieved for the final curtain, cries, "How glorious! How glorious! And what an escape!" Shaw calls the thesis of the play "trite," and of course its revenge motif and its celibacy motif have both been dealt with in the New Testament, but in modern comedies both are unusual.

In regard to *Pygmalion,* the issue has been sharply drawn by the desire of directors to sweep Eliza into the arms of Professor Higgins in an illogical and irrelevant final embrace. Shaw resisted this in his lifetime and wrote a full explanation showing the logic of the true ending, but there is more to it than logic. Like the ending of *King Lear,* which has also given offense, this one has poetry. The curtain falls on a new kind of consummation, a woman finding herself. These endings in which a woman (sometimes a man) finds herself instead of losing herself, even though they fit the standard Shavian pattern of reversal or paradox, are highly significant. In all the rest of literature there are few such findings. Colette ends *La Vagabonde* this way, but the ending carries far less conviction than Shaw's because Colette goes to great lengths to establish the reality of the love that has to be rejected in favor of the woman's self-realization. In realistic fiction the more strongly this point is made the more difficult it is to believe. The artistic problem is solved more satisfactorily in Kate Chopin's novella, *The Awakening* (1899), in which a nineteenth-century woman who has every advantage life can offer her, except for illusions about her feminine role, recognizes suicide as the only escape from her conflicts. The cold passion of this suicide makes it as different from those of Emma Bovary and Anna Karenina as such an act can be, but it hardly answers the question women are asking now: can a woman find herself (herself—not somebody's wife) without incurring death or disfigurement in doing so? Shaw's comedies say yes. They also say of course. They also say everybody knows it. Here, as in so much of contemporary writing about women, comedy is the mode that works best.

Even where the classic conclusion of comedy in a wedding takes place, the Shavian vision differs radically from tradition. None of these weddings is the simple ritual solution expected in comedy. To each the Shavian comedy of ideas imparts some meaning that gives comfort to the woman in rebellion against the marriage panacea. The question is met most explicitly in *Getting Married.* Here the subject of the play is actually the question: to marry or not to marry and why? In one sense the pattern is standard enough. An obstacle is placed in the way of the engaged couple, and that obstacle is eventually cleared away. Although Shaw claimed in a newspaper interview before the play opened that there is no plot but only an argument, the argument in this case functions as a plot and does just what a letter, an abduction or a mistaken identity would do in another play: it brings about the awaited wedding. But the wedding that follows this long exposition of the various impossibilities of marriage is accomplished with symbolic fitness away from all the ritual prepared for the other wedding that was to have taken place. It is as though the young couple had become different people after reading the pamphlet on the laws governing marriage that has so horrified them on their wedding morning, as though they had actually been prevented from marrying each other in the sense they first intended. Having lost their illusions before instead of after the wedding, the couple marry with less ceremony, and the changed meaning of that rite is made unmistakable by its changed position in the play. The announcement of the event is brief and prosaic; coming as it does just after Mrs. George's rhapsodic apostrophe to love (and complaint to men), it has a minimal effect, and the argument goes on for fourteen pages more. The final word on marriage in this play is Mrs. George's: "Hm! Like most men, you think you know everything a woman wants, don't you? But the thing one wants most has nothing to do with marriage at all." The question of what this is remains very properly suspended in the air among the many requirements the women in the play would like to make of marriage if they are to consent to it at all. The men, interestingly enough, find the status quo less intolerable. The bride has a Christlike objection to letting marriage interfere with her work for justice and salvation. Lesbia wants children but no husband. Leo wants a ménage à trois ("Well, I love them both.") or better: "I should like to marry a lot of men. I should like to have Rejjy for every day, and Sinjon for concerts and theatres and going out in the evenings, and some great austere saint for about once a year at the end of the season, and some perfectly blithering idiot of a boy to be quite wicked with. I so seldom feel wicked; and, when I do, it's such a pity to waste it merely because it's too silly to confess to a real grown-up man." And the bishop's opinion is that "most imaginative and cultivated young women feel like that."

Mrs. George, the mystic and philanderer, wants her marriage to stand like a rock while she flits off with various lovers and writes passionate letters to the Bishop about meeting him in heaven. Finally, the greengrocer's wife, the only woman in the play who accepts marriage and motherhood on the usual terms, is so thoroughly a wife and mother that her husband cannot talk to her and her children leave home as soon as possible.

When a wedding takes place in the midst of these discussions, it has very much the same effect on the meaning of the play as if no wedding had taken place at all. Interest has been focused on what will come after, and not on resolving the tangle that comes before. This is comedy of argument with a vengeance, and the subject of the argument is marriage, primarily woman's need to preserve a self in spite of marriage.

Man and Superman seems to be the chief stumbling block for feminists approaching Shaw. Here, of course, the outline of the plot is conventional to the point of parody. The curtain does indeed come down on one engagement announced, one secret marriage accepted. Ann does employ feminine wiles to get her man. And the author does in the Epistle Dedicatory speak of Woman as mother and say that "Ann is Everywoman." All this looks like male chauvinism and also like classic comedy. But not quite. Without taking the technical out provided by the author's saying this is "not a play, but a volume which contains a play," it is still possible to see an essential difference from traditional comedy, the very difference that the inclusion of the woman's viewpoint makes.

The pursuit of matrimony, running but never smooth, is again the center of the comic pattern. Octavius woos Ann, who woos Jack Tanner, who regards marriage as apostasy. Violet and Hector are secretly married and wooing Hector's father for support. Feminists naturally object to the implication that marriage is the natural goal of a woman's life, ignoring the fact that both Octavius and young Hector are as dedicated to that goal as the women, and that even Tanner, eloquent as he is on the subject, is no very reliable narrator of his own feelings on marriage or on the more pertinent subject of his feelings about Ann herself. The fact that both male and female are all for love is no departure from convention, but the nature of the obstacles certainly is. The resistance of Tanner, the Don Juan of the piece, is notorious, and his reasons are not very different from those of Shakespeare's Benedict. The resistance of Ann is less evident and more significant. Octavius is the man for whom Ann would be destined in a simpler story, as we know from *Don Giovanni* and from indications supplied by Shaw in his stage directions: "Mr. Robinson is really an uncommonly nice looking young fellow. He must, one thinks, be the jeune premier; for it is not in reason to suppose that a second such attractive male figure should appear in one story." Ann herself creates the complications without which there would be no play when she rejects this romantic whole-hearted lover. She does so because she is no longer the heroine of all female flesh and feminine caprice, but a person with ideas and conscious choice, a modern woman. Leaving aside the question of whether "Woman Immortal," one very provoking example of Shavian gamesmanship, is speaking through Ann, as Saint Joan's voices speak through her own unconscious mind, the mere mortal has quite decided ideas as distinct from simple impulses. Another unconventional touch is leaving the attractive Octavius unmated, in spite of the existence of a convenient sister whom any conventional plotting would have worked up into a fiancée. Besides, the subplot, with its suitably crasser subtheme (money), acts as a foil for the high ideas behind the figure of Ann. Violet, named for a flower that is a symbol of feminine modesty but actually grows like a weed, simply wants her Hector and his father's money, which is standard and all right. Empty and attractive, Violet and Hector are the pristine stuff of comedy. Their simplicity hints at the complexity of Ann's motives, which are explained in the Epistle Dedicatory.

Not only are the men as bent on marriage as the women, Tanner always excepted, but they are relegated to a passive role. This, of course, fits Shaw's reiterated view that women are the aggressors in sex, but it does reverse the sexual stereotypes, and in this respect Tanner is quite like Octavius and Hector and even the sentimental devil Mendoza. His moves are all reactions to Ann's actions. The women are enterprising, audacious, aggressive and self-assured, and it is they who secure all the desired outcomes through their wit and daring. Violet prevails against both her husband and his father to set up the marriage on her own terms with the necessary income. Ann prevails against both the man who says he wants to marry her and the one who says he does not, setting up just the arrangement that is best for all three. This Ann explains in the scene in which she rejects Octavius:

> ANN: [*with conviction*] Tavy. I wouldnt for worlds destroy your illusions. I can neither take you nor let you go. I can see exactly what will suit you. You must be a sentimental old bachelor for my sake.
>
> OCTAVIUS: [*desperately*] Ann: I'll kill myself.
>
> ANN: Oh no, you wont: that wouldnt be kind. You wont have a bad time. You will be very nice to women; and you will go a good deal to the opera.

A moment later she is explaining to Octavius why she does not dread disillusioning Jack: "I cant: he has no illusions about me. I shall surprise Jack the other way. Getting over an unfavorable impression is ever so much easier than living up to an ideal. Oh, I shall enrapture Jack sometimes!" There is every reason to believe in Ann's accuracy here. She does prevaricate, but she does not mistake.

A second feminist complaint against *Man and Superman* is that Ann employs feminine wiles to gain her end. What else can she do in her social context? Shaw's point here, as in his defense of Mrs. Warren's choice of profession, is that society is to blame for offering no workable alternative. Shaw says, with Tanner, "Forgive my brutalities, Ann. They are levelled at this wicked world, not at you." In this case as in others, criticism directed at action, character or any other dramatic element without regard to the social context and the thought has little or no validity. The act itself has no meaning. The act related to its occasion, its intention, its effects, its limiting context, does have meaning. Ann's deviousness is determined by society, which penalizes other methods in a woman, not by any feminine nature. Besides, Ann does not find deviousness congenial nor fool herself about what she is doing. She says:

> But I have a great respect for Violet. She gets her own way always.
>
> OCTAVIUS: [*sighing*] So do you.
>
> ANN: Yes; but somehow she gets it without coaxing—without having to make people sentimental about her.

Here Ann is voicing exactly the feminist objection to methods that trade on sexual attraction or the secondary sexual characteristics of helplessness, modesty and the like. The meaning of her behavior is therefore the opposite of what a simple plot summary would imply.

The third and most serious accusation of male chauvinism in this play rests on the idea of the mother-woman and the artist-man advanced in the Epistle Dedicatory. Shaw does set up the two goals in opposition and speaks of one as the man's and the other as the woman's. But to assume that he takes this to be an eternal principle is wrong, and to assume that woman is meant to be limited to this one role is equally wrong. In making Ann the mother-woman, he is speaking of "modern London life, a life in which as you know, the ordinary man's business is to get means to keep up the position and habits of a gentleman, and the ordinary woman's business is to get married." But this is the temporal and ordinary thing. He makes explicit reference to the complicated case in which the genius is a woman. I must admit that he goes on to say: "I state the extreme case, of course; but what is true of the great man who incarnates the philosophic consciousness of Life and the woman who incarnates its fecundity, is true in some degree of all geniuses and all women." This hyperbole seems to be part of the polemical rhythm, not of the real argument. Shaw's work argues always for freeing motherhood, not for forcing it, and even in this same Epistle there is a correction worth noting: "As I sat watching Everyman at the Charterhouse, I said to myself Why not Everywoman? Ann was the result: every woman is not Ann; but Ann is Everywoman." Then there is Tanner's little-noted question as he yields to destiny: "What have you grasped in me? Is there a father's heart as well as a mother's?"

Ann is taken too seriously most of the time. It is no wonder, considering the Everywoman business, but it does throw things out of kilter to take her more seriously than any other character in the play. She is a vital genius. The author says so. Yet she has her being in the light ironic mode, and her deviousness, her feminine wiles, the whole catalog of her faults must be interpreted accordingly. Look, for the parallel case, at Jack Tanner. Surely this parlor socialist, this talker, this ludicrously unconscious prey is not meant to represent the highest mark the philosopher-man can reach? Yet it is equally sure that his follies are not meant to discredit the tract he is supposed to have written. It is naive to forget that Ann is just as much a comic version of certain selected qualities, that though she is an incarnation of the divine spark she is a comic incarnation. She no more detracts from the value of the maternal function than Tanner detracts from the value of socialism, but she is a reminder that the Life Force may assume strange shapes to get its work done in our time.

The Millionairess, a late play that also ends with an engagement, shows the same kind of disparity between an apparently traditional comic pattern and an actually revolutionary and feminist structure. Its heroine is a walking catalog of the virtues the radical women's movement believes in. She is Boss incarnate and was created to be just that, as the Preface argues. Her methods are blunt and tough and by no means exclude physical violence. She has no scrap of modesty, guilt or dependence. She is in full possession of her own sexuality. Her first husband, whom she dumps without ceremony, is a handsome athlete without interest of mind or character, chosen primarily as a sex object. "He stripped well, unlike many handsome men," she says. But, as she explains to her lawyer: "I have made a very common mistake. I thought that this irresistible athlete would be an ardent lover. He was nothing of the kind. All his ardor was in his fists." Consigning him to the care of his mistress, she remarks, "His good looks will give you a pleasing sensation down your spine."

The Egyptian doctor on whom this free spirit fastens for her next husband, pursuing him by direct assault, without any feminine wiles, is finally undone, against his will, by her sexual vitality, as ruthless as her appetite for power, unless I entirely misread the capitulation that comes when he feels her pulse: "Ooooh!! I have never felt such a pulse. It is like a slow sledge hammer. . . . It is the will of Allah. . . . You are a terrible woman; but I love your pulse. I have never felt anything like it before." The courtships in *Village Wooing* and *Too True To Be Good* are even more explicit on this point. Again it is the woman as individual, full of force and particularity, that transforms the meaning of marriage as a conclusion. Conventionally, woman as female is passivity, a sex *object,* whereas Shavian woman is activity, a *subject* in sexual as in other matters. For the woman as female in literature, marriage and procreation have been treated as ends in themselves. In *The Millionairess,* the marriage is a goal, but it is only one goal, subsumed under the woman's main goal of having her own way about everything. Love never makes her forget herself or her principles. Here, as in most of Shaw's work, marriage may be part of a woman's life, as it may be part of a man's life, but it is destiny to the same extent for both.

Most of Shaw's plays make an even more complete break with the conventions of comedy. Weddings and matings recede from the center of interest and take their place along with other human concerns including social change and the survival of the species. In Shaw the assumption that society can and must change is as pervasive as the assumption in traditional comedy that the wheel will continue to go round. And that change is both embodied and symbolized in the new relation of woman to herself, to other people and to the universal. A glance at five plays having different emphases may indicate how the pattern plays itself out against different backgrounds.

Saint Joan might seem to be a fortuitous example of the importance of woman in transforming Shaw's drama, but I do not mean to argue from the simple fact that Joan was a female. In any case, plays like *Major Barbara, Pygmalion, Mrs. Warren's Profession* and *Misalliance* show that the woman protagonist is no historical accident. And there are elements in Joan's drama that show very well the conflict of the woman with her feminine role and the way that conflict epitomizes the drama of a new age. Her accusers dwell on witchcraft and unfeminine behavior. Her defense against these charges shows how necessary it is for women to unsex themselves to succeed in great enterprises, how the woman's role is a trap to be wary of and is, furthermore, the best example of the way all such traps as stereotypes work. These stereotypes claim to be roles but in fact are denials of role. Soldier is a role, bishop is a role, shepherd is a role (although shepherdess turns it into a mythological fancy), even saint is a role, but woman is an antirole and therefore a woman must be a rebel or nothing. The supposed role of woman is either a fiction or a negation. Mother is a role, cook is a role, typist is a role, but woman means only that one cannot be a soldier, cannot be a boxer, cannot be a bishop, cannot be a thousand other things without coming into conflict with the illogical role of woman. A real element in Joan's martyrdom is her inability to conform to the role assigned to her as a woman. Obedience to her father, domesticity, marriage, obedience to her husband—a different kind of martyr is made this way, but a woman like Joan has only a choice of martyrdoms. And to have any real role at all, she has had to learn the techniques of total subversion, for in her time no girl broke away with less.

In *Major Barbara* the initiative, the anguish and the enlightenment are primarily a woman's. Barbara Undershaft will have won her way through to be her father's heiress by right of her struggle, not by right of birth. She will marry Cusins, admittedly, and he will become the nominal heir, but only through her, through her rebellion, clearsightedness and courage. As a man, he had his role, professor of Greek. But as a woman, Barbara has had to blast her way out of the woman's role in order to have any real life at all. Having broken out of the old illusions, she is quite prepared to break out of any new ones that threaten her love affair with reality, and the impossibility of every last sacred cliché is the ironic heart of the play. Undershaft has succeeded because he does not confuse morality with business. Cusins will succeed because he does not confuse purity with virtue. Barbara succeeds because she does not confuse femininity with selfhood. The stories of the two men are rightly subsidiary to hers. Here, as elsewhere in his theatre, Shaw's socialism is subsidiary to his feminism. The woman, struggling through a swamp of deceptions and irrelevancies toward an idea of what she has to do in the world, is the heroic heart of the comedy.

As a test case, consider *Candida*. On the surface, a love triangle: married woman, romantic lover, dramatic confrontation, return to husband. Symbolically, the woman a Renaissance madonna, motherhood spiritualized at one period, again made flesh at another, and revived in the new religiosity of art—evidently a protean thing. The husband a pillar of society, in no ironic sense, a solid man. The lover an artist, fire and air. Such a triangle seems to promise a problem play, its real action in the interplay of forces like liberty, law, earth-mother, its outcome a lesson in the ranking of abstractions. Instead, the force of the play sheers off again to the issue of woman and the conflict with her ascribed role, a conflict to which the other characters acting upon her are only incidental. Candida has known and lived with her dilemma long before her husband and her lover duel verbally to possess her. There is no melodrama, no problem play, only an adroit comedy, yet a comedy of the new kind: centered in a woman, with inner conflict replacing outer obstacles, and with a smell of revolution in the air. In the climactic scene that plucks out the heart of the mystery, Candida reveals all the traditional relations in a strange new light. The husband's strength is weakness; the lover's weakness, strength. This paradox settles the outward events, which have ceased to matter. Whether she goes with one or remains with the other is no longer an interesting question. The interesting question is why. In writing his own version of *A Doll's House* and reversing the outcome, Shaw proves also that the importance of Nora's leaving is not the leaving itself but the reasons for it. In *Candida,* strength and weakness, principles of honor, all the used furniture of ideas about wifehood and motherhood and Love have been superseded by Candida's question: "Oh! I am to choose, am I? I suppose it is quite settled that I must belong to one or the other," and by Marchbanks, who translates: "She means that she belongs to herself." Whatever the secret in the poet's heart, that is the secret in the woman's.

In one way or another, that is the message of the plays. In *Heartbreak House* any mystical work is done by an old man aided by the Seventh Degree of Concentration (a rum concoction), but his daughters, Hesione and Ariadne, both declassicized versions of a feminine principle that once could redeem a male world, dominate the middle generation, their men being devoid of all epic quality. The entering wedge into the future, as a lost society founders, is the young Ellie Dunn, who falls in love with the handsome and false Hector Hushabye, plans to marry Boss Mangan and his millions for the sake of her helpless father and her expensive soul, and finally discovers her soulmate in old Captain Shotover's mad mysticism and sane questions. The women are without fear, as though masculine wars were only another football game, and they are hoping, as the curtain goes down, for the terror and beauty of another air raid.

It should be admitted that the dominance of the sisters over their weak men is one of the elements of decadence in *Heartbreak House,* yet the dominance is clearly healthier than the vacuum of submission that draws it forth. The women may prop up or tyrannize over the men, but the men have first been destroyed by something other than the women. Shaw never flinches from strong women. Where most men see in strong women a threat to themselves, Shaw sees in them a hope for the world. The destructive women, as Shaw recognizes, are the weak ones. Certainly in *Heartbreak House* the hope for any revival in a dying world lies in Ellie's quest for a sensible grail. The play again breaks the comic pattern without abandoning it, for the influence of Chekhov goes only so far. The woman sets aside romantic love to marry for money, sets that aside for a mystical marriage to reality in the old captain, and finally chooses danger, excitement and her own spirit. This pattern is radically different from the traditional comedy in which awareness of human folly, along with the right pairing off, can set a wobbling world spinning prettily again, but the Chekhovian pattern is not really followed either. The old world and its choices may be vanishing, but the self is still a reality and a source of strength. The new world that may emerge is evidently one in which the human spirit is androgynous. In this play, as in the Christian heaven, there is neither marrying nor giving in marriage, but there is redemption.

There is also a sense in which a play like *The Apple Cart* bears out my theory of a changed comedy and its relation to a changed role for women. The comedy is political and the vital genius a man, but the deployment of women is interesting. The scene moves from politics to playful love and back again, but King Magnus keeps the frivolity of his mistress firmly bracketed in the interlude. He returns almost on time to his work and his placid maternal wife whom Orinthia calls an old cabbage, with a remark no male chauvinist could have dreamed up: "Besides, all these old married cabbages were once roses; and, though young things like you dont remember that, their husbands do." In his cabinet King Magnus has only two dedicated, intelligent, honest public servants among the rabble of egotists, fools, frauds and babies. These two are the only two women.

ORINTHIA: And then you go back to your Amandas and Lysistratas: creatures whose idea of romance is a minister in love with a department, and whose bedside books are blue books.

MAGNUS: They are not always thinking of some man or other. That is a rather desirable extension of their interests, in my opinion. If Lysistrata had a lover I should not be interested in him in the least; and she would bore me to distraction if she could talk of nothing else. But I am very much interested in her department. Her devotion to it gives us a topic of endless interest.

These women are not the central characters in the comedy, but they are more important to it than the King's wife or his mistress, and they are effective because they have surpassed the feminine roles attributed to them. The main idea of the play is actually a variant on this feminine rebellion. One of the few men born, like a woman, with a role ready made for him is a constitutional monarch. Magnus is told over and over that he is supposed to be a rubber stamp, a figurehead. But this attributed character does not fit the man Magnus, and his refusal to accept it is exactly parallel to a woman's refusal to accept the role offered her by birth. Being a kingly king is like being a womanly woman: all right until it gets in your way.

On the womanly woman Shaw said the last word early in his career in *The Quintessence of Ibsenism,* and King Magnus is the proper test of those ideas, for Shaw recognized that woman's rebellion against her attributed role would be the model for all such rebellion against roles, against duty, against cant. He predicted then that the woman's revolt would come first because the woman's enslavement was more complete, but that man would learn subversion and come to understand the impossibility of "duty" in due course. But the exemplary case is that of the woman of spirit whose choice is to rebel or to die, and the particular comedy of our time is that in which a woman pits her spirit against a set of deadly mythologies, as in another age a man would pit his body against physical death, or a couple their desires against laws and fathers. Shaw is the creator of this kind of comedy, in which the emphasis is on fighting free of cant, and the implication is that by learning to see through one kind of cant women show men how to see through others. Seeing through newcant (the cant of one's own generation) is an art achieved only by the masters. Yet that is the art Shaw means to teach. Roebuck Ramsden, in *Man and Superman*, speaks with all the pride of middle age when he says, "I was an advanced man before you were born." With his name so weighted with masculinity, and a style so ineffectual in dealing with anything feminine, Ramsden is a perfect representative of the patriarchy, and his dedication to the newcant of his youth is typical of patriarchal illusions. Looking through the whole list of Shavian characters, it seems fair to say that most of the realists, those who have a grasp of the secret and need not repeat the nightmares of the past, are women. The only female equivalent of Ramsden seems to be Mrs. Clandon in *You Never Can Tell*, who liberates herself in the wrong direction by becoming more masculine. She has tried to reduce life to a science, but at least she has given birth to the fey twins and to Gloria, who finds out how to fall in love even though no one has ever taught her anything. Anyone who thinks to make life a science is no realist in Shaw's view.

Perhaps something of what Shaw values in woman can be deduced by looking at the men he selects to play Vital Genius in some plays. They are seldom husbands in the true sense. Husbands tend toward the bombastic or uxorious. Fathers and grandfathers come off much better. In *Major Barbara, Heartbreak House, Cashel Byron's Profession, The Millionairess*, and elsewhere, fathers show a certain verve. It is only a step from father to Caesar, who is paternal toward the infantile Cleopatra. Like the paternal, encouraging, instructive manner of King Magnus, his power, which is his detachment, which is his wisdom, is part of an androgynous consciousness. No conventional masculine traits like aggression, vengefulness, violence appear in the vital genius, just as no conventional feminine traits appear in the vital woman. Androgyny appears to be the key to the new humanity.[2]

If so, the remaining question would seem to be why women, so much more locked in a stereotyped sex role than men, should seem to represent the hope for the future. Perhaps because outsiders get a better training in realism. For them it has survival value, and miraculous attention goes into the lessons of survival. Also, where a culture places a high value on masculinity, repudiating that role is harder than repudiating the role of inferior. Whatever the reason, Shaw took the theme of woman's fate wherever he found it (and he found it everywhere) and made of it a mythogenic center.

Notes

1.   "As Bernard Shaw Sees Woman," *New York Times Magazine,* 19 June 1927, p. 2.

2.   For a valuable discussion of androgyny in literature and a distinction between feminist and androgynous works see Carolyn G. Heilbrun, *Toward a Recognition of Androgyny.*

Having the Last Word:
Plot and Counterplot
in Bernard Shaw

J. L. WISENTHAL

ELLIE:	This gentleman wants to know is he never to have the last word?
LADY UTTERWORD:	I should let him have it, my dear. The important thing is not to have the last word, but to have your own way.
MANGAN:	She wants both.
LADY UTTERWORD:	She wont get them, Mr Mangan. Providence always has the last word.

Heartbreak House, Act II[1]

I

Shaw's first play was a collaboration of sorts with William Archer, and one of his last was a collaboration of sorts with William Shakespeare. The play that eventually became *Widowers' Houses* began in 1884 with an agreement between Archer and Shaw that the former was to provide the plot and the latter the dialogue. The arrangement broke down after a few weeks when Shaw said to his collaborator, "Look here, I've written half of the first act of that comedy, and I've used up all your plot. Now I want some more to go on with."[2] Archer's plot was of the school that dominated the English theatre in the late nineteenth century, that of the French well-made play—the school of Scribe and Sardou, in which plot and incident are the essence of tightly constructed works. Shaw used Archer's plot, but in a way that made a mockery of the type of play Archer had in mind. In Bernard Dukore's words, "The entire play may be regarded as a demonic parody of the well-made play, whose features . . . it utilizes."[3] Whereas in Archer's plot the young man was virtuously and heroically to reject the father-in-law's tainted money, in Shaw's play Trench is made aware of the fact that he is just as guilty as the slum landlord and in the end he marries the daughter without rising to any heights of virtue or heroism. When Shaw

From *ELH* 50 (1): 175–96. Reprinted by permission of the Johns Hopkins University Press.

returned to his shorthand manuscript three years after the 1884 attempt, he gave the first two acts to Archer to read, warning him in advance that he had turned his plot into a different type of play. "The central notion is quite perfect; but the hallucinations with which you surround it are absent: you will have to put them in yourself," he wrote. "The bathing place is impossible; and I dont see how the long lost old woman is to be introduced without destroying the realism and freshness of the play: she would simply turn the thing into a plot, and ruin it. . . . You will perceive that my genius has brought the romantic notion which possessed you, into vivid contact with real life."[4] By the time Shaw added the third act in 1892, he was entirely on his own, without any pretence of a collaboration. He had taken Archer's scenario as a starting point, and had gone his own way from there.

In 1936, half a century after the attempted collaboration with Archer, Shaw provided a new final act for Shakespeare's *Cymbeline*. Once again he proved himself an awkward collaborator, who declined to respect the contribution of his partner. In his Foreword to his version of Act V, *Cymbeline Refinished*, he declared himself dissatisfied with the way in which Shakespeare resolved the complications of his plot by the revelation of Iachimo's deception and the true identities of the princes. "Having become interested in Iachimo, in Imogen, and even in the two long lost princes," Shaw said, "I wanted to know how their characters would react to the *éclaircissement* which follows the battle" (VII, 183). In Shaw's version the resolution of the plot is not the resolution of the human problems of the play; it is not so much an ending as the beginning of a new set of problems of conduct, and a potential new play that would be a sequel to *Cymbeline*. In the original *Cymbeline* Iachimo's confession leads to a reconciliation between Posthumus and Imogen, but Shaw's post-Ibsen Imogen is not so easily contented. "All is lost," says the disillusioned heroine near the end of the refinished act: "Shame, husband, happiness, and faith in Man./He is not even sorry"; and her last words in the play are, "I must go home and make the best of it/As other women must" (VII, 198–99). Just as Shaw's Imogen refuses to conform to the demands of Shakespeare's genre that there be general reconciliation, so do the princes refuse to accept their new roles as romance requires. They reject their position as heirs to Cymbeline's throne, and they reject Cymbeline himself as a father:

BELARIUS: . . .Come hither, boys, and pay
               Your loves and duties to your royal sire.
GUIDERIUS: We three are fullgrown men and perfect strangers.
               Can I change fathers as I'd change my shirt?
CYMBELINE: Unnatural whelp! What doth thy brother say?
ARVIRAGUS: I, royal sir? Well, we have reached an age
               When fathers' helps are felt as hindrances.

(VII, 196)

Shaw's Imogen, disgusted with Posthumus' behaviour towards her, exclaims bitterly: "My husband thinks that all is settled now/And this a happy ending!" (VII, 194).[5] Imogen is protesting here not only against Posthumus, but in effect against the type of play that Shakespeare put her into. In *Cymbeline Refinished,* as in *Widowers' Houses,* Shaw has used his collaborator as a sparring partner. In Elizabethan romance, as in the nineteenth-century well-made play, the plot works out the problems, and the characters unhesitatingly accept the solutions. In Shaw's versions of Shakespeare and Archer, the characters' vitality and originality assert themselves, and human will is not subject to the requirements of genre. Therefore, contrary to the plots that Shaw was working with—or working against—the threads are not all tied together at the end. When we reach the end of either *Widowers' Houses* or *Cymbeline Refinished* we are left with a feeling of dissatisfaction; the discords have not been harmoniously resolved, and more action seems to be required. In both works this effect is part of Shaw's dramatic strategy, to leave his audience feeling that the action is not complete and that any resolution is in their hands and is their responsibility.[6] Another part of the dramatic strategy in both works is to frustrate the audience's expectations. The audience of *Widowers' Houses* would not of course know Archer's exact original plot, but an audience in 1892 could certainly be relied upon to be familiar with the conventions of the well-made play. *Widowers' Houses* conforms sufficiently to these conventions to arouse expectations that the conflict between the slum landlord's money and the prospective son-in-law's conscience will be resolved by some device of plot, which would perhaps reveal the landlord as blameless or the young man as independently wealthy. But the third act of *Widowers' Houses* declines to follow such a course, and the play produces its fullest effect on an audience that is simultaneously aware of both the original genre and the Shavian reversals. In the case of *Cymbeline Refinished* this simultaneous awareness is more obvious, in that anyone who reads Shaw's version of Act V is likely to know Shakespeare's play. Although Shaw printed *Cymbeline Refinished* as a separate play in his collected works, it makes no sense outside its Shakespearean context.

Shaw seems to have found it congenial to take on the job of finishing other people's plays. His speciality as a refinisher was to tamper with the genre or the general effect of the original. One minor, partial instance of this practice occurred in 1909–10, when Harley Granville Barker needed a push to complete the penultimate act of *The Madras House.* Charles Frohman and J. M. Barrie, Shaw recounted, "appealed to me to reason with him. I took a shorter way by finishing the act myself and giving the woman the best of it (his sympathy was with the man). He was infuriated, and finished the act in his own way at once" (VII, 609). Another work reprinted among the "Uncollected Dramatic Writings" in the final volume of the Bodley Head *Collected Plays with Their Prefaces* is "A New Ending for Clemence Dane's *Cousin Muriel,*" which Shaw wrote for Edith Evans in 1940 (see VII, 652–57). Shaw gives the play a happy ending by allowing Muriel, who has been caught altering her employer's cheques, to argue her case and win him over. Here as in *Cymbeline Refinished* Shaw has transformed the ending of the original play by giving human will ascendancy over the revelations of plot.

And then there is Shaw's translation of Siegfried Trebitsch's *Frau Gittas Sühne*. In 1920–21 Shaw translated this play by his German translator as *Jitta's Atonement*—but given Shaw's proclivities with other people's plays we must think of the word "translate" both in its usual sense and in the sense of "change in form . . . transmute . . . transform, alter" (*OED*). For Shaw has taken the sad melodramatic plot and turned it into Shavian comedy by allowing the characters to exercise common sense and good humour. In particular, the ending has been altered to a point that would justify "Jitta Refinished" as a title for Shaw's work (which he included in the canon of his own plays, incidentally). Shaw achieves a happy ending not by manipulating the plot but by having the characters react differently—in a more human and less melodramatic way—to the situation in the original play.[7]

These are the clearest examples of Shaw's "collaborations," in which he has the last word at the expense of his collaborator's contribution. But in fact this type of collaboration can take more indirect forms, and it is a common feature of Shaw's work. Consider his relationship to Shakespeare, for example. *Cymbeline Refinished* does in an overt way what *Caesar and Cleopatra* does indirectly: both plays rewrite Shakespeare.[8] An intelligent response to *Caesar and Cleopatra* requires the audience to keep in mind Shakespeare's version of the two principals in *Julius Caesar* and *Antony and Cleopatra,* respectively. Shaw makes certain that an alert audience will not overlook the Shakespearean competitors. *Caesar and Cleopatra* has a number of allusions to *Antony and Cleopatra,* including references to Antony, Cleopatra's royal barge, and dolphins,[9] and we are reminded of *Julius Caesar* in this bit of dialogue in Act II:

CAESAR: Go, Ptolemy. Always take a throne when it is offered to you.

RUFIO: I hope you will have the good sense to follow your own advice when we return to Rome, Caesar.

(II, 202)

and in Rufio's reference in the final act to the dangerous daggers awaiting Caesar on his return to Rome (II, 288). As in *Cymbeline Refinished,* Shaw is trying to improve on Shakespeare, and in *Caesar and Cleopatra* he is correcting Shakespeare's portraits of Caesar and Cleopatra to bring out Caesar's greatness and Cleopatra's inferiority. One can see Shaw's play as a kind of prologue to *Julius Caesar* and *Antony and Cleopatra,* so that we have a Shavio-Shakespearean Roman trilogy in which the first play subverts the subsequent two.

Even without the Shakespearean allusions, a play about Julius Caesar and

Cleopatra is bound to direct our attention beyond itself to Shakespeare and to history, and to set up an outside frame of reference. This technique of the double perspective is characteristic of Shaw's work. In his early novel *An Unsocial Socialist,* the last word is given to the main character in the form of an appendix entitled "Letter to the Author from Mr. Sidney Trefusis." Trefusis tells the author, "I am sorry you made a novel of my story; for the effect has been almost as if you had misrepresented me from beginning to end."[10] He offers corrections and some indication of what has happened to him and other characters since the conclusion of the novel. Like the "Revolutionist's Handbook" appended to *Man and Superman* and the epilogue to *Pygmalion,* this appendix supplies a competing point of view, an outside perspective that takes us beyond the imagined world of the main work. In the case of *An Unsocial Socialist* Shaw invents his own collaborator, the central character who had provided the plot by giving the author permission to make use of his life story.

In *Man and Superman* (in its published form) the character John Tanner is given the last word in that his statement of faith, the "Revolutionist's Handbook," is printed in its entirety as an appendix to the play. Like Trefusis' letter to the author of *An Unsocial Socialist,* Tanner's "Revolutionist's Handbook" is at once part of the fiction and external to it. Another outside perspective is present within the play itself: the Hell Scene in Act III, which is Tanner's dream. Here he is given the last word in the sense that his vision goes outside the main action of the play and profoundly alters our response to the work as a whole. Yet another outside perspective is indicated in the stage direction that introduces Octavius in Act I: "Mr Robinson is really an uncommonly nice looking young fellow. He must, one thinks, be the jeune premier; for it is not in reason to suppose that a second such attractive male figure should appear in one story" (II, 535). This introduction is available only to the reader of the play, but Shaw presumably intends that a turn-of-the-century theatre audience familiar with Victorian stock-company stereotypes should be misled into thinking that this nice looking young fellow must be the Juvenile Lead.[11] Thus the audience's attention is directed towards a conventional alternative to *Man and Superman,* to which the action that follows serves as a corrective.

In *Pygmalion* too, the audience is expected to have another kind of play in mind, and here the counterpoint effect is central to Shaw's dramatic strategy. The nature of the submerged play is suggested by Shaw's subtitle: "A Romance in Five Acts." The sequel that follows Act V explains that the play is "called a romance because the transfiguration it records seems exceedingly improbable" (IV, 782), but even with respect to this meaning of "romance" Eliza resists the logic of the plot and thus rebels against the genre. Like the princes in *Cymbeline Refinished* who prosaically refuse to accept their transformation, so the "duchess" in *Pygmalion* protests (in Act IV) that she was better off as a flower girl, and she rejects the life for which the transformation has prepared her. And while in *Cymbeline Refinished* we have the challenge to romance when the obstacles to the love between Posthumus and Imogen are not completely removed (because of Imogen's continuing resentment), so in *Pygmalion* the marriage between Higgins and Eliza, which the genre calls for, fails to occur. The play goes as far as it can to frustrate the conventional expectations of an audience. It provides "a robust, vital, appetizing sort of man" as the eligible bachelor for Eliza, and throws out various suggestions of romantic or sexual involvement. There is the "seduction scene" in Act II, where Eliza is tempted with chocolates; there is Higgins' remark to his mother in Act III, "Ive picked up a girl" (IV, 722); there is Eliza's reference in Act IV to the ring Higgins bought her in Brighton; and there is Pickering's comment in Act V that the police inspector who has been called in to find Eliza "suspected us of some improper purpose" (IV, 758). All of this serves to remind the audience of the sort of play they are being denied—the play that is being subverted by *Pygmalion*. Then at the end of the play there is a marriage, and most of the characters go off happily to the wedding. But the marriage is that of the heroine's *father*: the ultimate slap in the face for the romantic conventions that an audience has been led to anticipate. The father is the traditional comedic obstacle to the fulfilment of young love, and here it is he rather than the daughter-heroine who marries at the end.

At the end of the play itself, that is—for as in *An Unsocial Socialist* and *Man and Superman* there is a passage of ambiguous status tacked on after the main work concludes. Here the playwright intrudes to disabuse the reader of any false expectations that he may still harbor. The point of this epilogue is what does *not* happen, and Shaw makes the ending of Eliza's story as remote from romantic comedy as possible. Eliza resists the genre of the submerged play to the extent that—for good, sensible, human reasons—she marries the insipid nonentity Freddy and opens a florist's and greengrocer's shop. The epilogue maintains the approach of the actual play in arousing expectations in order to defeat them: "Now here is a last opportunity for romance. Would you not like to be assured that the shop was an immense success, thanks to Eliza's charms and her early business experience in Covent Garden? Alas! the truth is the truth: the shop did not pay for a long time, simply because Eliza and her Freddy did not know how to keep it" (IV, 794). The assumption that underlies *Pygmalion* is that it is salutary for an audience to be disillusioned and compelled to think about human problems in a direct and original way, without the convenient mediating support of romantic conventions that distort human realities. Shaw's method in *Pygmalion* could be described as a type of collaboration. In order to bring the romantic notions which possess the audience into vivid contact with real life, he places behind the play itself an alternative that embodies our conventional preconceptions. Thus the play provokes the audience into seeing that the way of *Pygmalion* is that of life and humanity (in Shaw's view), while the way of the implied, background play is that of mechanism and illusion.

II

When Shaw told Archer in 1884 that he had written only the first part of their proposed play and had used up all of Archer's plot, he was not just indulging in a Shavian joke. He was unconsciously enunciating one of the structural principles of many of his subsequent works. He believed that "plot has always been the curse of serious drama, and indeed of serious literature of any kind" (Foreword to *Cymbeline Refinished* [VII, 182]). One of his structural principles, therefore, is to use up the plot and get on with the real drama. The serious dramatic interest lies in what happens afterwards—after the complications, contrivances, revelations, and explanations. As *Cymbeline Refinished* demonstrates, Shaw is more concerned with the way people respond to events than with the events themselves.[12] "The second-rate dramatist," he wrote in 1896, "always begins at the beginning of his play; the first-rate one begins in the middle; and the genius—Ibsen, for instance—begins at the end."[13] Shaw's complaint about some contemporary plays is like his objection to our truncated lives in *Back to Methuselah*: they never get beyond the trivial preliminaries, and they end just when they might become interesting. In 1895, in another of his theatre reviews, Shaw commented on a play entitled *The Divided Way*, objecting to the fact that the heroine commits suicide when faced with the dilemma that she is married to a man she does not love and is unable to marry the real object of her affections, his brother. If the playwright would bring his heroine back to life, Shaw suggests, "we should have a remarkably interesting play on top of the romantic one." Then we could see the woman facing her problems and trying to work them out, and we could see what happens when she leaves her husband and marries her brother-in-law. "Like all romantic plays which create a strong illusion," Shaw says, "this one irresistibly raises the question how its final situation would do for the starting-point of a realistic play. All Ibsen's later plays, from Pillars of Society to Little Eyolf, are continuations of this kind."[14] Or as Shaw wrote elsewhere, *A Doll's House* "began with the happy ending of all the drawing-room comedies in vogue at that time" (Author's Note on *Candida* [I, 599–600]).

This same attitude is evident in advice that Shaw gave privately to fellow writers about plays they had written. In 1894 Henry Arthur Jones, at the height of his reputation, published *Judah,* a melodramatic piece about a provincial nonconformist minister in love with a young woman faith healer who is exposed as a fraud. Shaw was not satisfied with the work. "Judah amused me," he wrote to Jones. "It consists of clever preliminaries; and when the real play begins with the matrimonial experiment of Judah and Vashti, down comes the curtain as usual."[15] Ibsen begins his plays at the end, while the lesser playwright ends at the beginning. Similarly, Shaw in 1911 gave Maurice Baring some advice on how to revise a play he had written (*The Double Game*), in an unpublished letter that is indirectly revealing about Shaw's own dramatic practice:

I have read the play, and ask you, as man to man, how you expect anybody to be satisfied with a play which stops violently at the beginning. . . . Nothing can be more interesting than the situation of the girl. She has proceeded on an ideal to which she believes her man corresponds. At a crucial point she finds out that he is what the English criminal classes call "a copper's nark." Now the expectation of seeing how she will readjust herself to this change in her outlook is quite thrilling. It is to this that the whole play has led up. If you are not equal to the occasion, there is nothing for you to do but shoot yourself. Instead of which, you shoot the girl, and say to the audience "Now that the girl is dead, there's no more to be said. Good night." There are no eggs rotten enough, no cats dead enough, to do justice to such a silly trick. You see it, dont you?

The true dramatic question, Shaw points out, is whether the girl will continue to love the man in spite of the revelation. "The scene in which this is answered is *the* scene of the play: without it there is no play: all that goes before is only the Scribean exposition by the butler and the housemaid more ingeniously done." Shaw challenges Baring in a way that is reminiscent of the collaboration with Archer twenty-seven years earlier: "If you can finish it, do. If not, sell it to me for five shillings; and I will finish it." The play must be resolved by the heroine's will, not by outside circumstances of plot. "There must be no murder and no suicide or regicide or Siberia or any other nonsense. You have ingeniously managed to set the girl absolutely free from the pressure of circumstances at the last moment; and she has therefore no excuse for not going through with her problem."[16]

In his own works Shaw often reveals what happens after the conventional plot reaches its conclusion, so that the heart of the work forms a kind of epilogue. In his second novel, written in 1880, the hero and heroine marry halfway through the book, and the rest of the novel explores the consequences of their misalliance. In a conventional novel the main characters might be parted in the middle and then marry at the end; in Shaw's *The Irrational Knot* they marry in the middle and part at the end.[17] When Shaw reread the book in 1905 he was pleased to discover that he had produced "a morally original study of a marriage" that anticipated *A Doll's House.*[18] In his next novel too, *Love among the Artists,* the two couples are married by the end of Book I, and Book II studies the consequences. In Shaw's first play, *Widowers' Houses,* the climax— the revelation of the father-in-law's sordid trade and the young man's unconscious complicity in it—comes at the end of the second act. The third act is a disappointment to the audience, but I think it is a deliberately administered one; the results of the revelation are dramatically and morally unsatisfactory, and the play's point is that such is the nature of real life in our present type of society.

The structure of *Mrs Warren's Profession* is similar to that of *Widowers' Houses,* in that the big recognition scene occurs at the end of Act II and then the rest of the play shows the characters reacting to the new situation. In a conventional well-made play the heroine might have rejected her mother in

Act II on discovering that she was a "fallen woman" and then would have come to accept her by the end of the play because she was a good woman in spite of everything. Shaw places the reconciliation scene in the middle of the play:

MRS WARREN:	[*fondly*] I brought you up well, didnt I, dearie?
VIVIE:	You did.
MRS WARREN:	And youll be good to your poor old mother for it, wont you?
VIVIE:	I will, dear. [*Kissing her*] Goodnight.
MRS WARREN:	[*with unction*] Blessings on my own dearie darling! a mother's blessing! *She embraces her daughter protectingly, instinctively looking upward for divine sanction.*

(I, 316)

In the submerged play that *Mrs Warren's Profession* is competing with, this would be a perfect final curtain scene, but for Shaw the revelation and reconciliation are at the beginning of the serious action, not the end. Vivie accepts her mother as a former brothel-keeper and then rejects her as a conventional mother: a nice reversal of traditional expectations. There is another reversal of expectation, too, that also takes the form of a false ending. In Act III Vivie discovers that she may be the half sister of Frank Gardner, the young man who wishes to marry her. Frank is carrying a rifle, which Vivie aims at herself after this revelation—but the episode, which would also make an excellent climax to the submerged melodramatic courtesan play, is insignificant in the development of Shaw's play. Shaw raises the issue of incest in order to tease the audience by dropping it as trivial and irrelevant.[19] *Mrs Warren's Profession,* after the "final curtains" of the second and third acts, proceeds to its main business, Vivie's self-liberation in Act IV. This final act can be seen as an ironic epilogue to the rest of the play, turning the melodramatic comedy of Act II and melodramatic tragedy of Act III into the tragicomedy of Vivie's common-sense rejection of her artistic acquaintance, her suitor, and her mother. As in *Cymbeline Refinished* and other plays for which Shaw provided endings, he transforms the mood and genre—except here he is refinishing his own play. Once the comic and tragic plots have been used up then the play goes off in its own direction.

    Candida, like *A Doll's House,* begins with the happy ending of all the drawing-room comedies in vogue in the late nineteenth century. The quarrel between the Christian Socialist clergyman and his capitalist father-in-law, which might have been the focus of someone else's play, has taken place three years before the play begins, and the happy marriage which might have concluded someone else's play is the opening situation of Shaw's. Thus *Candida* begins with a conventional happy ending, and then in Act III the plot ends just as the crucial part of the play begins. Ibsen in *A Doll's House,* Shaw wrote in a 1937 program note to *Candida,* defied the old-fashioned construction of the well-made play. "He made what was then an outstanding innovation by first finishing his story completely, and then, instead of bringing down the curtain as quickly as possible, making his characters sit down to discuss the play and draw the moral. Now this is what happens in Candida" (Author's Note, I, 600). In the final act Candida makes her choice between her husband and the young poet. This stagy scene, however, is not the climax but the preliminary: the real question is *why* she has chosen the husband and how the poet will respond to his rejection.

Although *Major Barbara* is a much more complex play—and a much greater one—its structure is similar in this respect to that of *Candida.* Conventionally, and in terms of plot, the big scene in *Major Barbara* is Cusins' revelation about his birth in the final act:

CUSINS:	Well, I have something to say which is in the nature of a confession.
SARAH: LADY BRITOMART: BARBARA: STEPHEN:	} Confession!
LOMAX:	Oh I say! . . .
CUSINS:	. . . then I stooped to deceive her about my birth.
BARBARA:	[*rising*] Dolly!
LADY BRITOMART:	Your birth! Now Adolphus, dont dare to make up a wicked story for the sake of these wretched cannons. Remember: I have seen photographs of your parents; and the Agent General for South Western Australia knows them personally and has assured me that they are most respectable married people.
CUSINS:	So they are in Australia; but here they are outcasts. Their marriage is legal in Australia, but not in England. My mother is my father's deceased wife's sister; and in this island I am consequently a foundling. [*Sensation*].

(III, 163–65)

Barbara's comment here is "Silly!"—and that is just the point. In the submerged play, the Victorian play about class barriers, this would be the climax, the culmination of the plot and the end of the play. Shaw, on the other hand, reduces it to the level of a silly joke that has no serious bearing on the real issues of the play (except thematically, as an instance of the relativity of moral codes). *Major Barbara* is a play of paradoxical reversals, and one reversal here is that whereas in Victorian drama (and in literature generally) characters would prove their legitimacy in order to gain their position in society, Cusins proves his illegitimacy in order to qualify as heir to the munitions works.[20] Furthermore, this supposedly shattering, culminating revelation does not end the play but in a sense begins it; the traditional conclusion is Shaw's point of departure. The heart of *Major Barbara* is the discussion that follows Cusins' confession. As in *Mrs Warren's Profession,* family relationships in themselves are insignificant: the illegitimacy here is no more important than the incest in the earlier play. As in *Cymbeline Refinished,* eligibility as heir on grounds of birth is insignificant too. Like the princes, Cusins is a reluctant heir. "There is an abyss of moral horror between me and your accursed aerial battleships," he tells Undershaft (III, 165). The question is not a technical one of the circumstances of one's birth, but a human one of the activity of one's will. Cusins must make up his *mind,* and it is mind—as opposed to mechanism—that Shaw's plays keep bringing us back to. And so the final twenty pages of the play are devoted to discussion and decision, and the essential part of the play comes after the conventional ending.[21]

The Shewing-up of Blanco Posnet has as its subtitle "A Sermon in Crude Melodrama," which in itself suggests the paradoxical juxtaposition of two genres, a Shavian technique that we looked at earlier. The melodramatic plot (as in *The Devil's Disciple*) has to do with a man on trial for his life who is saved at the last moment. The plot therefore ends when the trial ends, but the play does not end there. On the contrary, it is while the jurymen are leaving the box that Blanco suddenly rushes from the bar and jumps up on a table, declaring, "Boys, I'm going to preach you a sermon on the moral of this day's proceedings" (III, 795). Then comes the central part of the play.

Fanny's First Play carries further the structural principle of having the ending in the middle of the play. It does explicitly what many of Shaw's other plays do implicitly. Here the plot and the reaction to it are literally separate plays: Fanny's play and the frame that surrounds it. After the curtain comes down on Fanny's play the rest of *Fanny's First Play* is an epilogue devoted to a discussion of what we have just seen.

Back to Methuselah is structurally very different from Shaw's other plays, in that it is a cycle of five plays, roughly on the model of Wagner's *Ring of the Nibelung.* What is relevant to my present argument, though, is the fact that the goal of living 300 years, which is the basis of the cycle's overall plot, is achieved in the middle of the cycle. The middle play is entitled *The Thing Happens,* and the two succeeding plays explore the results. Once more in Shaw's dramatic world, it is what happens *after* the thing happens that is the real point.

Too True to be Good, like *Fanny's First Play,* is explicit about this principle. The first act in a sense brings the comic pattern to completion in that the Patient is liberated from her illness, from her illusions, and from the tyranny of her mother. This makes Acts II and III an epilogue about the results or aftermath of the Patient's escape. As soon as she leaves her bedroom, the Monster (the microbe whom she has infected) sits up and concludes the act as follows: "The play is now virtually over; but the characters will discuss it at great length for two acts more. The exit doors are all in order. Goodnight" (VI, 455–56). Here we have the outside perspective that takes us beyond the main play, the challenge to the audience's conceptions of dramatic structure, and the suggestion that the discussion—the human reactions—may be more important than the plot.

III

Shaw has been quoted as saying in an interview that critics should begin their interpretations of his work with the idea that "Mr. Shaw's plays begin where they end and end where they begin": "My plays [he explained] are interludes, as it were, between two greater realities. And the meaning of them lies in what has preceded them and in what follows them. The beginning of one of my plays takes place exactly where an unwritten play ended. And the ending of my written play concludes where another play begins. It is the two unwritten plays they should consider in order to get light upon the one that lies between."[22] We have been taking Shaw's advice in looking at his plays in relation to implied, unwritten ones, and in considering the significance of external frames of reference. We have seen that the beginning of one of his plays takes place exactly where an unwritten one ended, in the sense that he disposes of the unwritten play and then proceeds with his own, or with the central part of his own. What then of the unwritten play that follows the ending of Shaw's play? Let us look at *Candida* again. As we have noticed, it begins where an unwritten play ended in that the conflict with the woman's father is in the past, and the happy marriage is well under way, and also in that the conventional ending of the woman's choice is Shaw's beginning of the crucial and final scene of his play. The play has yet another false ending, however. In the final lines the poet leaves the house, and the husband and wife embrace by their cosy domestic hearth. But then comes another of those passages of ambiguous status, an intrusion that is part of the fiction but not part of the fiction. This time it is the notorious stage direction that concludes the play, which gives the playwright the last word: "They embrace. But they do not know the secret in the poet's heart" (I, 594). As in the case of the epilogue to *Pygmalion*, this stage direction merely confirms what is in any case dramatized in the final scene of the play that the audience sees on the stage. Marchbanks has outgrown Candida and the romantic domestic bliss that she represents; he is headed for greater things. The stage direction emphasizes the fact that the static, conclusive ending of the domestic tableau is illusory. The stage direction draws our attention away from the domestic drawing room to the night outside, away from the problem that has (perhaps) been resolved to the dynamic principle of growth and development inherent in the poet Marchbanks. Thus the ending of *Candida* turns the play into a prologue to a work about Marchbanks: what will he do with his "man's voice"? In *Pygmalion*, the play in a way becomes the prologue to a short story about what Eliza will do once she becomes a woman. *Candida* leaves its sequel unwritten.

These endings that are beginnings are very much part of Shaw's general outlook. In his Hegelian view of history, process never stops; every dialectical resolution is merely a resting place or jumping-off point. There is no finality in life or history; every ending is a new beginning; there is always something to add. In Shaw's evolutionary universe the Day of Judgment is not the end of history but rather a beginning. In *The Simpleton of the Unexpected Isles* the Angel announces that "This is the Judgment Day."

MRS HYERING: But where does the end of the world come in?

THE ANGEL: The Day of Judgment is not the end of the world, but the end of its childhood and the beginning of its responsible maturity.

(VI, 821, 825)

Even if the human race should come to an end, Shaw suggests repeatedly, the Life Force would then try a new experiment and life would go on to another stage.

For Shaw there is always something to add. There is always a last word because there is never a last word. This is true of his view of history and it also expresses itself in other ways. Shaw writes a play and then has the last word by writing a preface later for its publication. Then he quite often adds a postscript to the preface, to bring it up to date or to include an afterthought. The Preface to the original 1907 edition of *John Bull's Other Island,* for example, has a postscript written after the sheets had passed through the press, then another postscript headed "A Year Later," and then there is a preface to the original preface, which Shaw wrote for the 1912 publication of the play, and a further postscript in 1929, headed "Twenty-four Years Later." There is a similar series of epilogues in the Constable Standard Edition volume (put together by Shaw himself) entitled *Essays in Fabian Socialism:* the last two sections are headed "Fabian Essays Twenty Years Later," Shaw's Preface to the 1908 edition of *Fabian Essays in Socialism;* and "Fabian Essays Forty Years Later: What They Overlooked," his Preface to the 1931 edition.

Shaw's sense that there is always another last word to be had is an important element in his dramaturgy. Every drama must present a conflict, he wrote in the Preface to *Plays Pleasant,* and "The end may be reconciliation or destruction; or, as in life itself, there may be no end" (I, 373).[23] Shaw's plays are open, living, growing structures, and they cannot be concluded with neat mechanical precision. Some of his plays have no ending at all, and just stop in the middle of a conversation or speech, with the implication that the discussion will continue later. At the end of *Getting Married,* for example, Mrs George refers to the thing that a woman wants most from marriage. Considering her authoritative role in the play as a kind of inspired prophetess, her view would be highly relevant to the discussion. But she asks the ascetic chaplain for his view:

MRS GEORGE: . . . Perhaps Anthony here has a glimmering of it. Eh, Anthony?

SOAMES: Christian fellowship?

MRS GEORGE: You call it that, do you?

SOAMES: What do you call it?

(III, 661)

And that is the last we hear of the matter, for Mrs George is called away before she can answer, leaving the question hanging in the air. Here Shaw is again teasing his audience and directing our attention beyond the play to an unwritten one that would continue the discussion.

Too True to be Good ends in the middle of the preacher's concluding sermon. His last words are in the printed text but are not meant to be heard distinctly by the audience in the theatre.[24] The speaker is enveloped by fog, and his sermon just drifts off into nothing. Then the playwright gives himself the last word in a substantial stage direction in which he says that although "he has given the rascal [i.e., the preacher] the last word" his own favorite is the woman of action. Here the outside perspective undermines the final speech even further than the stage action does, and it refers us to the possibility of action beyond the play.

Many of Shaw's plays, like *Candida,* have the suggestion of action beyond the play in an unwritten epilogue or sequel. In *The Man of Destiny,* for example, the sequel is Napoleon's subsequent career in history, to which the play is a prologue, while in *The Apple Cart, On the Rocks,* and *Geneva* the epilogue (at the time of the respective plays' composition) is not only unwritten but unknown; the plays remain to be continued by history. At the end of *Major Barbara* Undershaft has the last word, but any last word is only provisional, and the ending can be seen as a prologue to the sequel that would reveal whether Cusins and Barbara are able to accomplish their intentions as inheritors of the munitions works. At the end of *Androcles and the Lion* Androcles' safety is assured, but the real subject of the play is not this question of plot but rather the larger issue of emerging Christianity. Lavinia proclaims her intention to "strive for the coming of the God who is not yet" and we learn that her arguments with the Roman captain will continue after the final curtain (IV, 634). In *Heartbreak House* Providence has the last word, as Lady Utterword claimed it does, but this last word is a growl of disgust in the form of enemy bombs. In another sense the last word of the play (apart from Randall's flute) is the final lines of dialogue:

MRS HUSHABYE: But what a glorious experience! I hope theyll come again tomorrow night.

ELLIE: [*radiant at the prospect*] Oh, I *hope* so.

(V, 181)

These characters, like Lavinia in *Androcles,* have their minds on the future, and what the future will bring at the end of *Heartbreak House* is unknown.

The last word of *Back to Methuselah* is "beyond." The play seeks to cover human history from beginning to end, but the end is another beginning. The final play of the cycle, entitled *As Far as Thought Can Reach,* takes place 30,000 years hence, and when it ends we are taken back to the beginning with the reappearance of Adam, Eve, the Serpent, and Cain, and then we are taken further back to Lilith, who preceded them in time. But this does not imply the cyclical pattern it appears to, for Lilith speaks not of the past but the future. After all the progress that *Back to Methuselah* has depicted, life is still in its infancy, Lilith declares, and she concludes: "It is enough that there *is* a beyond" (V, 630–31). One might set next to this phrase the last lines of *The Simpleton of the Unexpected Isles:*

PRA: All hail, then, the life to come!
PROLA: All Hail. Let it come.

(VI, 840)

Shaw's final play, *Why She Would Not,* written in July 1950 a few months before his death, has (in one draft, at any rate) this as the conclusion to its last speech: "We must leave the world better than we found it or this war-ravaged world will fall to pieces about our ears" (VII, 679). It is fitting that Shaw's last word, dramatically speaking, should look to the future and impose a responsibility on his audience as his legacy.

The Preface to *Pygmalion* begins, "As will be seen later on, Pygmalion needs, not a preface, but a sequel, which I have supplied in its due place" (IV, 659). Sometimes the ending of Shaw's written play concludes quite literally where another work begins. *Pygmalion's* sequel is a short story, and *Androcles and the Lion* has an epilogue at the end in the form of an essay on the timelessness of the play's theme of martyrdom: another of the author's intrusions that introduce a new perspective. The fifth act of *The Doctor's Dilemma* is an epilogue in dramatic form, which takes place well after the main action of the play and reverses the position of Sir Colenso Ridgeon, who has been victorious in the first four acts but is now humiliated. And *"In Good King Charles's Golden Days"* has a kind of epilogue, in that after the long discussion in Sir Isaac Newton's house in Act I there is a brief domestic second (and final) act that shows Charles in a very different light, as the faithful husband of Catherine of Braganza.

Shaw does of course have one play with an explicit epilogue. *Saint Joan* exhibits many of the characteristics of Shaw's dramatic art that I have been discussing, and I believe that the structure of *Saint Joan* can be most fully understood and appreciated in the light of the issues I have raised. We have seen, for example, that *Cymbeline Refinished* and *Pygmalion* reject the conventions of their genre by taking the story further than the conventions of romance permit. Now the structure of *Saint Joan* is suggested in a sentence in the Preface to the play: "The romance of her rise, the tragedy of her execution, and the comedy of the attempts of posterity to make amends for the execution, belong to my play and not to my preface, which must be confined to a sober essay on the facts" (VI, 66). *Saint Joan* exhibits in a striking way the mixing of genres that we have seen in *Mrs Warren's Profession* and elsewhere in Shaw's work. The romance of the early scenes is not enough,[25] and the play goes on to show the struggle and defeat that result from Joan's rapid rise. It is true that the historical record demands that her story be taken further than her successes at Orléans and Rheims, but the point is that in *Saint Joan* the historical record and Shaw's genius find a remarkable meeting ground (in this respect and in others too). The historical record, however, does not require the play's next—and much more jarring—reversal. The romance of her rise is not enough for Shaw, and neither is the tragedy of her execution. On the whole *Saint Joan* without its Epilogue looks most like a tragedy, and it is characteristic of Shaw to undermine the generic conventions of his submerged play. In *Major Barbara* the submerged comedy should end with the union of Barbara and Cusins after Cusins' revelation about his birth. The play does end with the union of the young couple, but this is really just a detail that is overwhelmed by the big issues of the discussion in Act III, which widens the context and makes the future of society predominate as an issue over the present personal happiness of Barbara and Cusins. In the submerged tragedy of *Saint Joan* death should be the end. And the play proper does end with Joan's death. Shaw is consistent with his usual practice, however, in arousing expectations of tragedy in order to defeat them. That is why he has the Archbishop say in the Cathedral scene, "The old Greek tragedy is rising among us. It is the chastisement of hubris" (VI, 146). Here our attention is drawn away from the play itself to the dramatic tradition of which it is supposed to be a part. But the play surprises and challenges us by moving beyond tragedy. The play that precedes *Saint Joan* in the Shaw canon is *Jitta's Atonement,* completed less than two years before *Saint Joan* was begun. Needless to say they have little in common, but there is this one point of contact. In both plays Shaw has taken the somber and tragic and turned it into the colloquial and comedic. He has taken a genre and style and then has deliberately proceeded to distort them. Thus we move in *Saint Joan* from the formal trial scene in the hall of the castle to the informal atmosphere of Charles's bedroom, with the king "reading in bed, or rather looking at the pictures in Fouquet's Boccaccio with his knees doubled up to make a reading desk" (VI, 190).

In *Major Barbara* marriage does not have the last word; there is more to be said after the comedic pattern is fulfilled. In *Saint Joan* death does not have the last word; there is more to be said after the tragic pattern is fulfilled. Both plays—like so many others of Shaw's—go on after the plot has been used up. The plot of *Saint Joan* ends with the burning, but as usual Shaw wants to examine the results of the event rather than remaining satisfied with the event itself. As usual Shaw treats the conventional ending as his point of departure. "As to the epilogue," he protests in his Preface, "I could hardly be expected to stultify myself by implying that Joan's history in the world ended unhappily with her execution, instead of beginning there" (VI, 75). In the play itself, after the burning, Warwick meets Ladvenu as the latter returns from the execution:

WARWICK: I am informed that it is all over, Brother Martin.

LADVENU: [*enigmatically*] We do not know, my lord. It may have only just begun.

(VI, 189)

And Ladvenu concludes his account of the execution by saying with conviction: "This is not the end for her, but the beginning" (VI, 189). When the executioner assures Warwick, "You have heard the last of her," Warwick has the last word in the scene: "The last of her? Hm! I wonder!" (VI, 190).

The Epilogue to *Saint Joan,* like the Hell Scene of *Man and Superman,* creates a fresh perspective and makes us see the action of the main play in a new way. In both cases our vision is extended so that our context is now the whole of history and not just turn-of-the-century London or late mediaeval France. (The same is true in a minor way of the little "epilogue" to *Androcles and the Lion.*) In these plays we are made to look ahead. Joan's death is not an ending but a beginning, and indeed the Epilogue itself is not an ending but a beginning. The last word is given to Joan, after her admirers have slipped away when she refuses to accept her role as dead saint and talks about returning to earth as a living woman: "O God that madest this beautiful earth, when will it be ready to receive Thy saints? How long, O Lord, how long?" (VI, 208). The Epilogue offers no resolution, but points us to the future. The issue finally is not what has happened to Joan but what will happen to her: when will the earth be ready to receive such a person? The play ends with a question, and as in Shaw's other plays the last word is that there is no last word.

Notes

1.   *The Bodley Head Bernard Shaw: Collected Plays with Their Prefaces* (7 vols. London: Max Rheinhardt, The Bodley Head, 1970–74), 5.130. Subsequent quotations from Shaw's plays, prefaces, and related articles are from this edition, with volume and page numbers indicated parenthetically in my text.

2.   Shaw is being quoted here by Archer, in an 1892 newspaper piece that Shaw used in

his Preface to the 1893 edition of *Widowers' Houses* (1.38). Shaw's own account in this Preface is similar, except that he says he was in the middle of the second act when he needed more story to go on with. Cf. "How William Archer Impressed Bernard Shaw" (1927), *Pen Portraits and Reviews* (London: Constable, 1949), pp. 21–22. For a more detailed account of the collaboration between Shaw and Archer, see Jerald E. Bringle's Introduction to *Widowers' Houses: Facsimiles of the Shorthand and Holograph Manuscripts and the 1893 Published Text* (New York: Garland, 1981).

3.   Bernard F. Dukore, *Bernard Shaw, Playwright: Aspects of Shavian Drama* (Columbia: Univ. of Missouri Press, 1973), p. 280n. Dukore lists features of the well-made play that are found in *Widowers' Houses*. See also Eric Bentley, "The Making of a Dramatist (1892–1903)," in *G. B. Shaw: A Collection of Critical Essays,* ed. R. J. Kaufmann (Englewood Cliffs, NJ: Prentice-Hall, 1965), pp. 59–62.

4.   Shaw to William Archer, Oct. 4 1887, in Bernard Shaw, *Collected Letters 1874–1897,* ed. Dan H. Laurence (New York: Dodd, Mead, 1965), p. 176.

5.   Cf. Grace Tranfield near the end of *The Philanderer:* "They think this a happy ending, Julia, these men: our lords and masters!" (1.225).

6.   Cf. Brecht's Epilogue to *The Good Person of Szechwan:*

> Ladies and gentlemen, don't feel let down;
> We know this ending makes some people frown.
> We had in mind a sort of golden myth
> Then found the finish had been tampered with.
> Indeed it is a curious way of coping:
> To close the play, leaving the issue open. . . .

(*Plays* 2, tr. John Willett [London: Methuen, 1962], 311.)

7.   *Jitta's Atonement* is in Vol. 5 of the Bodley Head *Collected Plays with Their Prefaces,* with a Translator's Note. A straight non-Shavian translation of Trebitsch's play has been published as *Jitta's Atonement: Shaw's Adaptation and the Translation of Trebitsch's Original* (Ann Arbor: University Microfilms International, 1979), with an introduction comparing the translation with the German original. Dukore (pp. 203–11) also discusses *Jitta's Atonement* in relation to the original.

8.   Shaw may also have felt tempted to try his hand with *Othello.* He said to Maurice Baring about this play, "You always want to get up and shout that the handkerchief is a plant, and that what you really want to know is how the miscegenation will turn out if it gets fair play" (Feb. 27, 1918, Humanities Research Center, University of Texas at Austin.© The Bernard Shaw texts 1983 The Trustees of the British Museum, The Governors and Guardians of the National Gallery of Ireland and Royal Academy of Dramatic Art). It is worth noting here, too, that the play of Shakespeare's to which Shaw responded most fully was *Hamlet,* which transforms the Elizabethan revenge-play convention in a way that anticipates Shaw's reworkings of the dramatic traditions he exploits.

9.   See my introduction to Bernard Shaw, *The Man of Destiny and Caesar and Cleopatra: Facsimiles of the Holograph Manuscripts* (New York: Garland, 1981), pp. xiv–xv. The title of *Caesar and Cleopatra* itself constitutes a direct challenge to *Antony and Cleopatra;* Shaw wrote in 1913 in defence of his unerotic Caesar that "the very first consideration that must occur to any English dramatic expert in this connection is that Caesar was not Antony" ("*Caesar and Cleopatra,* by the Author of the Play" [2.314]).

10.   *An Unsocial Socialist* (London: Constable, 1932), p. 255.

11.   This stage direction is briefly discussed in Martin Meisel, *Shaw and the Nineteenth-Century Theater* (1963; rpt. Princeton: Princeton Univ. Press, 1968), p. 35. Much of Meisel's

commentary on Shaw's use of nineteenth-century dramatic genres is relevant to the issues I am exploring here.

12. Cf. Dukore, p. 215.

13. *Our Theatres in the Nineties* (3 vols. London: Constable, 1948), 2.84.

14. *Our Theatres in the Nineties,* 1.258.

15. Shaw to H. A. Jones, Nov. 19, 1894, *Collected Letters 1874–97,* p. 459.

16. Shaw to Maurice Baring, March 4, 1911, Humanities Research Center, University of Texas at Austin. Cf. Shaw's advice to Frank Harris about his play *Mr and Mrs Daventry:* "Fortunately for you, the play is a real beginning. You have hardly dug a foot into the vein as yet. The husband's suicide is all my eye. What you must do now is to begin a sequel to the play as follows:—" and Shaw offers a scenario in which the husband's shot is not fatal and the situation develops as a problem of conduct (Shaw to Frank Harris, Nov. 4, 1900, *Collected Letters 1898–1910,* ed. Dan H. Laurence [New York: Dodd, Mead, 1972], pp. 194–95).

17. See Stanley Weintraub's introduction to Bernard Shaw, *An Unfinished Novel* (London: Constable, 1958), p. 7.

18. Preface to *The Irrational Knot* (London: Constable, 1950), p. xix.

19. See Meisel, p. 145. His whole chapter on *Mrs Warren's Profession* in relation to the late Victorian courtesan play (pp. 141–59) has a bearing on my argument.

20. Meisel, p. 296n.

21. Cf. Dukore, p. 85: "If plot were all, as it is in the well-made play, the resolution of the technical details might end the play. But with social and moral questions paramount, the plot cannot be so easily resolved."

22. Paul Green, *Dramatic Heritage* (New York: Samuel French, 1953), pp. 125–26.

23. I have touched on this matter of endings in *The Marriage of Contraries: Bernard Shaw's Middle Plays* (Cambridge, MA: Harvard Univ. Press, 1974), pp. 20–21.

24. Dukore reveals that the final lines of this speech were added during rehearsals when it was found that the curtain would not come down quickly enough to cut the speaker off (p. 25).

25. "It was a great experience hearing G.B.S. read *Saint Joan* for the first time, to me, Lewis Casson and Cherry-Garrard (of the Antarctic). The first scene took one's breath away by its audacity. . . . Three scenes followed, full, crammed full of thought, of daring imagination, until the wind changed on the Loire and we all gasped. G.B.S. said: "That's all flapdoodle up to there—just "theatre" to get you interested—now the play begins' " (Sybil Thorndike, "Thanks to Bernard Shaw," in Raymond Mander and Joe Mitchenson, *Theatrical Companion to Shaw* [London: Rockcliff, 1954], p. 14).

Deconstruction as Devil's Advocacy:
A Shavian Alternative

RICHARD F. DIETRICH

The contention in this essay is that while Bernard Shaw could not be called a deconstructionist, at least nothing a Derridean would so call, nevertheless there is deconstructive activity of a significant kind and degree in his work, worthy of investigation for its own sake. In the Shavian quality of devil's advocacy to be found within such activity may also lie a clue to the future of deconstruction, one, in fact, already adumbrated in the accounts of such critics as Christopher Norris and Jonathan Cullers.

The question at first is whether Shavian deconstruction as devil's advocacy is a completely realized action or one of those many half-realized ideas that characterizes the work of a man unable to develop all the ideas that occurred to him. Considering the latter first, one is reminded of that "modest" prophecy with which Shaw, who had not yet written most of his masterpieces, closed the "Preface" to *Three Plays for Puritans* (1900)—"I shall perhaps enjoy a few years of immortality. But the whirligig of time will soon bring my audiences to my own point of view; and then the next Shakespear that comes along will turn these petty tentatives of mine into masterpieces final for their epoch."[1] One supposes that the "petty tentatives" Shaw had in mind were certain innovations of dramatic theme and technique that he knew he had not fully developed; and so we now have articles, for example, that show how Shaw anticipated The Theatre of the Absurd and other avant-garde theatre, certain "tentatives" of Shaw's anti-realistic dramaturgy being more completely realized by Brecht, Ionesco, Beckett, and others.[2] If Shavian deconstruction is another such "tentative," then its anticipation of another kind of contemporary avant-garde, that of today's literary critic, should be equally worthy of study for its own sake. Post-modern criticism seems tailor-made for Shaw, and, further, this criticism can be viewed as the full flowering of an attitude towards writing that Shaw was among the first to attempt. Long before Derrida was dreamed of, Shaw struggled, in a world much less sophisticated in linguistics, to analyze texts in a way that saw through surfaces to the competing components beneath, in the deconstructionist manner. Yet this could be called "tentative" because his

From *Modern Drama* 29 (September 1986). Reprinted by permission of *Modern Drama*.

approach, artistic-critical rather than scholarly-critical, was far less systematic and far more figurative than that of most deconstructionists. Moreover, it is difficult to identify deconstructive activity in his writings because, as a practitioner working without a theory, unaware of deconstruction as a single thing, Shaw combined deconstruction with more traditional methods of analyzing arguments.

But these are considerations only if we think of Shaw's deconstruction as "tentative." Another possibility is that Shaw's use of it was as complete as he wanted it to be (or perhaps even as it can be, as will be argued later). Using deconstruction as "devil's advocacy" to test the outer limits of truth and order, Shaw perhaps deliberately avoided the most extreme forms of deconstruction (for which Shaw would probably not object to the name of "Derridadaism") to adopt a more positive position. The problem, then, is to show that Shaw's deconstructive strategy is not, as a Derridean might argue, "mere" devil's advocacy, a half-hearted version of the real thing, but a fully realized action.

Shaw is compared here mainly to the Anglo-American variety of deconstruction, for its modified version of Derrida (a "tamer" version, some would say) is more in keeping with Shaw's pioneering attempts; its greater sensitivity to the charge that deconstruction left to itself is a critical dead-end has forced it to consider, or reconsider, more moderate positions. Avoiding deconstruction at its most reductive and jargonish, as well as its most radical, then, this study will focus rather on how the general ideas of domestic deconstruction help us understand a certain bent of Shaw's writing, particularly in the works that analyze or react to texts. Although it should come as no surprise that Shaw, as a dedicated anti-academic, was never content to analyze a text for its own sake, his deconstruction usually rises out of the text to a more important consideration of the socio-political context and to proposals for positive action, a consideration which, from the Derridean point of view, often compromises his deconstruction and renders it "mere" devil's advocacy. With Shaw as with some Anglo-American deconstructionists, deconstruction is a *temporary* strategy, as all devil's advocacy necessarily is. And with Shaw it is apparently an ironic strategy as well, for Shaw's devil's advocates are never really devils—they only appear so, for a time.

Devil's advocacy will be defined gradually, and emphasized at the conclusion; we need first to see as much evidence of deconstructive activity in Shaw as possible. Perhaps "activity" is a good word to start with. Christopher Norris, explaining Derrida, insists that deconstruction is not a method but an activity, the deconstructionist opposing the very idea of a static method with an ABC of fixed values.[3] This is a very Shavian attitude as well, for one would be as hard-pressed to reduce Shaw's analytical process to a formula as Belsey, Cullers, Eagleton, Norris, and others have been to summarize Derrida's. But that the attitude is similar suggests that the most useful thing to do at this point is to establish a general field of like-mindedness. Establishing like-mindedness is of course not the same as establishing influence; rather the object is to contribute to the evidence of a *Zeitgeist* (a "spirit of the times" being one of Shaw's favorite concepts, by the way), assuming that it is always valuable to the history of ideas to note the first strugglings of an idea to assert itself. While it may be true that one can also find evidence of deconstructive activity in many of Shaw's Victorian and Edwardian contemporaries, it would seem worthwhile to point this out only in the case of those who, like Shaw, have developed it to the point of a conscious, consistent, and *characteristic* strategy.

One might begin by checking Shaw's practice at an early point of his career. An indication that Shaw was rather vaguely working toward a basic tenet of deconstruction is to be found in his first full-length essay, *The Quintessence of Ibsenism*, written in 1890 as a lecture for the Fabian Society (with revisions in 1913 and 1922). *The Quintessence* mainly examines texts—mostly Ibsen's plays and the critical response to those plays. Most of what could be identified as deconstructive activity is not of the debunking or unravelling type, for Shaw treats Ibsen as a *self*-deconstructor who used his own contradictions to fuel his creativity, to further his art. His reading of Ibsen's plays finds a general pattern in which most plays contain a small "difficulty" (what the deconstructionist would call a marginal "contradiction") that is artistically transmuted into the major theme of a later play:

> I have shewn how the plays, as they succeed one another, are parts of a continuous discussion; how the difficulty left by one is dealt with in the next; how Mrs. Alving is a reply to your hasty remark that Nora Helmer ought to be ashamed of herself for leaving her husband; how Gregers Werle warns you not to be as great a fool in your admiration of Lona Hessel as of Patient Grisel. The plays should, like Wagner's Ring, be performed in cycles; so that Ibsen may hunt you down from position to position until you are finally cornered.[4]

It seems that there are several things wrong with this as a deconstruction. First, Shaw talks about characters rather than codes of meaning, though the former might very well be translated into the latter (as I'll show later). Secondly, he projects Ibsen's contradictoriness upon his audience (although Shaw concedes elsewhere that it was also himself Ibsen hunted down). Thirdly, his treating of this contradictoriness as being the result of Ibsen's realization that language, especially formulaic language, is incommensurate with experience, is not quite the same as finding that a writer's language is torn by "warring forces of signification."[5] Lastly, Shaw's conclusion is close to a deconstructionist position only by implication—the quintessence of Ibsenism is that there is no quintessence, for Ibsen arrives at no easy formula for living life; rather, "conduct must justify itself by its effect upon life and not by its conformity to any rule or ideal."[6] That is, the unstated assumption is that Ibsen's texts, unable to synthesize all the codes that comprise them, do not possess any unifying principle that could be abstracted as a motto for living life. Typically, in Shaw deconstructive activity is used to point a moral at life rather than at the text, the moral being that there is no moral, and the moral perhaps being as much existentialist as deconstructive. From today's perspective, this is a rather unsatisfying stab at deconstruction. To see a clearer affinity between Shaw and deconstruction, we need to back off from the critical practice to see the ideas behind it.

One could summarize Shaw's affinity by referring to the "Maxims for Revolutionists" Shaw appended to *Man and Superman*—just as the quintessence of Ibsenism is that there is no quintessence, so, more broadly, "the golden rule is that there are no golden rules."[7] This position has been mistaken for anarchism, as deconstruction has been mistaken for anarchism, but it merely conveys Shaw's skepticism about language and its ability to express absolute truth. The biblical golden rule of "Do unto others as you would have them do unto you" is a good example of language that fails us by being vague, too general, and inviting of contradiction, and so a skeptical Shaw puckishly inverts the rule—in the "Maxims for Revolutionists" we also find, "Do *not* do unto others as you would that they should do unto you. Their tastes may not be the same."[8] [My italics]

This skepticism is the primary element in the like-mindedness of Shaw and the deconstructionists, a limited skepticism aimed at the way language operates as a system of meaning, a system that is more out of control than not, that uses people more than people use it. Shaw's favorite example of language in control of people was in the criticism of drama critics. Strangely, Shaw noticed, even most of the critics who favored "realism" (such as Clement Scott of *The Daily Telegraph*) had in common with those who didn't the characteristic that their conception of life was largely literary and artificial, based on stage convention, and on texts that romanticized, sentimentalized, and idealized existence. As he was totally unprepared by such habits to accept Ibsen's grimmer account of reality, it is no wonder that Clement Scott reviewed *Ghosts* hysterically. But it was also a matter of the critics ignoring how the reality of contemporary play construction contradicted their own critical idealism—"It is a striking and melancholy example of the preoccupation of critics with phrases and formulas to which they have given life by taking them into the tissue of their own living minds, and which therefore seem and feel vital and important to them whilst they are to everybody else the deadest and dreariest rubbish. . . ."[9]

No wonder too that Shaw's plays came as such a shock in the nineties, for they not only attacked conventional notions of reality through plot and character inversions, as did Ibsen, but unlike Ibsen, they also employed *verbal* inversion (more telling than Gilbert & Sullivan's merely cynical "topsy-turvyisms") to dismantle the familiar linguistic structures people professed as creeds, revealing the contradictions within and between creeds, and between creed and actual behavior. As Shaw said, "I . . . deal in the tragi-comic irony of the conflict between real life and the romantic imagination,"[10] his typical method being verbal shock—devil's advocacy—aimed at the cliché thinking of the idealist mind. A second thing Shaw has in common with deconstruction-ists, then, is a technique of defamiliarization. In showing the process by which a text was constructed and pointing up its contradictions, the deconstructor wrenches the reader out of a certain habit of reading and forces a more thoughtful response to language. Shaw employed the more provoking method of outrageous overstatement, but the intent was similar.[11]

This points to a third thing Shaw has in common with deconstruc-tionists—a healthy respect for language as a primary reality of human existence and an understanding that everything in that reality is "text." As Shaw's frequent practice was to treat "text" as something more than just "writing" in the usual sense, one wonders about this as an anticipation of Derrida.

Derrida's idea of "text" derives from Saussure's concept of *"différance,"* the principle that language is a differential network of meaning. Both a word and the concept it describes, as Norris sums it up, "are caught in a play of distinctive features where differences of sound and sense are the only markers of meaning."[12] But, as Norris notes, for Derrida the sense of the word *"différance"* is suspended between two French verbs meaning "to differ" and "to defer," the second sense adding to Saussure's concept of differentiation the idea that "meaning is always *deferred,* perhaps to the point of endless supplementarity, by the play of signification."[13] Derrida, then, in a radical definition, himself playing with words, employs the word "writing" to designate the inscription of a surplus of meaning that enforces a constant shifting of signifieds; therefore the differences between words are never fixed differences, as each play of significa-tion creates a surplus of meaning that spills over into new meaning and forces a chain reaction over a certain range of vocabulary. Thinking of "writing" in this broad sense as the origin of language, Derrida calls it "writing" because it is "inscribed," but "inscribed" he must mean metaphorically, as in the old expression, "It is written," referring to something not literally inscribed but to something "built in" from the beginning and inescapable, a causal force. To distinguish what we ordinarily mean by "writing" from this much broader application, which includes speech as well, Derrida calls the latter "protowriting." Protowriting can perhaps be understood as the program "written," so to speak, in our neural mechanism that, in the right circum-stances, forces us to play with signification, to invent differences among words, and that forces words into separate molds, but allows every mold to be breakable or subject to an overflow of meaning. It is "written" that it should be so. It is in that broad and metaphorical sense then that, as was said, everything in the realm of language is "text," whether graphic, spoken, thought, or suspended in the structures of the mind. This combination Derrida calls "the general text."

Although Shaw of course never used the Derridean language of "the general text" and "protowriting," he nevertheless seems on the way towards Derrida's radical view of things, for, like Derrida, he treats as "text" not just that which is graphically inscribed, but speech as well (what Derrida calls "vocal writing"), and beyond that something more fundamental: some construct that simply exists in what Shaw variously called "the popular imagination," "the romantic imagination," "the tissue of their own living minds," or "the mental fabric of my readers." Shaw's notorious attack on Shakespeare, for example, was directed much less at Shakespearean texts than at "Shakespeare" as a construct of "the general text." It was the "Shakespeare" in people's heads that he was after.

Shaw seemed to have an intuitive grasp of a central principle of modern linguistics—namely, that language precedes people and shapes their thoughts, even that language *is* thought.[14] Because he sensed the importance of language to belief systems and yet was not fatalistic about language, Shaw's central thrust in his polemics and his analyses of texts was to attack, especially at the points of self-contradiction, an aspect of the verbal molding process, which he called "idealism." Shaw's reading of Ibsen in *The Quintessence* is precisely that Ibsen was an iconoclast of life-denying linguistic molds, or ideals, ideals that were unhealthy because they attempted to stop the play of signification, which is to stop human growth.

The principal thrust of *The Quintessence* is Shaw's indictment of what he calls "idealism," and his analysis of Ibsen's plays and Ibsen's critics is handmaiden to that. (Shaw here follows another deconstructionist principle, by the way, in writing his own Ibsen, so that everywhere Ibsen goes *The Quintessence* is sure to follow, not as definitive interpretation but as a most interesting graft upon Ibsen's texts, to the greater glory of Derridean intertextuality.) Shaw defines "idealism" by contrasting it with two other modes of thinking—"realism" and "Philistinism," "realism" being of the visionary rather than the verisimilar kind.

Shaw presents his three types—realist, idealist, and Philistine— seemingly as sociological groups, and he uses their different reactions to conventional marriage and family arrangements as his example of typical behavior: the easy-going, comfort-loving Philistines go along with things for the sake of convenience; the idealists, though failures in marriage, idealize marriage as "made in heaven" and the family "as a beautiful and holy natural institution,"[15] insisting guiltily on suppressing any attack on the institutions; the rare realist, seeing more clearly, behind appearances, insists not only that institutions are man-made, temporary, and relative to culture, but that they *must* be changed periodically in order to keep pace with human evolution and the growth of will.

Further investigation reveals that Shaw meant these three types to be taken also as elements within the psyche of every human being; indeed Shaw treats them that way in his plays, where you will find characters, when not dominated by a single psychic principle, torn by warring psychic principles, not the familiar id, ego, and superego of Freudian psychology, but the realist, idealist, and Philistine principles of Shavian psychology.[16] Shaw also was able to treat the three principles as sociological types because one of the three tends to dominate the personality at crucial times *in society* and become one's character note. These principles become relevant to deconstruction when Shaw shows the conflicting elements of the psyche as deriving from "the general text." That is, the conflicting components of our psychological make-up are the correlatives of the competing codes of our language, the former apparently produced by some action of the latter upon human personality. Realism, idealism, and Philistin-ism are modes of thought, and thought is language. This suggests that, whatever other systems of categorizing are valid, codes of meaning could also be identified as realist, idealist, and Philistine codes. If that is possible, then not only is Shavian drama illustrative of deconstructive principles, but a closer look at *The Quintessence* reveals that Shaw's discussion of characters rather than codes of meaning is due to the fact that, for him, the characters *are* the codes, when viewed as social types, or are composites of codes, when the character is viewed as composed of psychic principles. Ibsen's characters are shown to be torn by internal conflict. In pointing to the conflict within Ibsen's characters between realist and idealist principles (the Julian of *Emperor and Galilean,* for example), Shaw is directing attention to the warring forces of signification within the language that provides the thought-matrix of their individual beings. These warring forces within individuals are also referred to in such later maxims as, "What a man believes may be ascertained, not from his creed, but from the assumptions on which he habitually acts."[17] For such assumptions are as language-based, in thought at least, as any professed creed. With such attention to conflicting codes of meaning within a single language matrix, Shavian deconstruction in *The Quintessence* is thus more prevalent than at first seems the case.

To draw out Shaw's affinity with deconstruction further, consider the idea that Shaw's three types may serve not only as sociological and psychological categories, correlative with codes of meaning, but as psycholinguistic categories as well. One of the principal things that differentiates the three types, as types, is their use of and attitude toward language.

Shaw's idealists are characterized, psycholinguistically, by their attitude toward the play of signification that is the normal, healthy way with language. Idealists, anti-deconstruction to the core, imagine that once certain favored words are received within certain molds, the play of signification can be stopped, frozen for all time. Notoriously lacking a sense of humor in the area of their ideal, idealists even try to "police" the language to enforce this view. Treating the favored text as sacrosanct, absolute, and unified, they will allow no text to be created that is not conventional at heart or that would be a rival to the sacred text. On the stage, for instance, for two centuries between the time of Congreve and Wycherly and that of Wilde and Shaw, bourgeois marital idealists largely succeeded in discouraging any drama that did not fulfill the conventional pattern of idealized love and marriage, with its "happily ever after" dénouement. No problematics were allowed, except phoney problems that could be mechanically resolved by a *deus ex machina* or an improbable plot twist. The presence of such problematics in Ibsen's plays, in part, drove the idealist critics crazy, as Shaw points out.

The Philistines are characterized, psycholinguistically, by their easy-going, good-natured conformity to whatever the idealists want in the way of language, as long as this conformity is spiced with a good deal of compensating public entertainment (formulaically manufactured by the idealists of course) and salted with a good deal of private joke-telling at the expense of the idealists. However, though idealists are frequently the butt of Philistine jokes, the joke-telling isn't really subversive because it merely relieves hostility rather than transforms it into reformist zeal—like the old joke upon the Victorian ideal that man is the pursuer, woman the pursued; the Philistine punch line is, "but most women take care not to outrun their pursuers." The joke enjoyed, there's no harm done to either the ideal or the sexual double standard underlying it. A certain play of signification is threatened by the joke, but is quickly dissipated in the guffaw that relieves the pressure. And no doubt that is why some critics view comedy as fundamentally conservative. But there's more than one kind of comedy, and another kind is illustrated by Shaw's *Man and Superman,* in which Shaw inverts not only the Victorian ideal but the Philistine joke upon the ideal, as coy Jack Tanner runs from Ann Whitefield but takes care not to get so lost she can't find him.[18] The play ends with a marriage pending, conventionally enough, but what a marriage it will be! The love that inspired it is primarily biological, the honeymoon will be spent at a socialist convention, and the possibility of a "happily ever after" ending is cancelled by our understanding that this marriage will be more like a debating society than an idyll of domestic bliss. And when we remember that Tanner was persuaded to capitulate to Ann by his dream of "Don Juan in Hell," we conclude that this marriage was made in Hell, not Heaven. The further joke is that Shaw believes "Hell" to be the proper place for marriages to be made.

This is the sort of comedy that tickles the fancy of Shaw's "realist," for the realist loves the play of signification set loose by such subversive comedy. The realist is characterized, psycholinguistically, by his view that, to paraphrase Shaw, "the Bible is that there is no Bible." That is, there is no text so authoritative or unified that it cannot be deconstructed. The realist sees that beyond appearances all texts have ideologies behind them, that frequently coercive institutions stand behind the ideologies, and that their intent or effect is to freeze human development by controlling language. He also sees that such efforts are self-defeating, for the more idealists try to suppress the play of signification, the greater grows the desire to break the suppression with a burst of contradictory creativity, even within the idealist text itself, as the realist potential within the idealist begins to rebel (thus providing another reason why texts are torn by warring forces of signification). The realist sees that life over the long term involves a growth of will, apparently of an evolutionary sort, and that to frustrate that will by suppressing the play of signification which must accompany it is to invite personal and social disaster. If Derrida is right in his assertion that all language begins as metaphor, then "dead metaphor" must make up the bulk of language, its figurative sense largely forgotten. In so far as this language has any life at all beyond the purely functional, it must get it through the play of signification that puts it in new contexts, perhaps mixed with new language. Realizing that if our language dies, in some sense we die, Shaw's realist adopts a strategy of enlivening and freshening the language, partly through the redefining of words to make them relevant, but more through verbal shock tactics—devil's advocacy—which set loose the play of signification. When Shaw was young, the world of Victorian convention looked unmovable, requiring nothing less than dynamite. The extremity of Shaw's rhetoric is always relative to Victorian stolidity and absolutism.

In his characterization of the realist's view of the human will as growing, the growth stimulated by conflict, Shaw seems especially in tune with the post-modern view, as summed up by Catherine Belsey: "Unfixed, unsatisfied, the human being is not a unity, not autonomous, but a process, perpetually in construction, perpetually contradictory, perpetually open to change." She goes on to quote Lacan to the effect that "linguistic change, therefore, any alteration of the relationship between man and the signifier, 'changes the whole course of history by modifying the moorings that anchor his being.' "[19] "Modifying the moorings" is exactly what Shaw's realist is up to. And one need only compare today's marriage and family practices with those of the Victorians to see the results.

But domestic conflict is not the extent of Shaw's concern in analyzing the texts of idealism. Shaw's 1922 "Preface" to *The Quintessence* reveals how he himself had grown in his realization of the applicability of his three psychosocial principles, and it gives us a further way to convert these principles into codes of meaning. Looking back on the wreck of Western civilization, Shaw sees that the Great War was "a war of ideals": "Liberal ideals, Feudal ideals, National ideals, Dynastic ideals, Republican ideals, Church ideals, State ideals, and Class ideals, bourgeois and proletarian, all heaped up into a gigantic pile of spiritual high explosive, and then shoveled daily into every house with the morning milk by the newspapers, needed only a bomb thrown at Serajevo by a handful of regicide idealists to blow the centre out of Europe. Men with empty phrases in their mouths and foolish fables in their heads have seen each other, not as fellow-creatures, but as dragons and devils, and have slaughtered each other accordingly."[20] Denouncing the post-war "reaction from Militarist idealism into Pacifist idealism" as simply a way of avoiding self-criticism, Shaw presents the "prophecy" of his *Quintessence* as once again highly relevant.[21] The interesting thing, for this article, is how Shaw visualizes the various idealisms as coded linguistic fragments—"phrases in their mouths and foolish fables in their heads," "a phrase in a newspaper article, or in the speech of a politician on a vote-catching expedition"[22]—that turn into warring forces of signification. Shaw's "war of ideals" is only just short of being as explicitly presented as a war of competing codes as a deconstructionist would like. It might indeed make an interesting contribution to both psycholinguistics and structuralism if it could be found that codes of meaning are in fact identifiable as realist, idealist, and Philistine codes, and that these in turn can be broken down into several varieties of each.

Codes of meaning are of further interest to deconstructionists as they form into, as Cullers puts it, "value-laden hierarch[ies], in which one term is promoted at the expense of the other."[23] A good example of the deconstructive approach to such hierarchies is in Shaw's inversion of the standard Victorian hierarchy of idealists as the most admirable, Philistines as the salt-of-the-earth "silent majority" in the middle, and the realist (whom they mistakenly would have called "cynic") as the lowest of the low, a "beastly" trouble-maker. Shaw astonishes Victorian idealists by putting them lower on the ladder of evolution than the realist. On the assumption that all hierarchies are linguistic cover-ups of ideological power struggles, deconstruction systematically demonstrates that all such hierarchies can be inverted, and should be, not for the sake of establishing new hierarchies but to contribute to the understanding that all hierarchies are arbitrary and relative.[24] It is true that *The Quintessence* seems merely to replace an old hierarchy with a new hierarchy, but more likely that is a characteristic Shavian overstatement, operating as a balancing device.

Shaw's career as both dramatist and essayist seems based on a consistent strategy of attacking conventional hierarchies, frequently by inversion, but the object was not to institute new ones but to restore the play of signification by drawing attention to the arbitrariness of all hierarchies. In *Man and Superman,* for example, the inversion of the Victorian sexual hierarchy in the play's main action, woman being the pursuer in the sex chase, does not deny its opposite, for Octavius, Ramsden, and Mendoza are still or have been pursuers of women, though hopelessly idealistic ones. And, further, Tanner's running away is "coy." That is, neither the old hierarchy of the dominant male in pursuit of "the weaker sex" nor the new hierarchy of the dominant mother-woman in pursuit of the helpless male is presented as exclusive or absolute. Rather each construct of meaning is necessary for the other to exist, and the spark of their interaction contributes to the endless play of signification that enriches our sexual codes over the centuries.

Sometimes Shaw sought to restore balance by simply attacking established hierarchies, sometimes by providing a rival hierarchy that inverted the established one, and sometimes he maintained opposing hierarchies in dialectical tension. As an example of the latter, there runs throughout his work a nice balancing act between his Ibsenism (self over society) and his socialism (society over self), and frequently they appear in the same work. A good example of the balancing of the hierarchies of self and society is the previously mentioned golden rule. The biblical golden rule establishes a hierarchy of values that places socially thoughtful behavior over selfish, individualistic behavior. Shaw's Ibsenist inversion reminds us that because individual tastes are frequently and rightfully a determining factor in how one treats others, one could just as easily argue for the primacy of self over society. But Shaw's inversion, true to deconstructionist principles, does not cancel out the original golden rule. As a socialist who argued for equality of income in a neighborly society, Shaw knew that the biblical dictum still may work, but only if we are aware of to what degree and in what circumstances, and it is to such relative circumstances, and to the play of signification that constantly alters the circumstances, that Shaw's verbal inversion calls attention. Such "word play" is precisely that—"play"—a long-acknowledged force for the liberation and rejuvenation of the human spirit. So too the play between a world in which rules are needed and a world in which rules sometimes need to be ignored, which is what Shaw's inversion of the golden rule more generally refers to, produces a creative tension, as neither cancels out the other, but the play of the polarization generates new meaning. Further, the polar opposition establishes a range of meaning within which one can roam in search of meaning pertinent to oneself. The effect of inverting an established hierarchy, then, is to restore balance, define limits, and to allow for a freer play of signification which will arise from that balance and operate within those limits. The objective might be to create a cultural atmosphere in which no one would even think of asserting the absolute truth of any hierarchy of meaning, but would be stimulated by the play of signification between hierarchies to create a synthesis to suit the case. Of course such talk of "balance" and "creative tension" makes Derrideans nervous, for it reminds them of the New Criticism they seek to discredit, but I am not claiming here that Shaw is a Derridean; in fact, this is precisely where Shaw gets off. He is with Derrida in wishing to free us of absolutisms, but he does not suspect the temporary harmony of a "creative tension" of harboring such absolutisms.

The reason for discouraging absolutism is that at the root of modern linguistic theory is the belief that language is an expression of will—a struggle for power sits at the base of all linguistic invention and use. Reviewing Nietzsche's contribution to linguistics, Christopher Norris sums up the philosopher's view "that Socrates himself is a wily rhetorician who scores his points by sheer tactical cunning. Behind all the big guns of reason and morality is a fundamental will to persuade which craftily disguises its workings by imputing them always to the adversary camp. Truth is simply the honorific title assumed by an argument which has got the upper hand—and kept it—in this war of competing persuasions. If anything, the sophist comes closer to wisdom by implicitly acknowledging what Socrates has to deny: that thinking is always and inseparably bound to the rhetorical devices that support it."[25] And what is true of the creation of texts is also true of the reading of texts—"Texts are in and of the world because they lend themselves to strategies of reading whose intent is always part of a struggle for interpretative power . . . texts exist from the outset as ground to be competed for by various strategies of self-promoting knowledge."[26] And Jonathan Cullers quotes Derrida to the effect that deconstruction itself is not immune to such willfulness and is certainly not to be some sort of ivory tower method of escaping the conflict of wills. Citing Derrida's own political involvement, Cullers writes that "the realities with which politics is concerned, and the forms in which they are manipulated, are inseparable from discursive structures and systems of signification, or what Derrida calls 'the general text.' "[27] All of this could have been written with *The Quintessence* as source, for Shaw's three psycho-social types are classified precisely on the basis of their response to will, which Shaw defines as "the prime motor" of human activity.[28]

Concerned as always to make connections between old language and new as part of his own reading strategy and contribution to the play of signification, Shaw identifies the will as "our old friend the soul or spirit of man" and says that "all valid human institutions are constructed to fulfill man's will."[29] But Shaw is not advocating abandonment to will, for will is only the motor—it must be fueled by imagination and steered by informed intelligence, and *Man and Superman* is only one of several plays that make steering versus drifting a primary metaphorical conflict. As Shaw says in *The Quintessence,* "ability to reason accurately is as desirable as ever; for by accurate reasoning only can we calculate our actions so as to do what we intend to do: that is, to fulfil our will."[30] Note that even in this early text emotion and reason are both conceived of as serving the will; it was not long before Shaw came to see no distinction between thinking and feeling, reason and passion, except one of degree. Accepting the will as prime motor and language as its medium, Shaw ended by declaring that thought is a passion.[31]

As soon as you declare that thought is a passion, you put yourself in line with that modern linguistic theory that sees the creation and development of language as a consequence of the passionate thinking of the willful human mind. And that is why Shaw laughed at the academic ideal of rational discourse, preferring instead to write in a way that was frankly polemical (for polemics is beneath all writing), and to reach more for affective levels of communication, where persuasiveness is more effective. As he summed it up. "It is not my habit . . . to begin by definitions, and when I do, I decline to be held by them. I do not address myself to your logical faculties, but as one human mind trying to put himself in contact with other human minds."[32] Rationalists may only shake their heads, but Shaw knew that words were shifting counters of passionate thought, with almost tactile properties if properly delivered, and that what mattered was not the logical consistency of his discourse (he enjoyed quoting Emerson's "A foolish consistency is the hobgoblin of little minds") but the degree to which he could "touch" other human minds with his words.

This assumption that thought is a passion also explains Shaw's insistence on being a propagandist. Having no illusions about his own neutrality or the neutrality of language, he would let his readers have none either, clearly signalling his bias. Using his drama criticism to discountenance the old drama and to make way for the new, he spoke of how his reviews were "not a series of judgments aiming at impartiality, but a siege laid to the theatre of the XIXth Century by an author who had to cut his own way into it at the point of a pen, and throw some of its defenders into the moat."[33] And so Shaw's readers were usually not left any doubts that the writer who was, so to speak, twisting their arms, meant to persuade them of his point of view, though his simultaneous pulling their legs and his habitual use of irony, paradox, and overstatement required considerable sophistication to understand.

And thus it is that "truth" in Shaw's writings is difficult to locate, for it is embedded in the interplay between propagandists and competing ideologies, and cannot easily be summed up. Shaw's particular genius was that he was so good at drawing out and making explicit the notions that ideology lurks everywhere and that Everyman is a propagandist (if only unwittingly in most cases)—it is in this sense that "drama of ideas" is a good term for his plays, for what animates most of Shaw's characters is exactly the compulsion to propagate a self-justifying ideology, a compulsion Shaw thought "divine" in origin, however distortedly it comes out, while the competing codes that verbalize their divided selves trip them up, revealing self-contradiction in the midst of self-justification. But Shaw's is a "divine comedy" in that it shows verbal prat-falling to be in the interest of human ascent.

Consider now an example of Shaw's seemingly proto-deconstructive view that "the Bible is that there is no Bible" that, by falling short as "mere" devil's advocacy, as strict Derrideans would view it, also provides us with an instructive contrast with Derridean deconstruction. What better example than Shaw's reading of the Bible itself, as we find it in the "Preface" to *Androcles and the Lion?*

This Preface finds Shaw ostensibly taking a different tack in that he presumes to give us "the Gospels without prejudice."[34] But in light of its date—1915—when Shaw's insistence on being prejudiced and propagandist was well known, the pose of neutrality can only be taken as a joke, aimed at the academic ideal of neutrality. This amusing persona might disconcert someone who reads the Preface out of context, or without knowledge of Shaw, but that is the risk in any ironic rhetorical strategy. Proof that Shaw assumed knowledge-able readers is in his tricky beginning, definitely not for beginners—after his opening declaration that Jesus was right and his way should be tried, he counters this affirmation of ancient religious teaching with an ironic assurance: "I can assure you I am as skeptical and scientific and modern a thinker as you will find anywhere."[35] Certainly Shaw does not disappoint those who expect him to debunk Jesus from a modern perspective, but the surprise is the degree to which he balances this with an affirmation of religious values, attacking those who have strayed from the path pointed out by Jesus. This Preface like so many others can be seen as the typical Shavian balancing act between opposing hierarchies, skepticism and belief forming one of the more important sets of hierarchies and exchanging positions in their respective hierarchies according to Shaw's place in the argument and the stress he is placing.

Although Shaw will eventually take the "Higher Criticism" of the Bible to task, it is obvious that criticism has been the source for his reading. His account is dotted with remarks about "grafts," "interpolations," "inscriptions," "accretions," and the "jerry-building" of unrelated traditions and doctrines,[36] which shows his responsiveness to modern biblical criticism in its analytical and disintegrative phase, and which reminds us too that the vocabulary of deconstruction was partly anticipated by the "Higher Criticism," for its practitioners were among the first to call our attention to the fact that texts are composed of competing codes. Did Shaw add anything to what the "Higher Criticism" thought it had established?

It might seem that he did not, for mostly he follows the "Higher Criticism" in its strategy of divide and conquer. The Gospel of John is shown to testify quite differently from the Synoptic Gospels (so much for the unity of the New Testament), the Synoptics themselves, written by quite different men in different times and circumstances, are shown not to be all that "synoptic" (so much for the unity of the Synoptics), and contradictions within each gospel are duly noted (so much for the unity of the individual gospels). This is all standard stuff. But Shaw contributes to this process in characteristic ways that gradually alters the standard line.

First, he offers the unique perspective of a "popular" writer. This is no dry-as-dust scholarly presentation; he has a feel for what it was like to write the Gospels that only a "popularizer" like himself could have. And he has a sense of narrative that allows him to appreciate the challenges of storytelling presented to the gospellers by their material. Secondly, he contributes his usual anachronistic approach to texts, finding contemporaneity in biblical times, such as his characterization of Luke as a Parisian romancer and of Jesus as a communist. But his major contribution is to take Jesus off the cross and out of the dusty tomes of history and scholarship and make him work again as a living force. And to do that he had to aim his deconstructive activity less at texts than at the institutions derived from and protective of texts, pointing out, for example, how "Barrabas," the people's choice, contradicts by his behavior the institutions (as well as the instituted texts) of that very Christendom he now presumes to represent. That is, as usual Shaw identifies codes of meaning by the names of characters—"Jesus" and "Barrabas" being the principals.

Here as elsewhere Shaw's principal deconstructive thrust is aimed less at specific texts than at "the general text," and less at "the general text" than at its socio-political context. From text to general text to context and back again is Shaw's typical polemical movement. From the Gospels as specific texts to the general ideas about Christ and Christianity to be found in "the mental fabric of my readers" (as Shaw here designates "the general text"), to the embodiment of those ideas in the socio-political structures of institutional Christendom, these constitute the three basic levels at which Shaw conducts his argument.

And it is the socio-political level, the world of action, that is primary. Shaw principally shows how human beings who call themselves Christians behave only partially, some minimally, according to the codes of their professed creed. Shaw's analysis of language-based human behavior is analogous to the deconstructive reading of a text—human beings are like texts in being driven by competing codes, the codes one is conscious of and subscribes to being undermined by other codes that work secretly, perhaps even to the extent that the secret codes constitute the assumptions on which one habitually acts. Even the most scrupulously "correct" person thus falls short of perfect unity by virtue of embedded contradictions. The contradictions are not evidence of villainous hypocrisy but of standard, language-controlled human nature. Awareness of the contradictions and subsequent *self*-deconstruction, as in the case of Ibsen, can lead to fruitful development. Living in blithe ignorance is Shaw's *bête noire*. Being aware of the contradiction between one's professed creed of "brotherly love" and one's capitalistic, Barrabas-like behavior (the secret creed of "every man for himself") might fruitfully lead to the arrangement of a better sort of society, one closer to the communal ideal of Jesus and his disciples. Not that capitalism has it all wrong—"money *is* the root of all good," after all; it's just that the hierarchy that places "money" at the top needs to be balanced with the hierarchy that places "money" at the bottom (as in "Money is the root of all evil"). If the hierarchies are properly balanced, the pursuit of the more abundant life sought by the Life Force may produce "riches" of both kinds, spiritual and material, which better answer the needs of our dual nature.

"The Uncrucifying of Christ," to borrow an apt phrase suggested by John Fowles's *The French Lieutenant's Woman*,[37] which Shaw effects in this Preface by debunking the crucified Christ of "Crosstianity," is an effort to return Christ and attendant spiritual values to a world which had shelved him and them in favor of a wholly materialistic pursuit, and the only means of achieving this in a secularized world lies in emphasizing the humanity of Jesus, a man acting and doing in the real world, asserting his will according to principles he alone understood clearly, principles which Shaw takes great pains to make more clear to everyone.

Following from the idea that Jesus was a man of action, one of those principles is that "the open mind never acts: when we have done our utmost to arrive at a reasonable conclusion, we still, when we can reason and investigate no more, must close our minds for the moment with a snap, and act dogmatically on our conclusions."[38] Again mocking the academic ideal of neutrality, Shaw closes his argument with a high-wire act that balances between heterogeneity and orthodoxy, the open mind and the closed mind, tilting at the end in favor of establishing and following a dogma, no doubt aimed at all those noble-souled but ineffectual types who would soon inhabit the pages of his *Heartbreak House*, those higher souls who looked with paralyzed horror at the brutalization of the world by those less shy of "taking action." It is interesting that a similar attitude is emerging among deconstructionists, some of whom are coming to realize that one can't spend all day in deconstructive activity. As Norris puts it, "there must be an end-point to this dizzying regress. It is reached at the moment when skepticism encounters a figural will to power beyond reach of further deconstruction."[39] Unless the goal of deconstruction is to contribute to a new unity (as the splitting of the atom may lead to a unified field theory), it can proceed only in endless reductionism or end in paralysis. We must be skeptical about language, but we must use it anyway, and the moment comes when we must act on it. As Norris says, "deconstruction is . . . an activity of thought which cannot be consistently acted on—that way madness lies . . ."[40] Also, "deconstruction neither denies nor really affects the common-sense view that language exists to communicate. It *suspends* that view for its own specific purpose of seeing what happens when the writs of convention no longer run. . . . But language continues to communicate, as life goes on, despite all the problems thrown up by skeptical thought."[41]

It is because skepticism has its limits that Shaw concludes his Preface with a critique of that very "Higher Criticism" on which he has leaned so hard to this point. To encourage constructive action, rather than further deconstruction, Shaw ends by saying that the disintegrations of the "Higher Criticism," "though technically interesting to scholars . . . have hardly anything to do with the purpose of these pages. . . . What I am engaged in is a criticism (in the Kantian sense) of an established body of belief which has become an actual part of the mental fabric of my readers. . . . For good or evil, we have made a synthesis out of the literature we call the Bible. . . . I have taken the synthesis as it really lives and works in men."[42] Arguing that the fundamental emotional unity of the Bible overwhelms its more superficial contradictions, Shaw, dropping his devil's advocacy, finds a unity there which transcends the logical-linguistic contradictions sought after by deconstruction.[43] That this emotional unity is a more powerful force in history than all the disintegrative criticism in the world contains an important lesson, perhaps, for contemporary criticism.

In contrast to the persistent negativity of deconstruction at its most extreme, Shaw, after the devil has been given his due, typically accentuates the positive, emphasizing the author's triumph over contradiction in synthesizing most of the codes employed. Shavian negation tends to stop at the point where he encounters, to quote Norris again, "a figural will to power beyond reach of further deconstruction." Sensing that he has reached that point in his reading of the Bible, Shaw pulls back from the "Higher Criticism" when he sees it operating too mechanically in pursuit of mere rational consistency. A text passes some sort of truth test when the will of the text is greater than that of the analyzing critic. And so, for many people, Shaw's treatment of the New Testament has saved it as a powerful literary unity, nourished by its own contradictions. And when we add to this his comments on the Old Testament (as in *The Adventures of the Black Girl in her Search for God*), we see that what Shaw ultimately shows is how "contradiction" served, as it did for Ibsen, as a creative force for the evolution of the unity, as the various codes of the Bible struggled against each other to push toward the common goal of becoming a testament of man's spiritual growth. To be sure, from the point of view of the devil's advocate, "the Bible is that there is no Bible," but such advocacy is by its nature a temporary putting of the case against, to test the truth of the case. The truth is that, despite its flaws, the Bible *acts* as a unit, and such factuality Shaw knew better than to deny. And only someone "hell bent" on deconstruction for its own sake, oblivious to history, would so deny.

In a recent issue of *College English,* William E. Cain, in reviewing four books on deconstruction, sees deconstruction as no longer the frightening bogey man it once seemed but as a respectable and necessary complement to New Criticism and other methods.[44] Deconstruction discredits New Criticism only as a complete method, absolute unto itself, not as a component of a total method, not yet entirely realized, of which deconstruction is another component. Strict Derrideans may not like this attempt to domesticate deconstruction or to see it as a dependent part of a whole, but one of their own most fervently held tenets—that nothing stands still—is so demonstrated. The rising tide of voices calling for deconstruction to arrive at a more positive philosophy that will allow it to be used for something besides destruction is also inevitable. As Cain puts it:

> When we capitalize upon deconstruction in this manner, we are involving it in historical inquiry, drawing upon it in order to discover how central, formative distinctions develop, why they endure, and through what means we can refashion them to help construct a better future. For deconstruction to be a truly "critical" method, for it to define itself as something more than just another academic field, for it to pass productively "beyond interpretation," it must enter forcefully into the positive *reconstruction* of politics, institutional practice, and history. These are the demanding tasks that await the next phalanx of guides and commentators.[45]

And thus one of the aims of this article is to remind criticism of Shaw's work, for in its particular use of deconstruction may lie, as was said at the beginning, a clue to the future of deconstruction. As the career of his own John Tanner shows, Shaw well understood the natural process by which today's radicals become tomorrow's domesticated. One can play the devil's advocate only so long. One may question and debunk all one likes, but sooner or later one must act, from a dogma (known or hidden), and there is no action that does not meet reaction, from another dogma (known or hidden), resulting in compromise, a "taming" of the original impulse. Further, the fact that deconstruction is being encircled by other methods is probably a prelude to its being absorbed by them as a necessary component of some larger unit. The wise deconstructionist, perhaps, will not resist but simply play his or her part—the obvious role of devil's advocate, a role that, as Shaw shows, can be played to the hilt, with no half-measures or half-heartedness about it. And when deconstructionists awaken to the *total* context of their deconstructive activity, they may discover that "devil's advocacy" is not "mere" devil's advocacy but really all that they can or should do with deconstruction, the only role they can play in the greater drama. If so, Shaw has given us examples of how to exercise deconstruction while containing its negative charge within a larger perspective.

Shaw's larger perspective may be a stumbling block, however, for while its evolutionary view of things is not inimical to deconstruction, it yet may not entirely satisfy the contemporary secular-scientific mind. But in the hope of at least inspiring fruitful comparisons and contrasts, I will conclude with a description of the Shavian metaphysic, which might serve as an alternative to current practice.

Shaw's metaphysic both explains the source of linguistic stress and development in terms larger than usually given and, following from that, even beyond what has already been suggested, shows how to be deconstructive without being destructive. As a dramatist by temperament Shaw was fascinated by conflict and contradiction, but unlike a lot of dramatists he sought out a metaphysic that would explain the conflict and contradiction as part of a larger unity, that would make conflict and contradiction cause for rejoicing rather than cause for despair. Whatever one thinks of Shaw's religion of Creative Evolution, it at least makes sense of that linguistic theory that follows from the Schopenhauerian-Nietzschean philosophy of the will to power. Words are agents of survival and potency, and their development in language according to the Saussurean principle of *différance* can also be explained by the principle of trial and error that Shaw's Life Force uses to ascend along an evolutionary path toward godhead. Small wonder that our language is composed of competing codes, for, in Shaw's understanding, our linguistic history is the record of billions of individual attempts, in small and large ways, by realist, idealist, and Philistine principles, to achieve godhead through the consciousness-raising device of language play. To invent a language difference is to add power to oneself but also consciousness and thought capability to the species. One of the principal spurs to such creativity is the development of opposing systems of signification by others, and from that follows the struggle to institute universal, or at least more common, systems of signification. But the system is never completed, conceptual closure never achieved, because the restless will, imbued with longings for the divine, seeks ever higher levels of consciousness in search of its ultimate fulfillment. One of the principal tasks of the devil's advocate is precisely to challenge attempts at closure and to point to fissures by which new ideas may enter. One is reminded of the way Shaw used to dismay his fellow socialists by looking forward to the day when, before socialism had completed its conquest of the planet, a new system would come along to contest and replace it.[46] Nothing could be more typical of Shaw's imagination than the way it reached ahead, with more interest in the destroyer of his own system than in those who would bring about its triumph. In works such as "The Illusions of Socialism" he even pointed to the loose threads in the socialist design, in case any one wanted to pull them. In Shaw's view, the unifying force of an ideology is necessary, but simultaneously problematical and temporary. As Cullers writes, "Deconstruction leads not to a brave new world in which unity never figures but to the identification of unity as a problematical figure."[47] Shaw goes further in arguing that unity ends in dogma, but he also urges that dogma be acted upon within broad limits of toleration, so that the destroyer of the stale system and the creator of the new system have room to breathe.

Something like this metaphysical underpinning is desperately needed to rescue deconstruction from the abyss. And when the metaphysic is found, perhaps from that will issue, as it has in Shaw's case, the discovery of a new unity that transcends the disintegrative actions of deconstruction. Shaw saw the new unity in a realization that language's fundamental reference is to fears and aspirations that are consistent on their own alogical level because unified by the evolutionary drive, language being a code of codes, speaking, beneath the competing codes nearer the surface, of the universal struggle for a more abundant life. So believing, Shaw could devilishly deconstruct a valued "text" without fear that he was destroying its life, for he believed as well that the life of a great text is largely subterranean, feeding on its own contradictions, nourished by the struggle for verbal agreement, and that the life of a great text is also in the interaction between the text itself and the never-ending commentary upon it, words without end. And he also believed that the devil's advocate of deconstruction is an angel in disguise, leading the way to a better future, helping in the struggle to synthesize the competing codes, to heal the fissures pointed out by deconstruction, providing the dynamics for evolution. But while this "faith" may have satisfied Shaw, whether it can serve to clothe deconstruction in a valid metaphysic remains to be seen. In the meantime, the idea of using deconstruction as devil's advocacy, to be circumscribed by complementary methods, even by dogma (as the original devil's advocate served a church), may be an alternative to current practice worth pursuing.

Notes

1. *The Bodley Head Bernard Shaw: Collected Plays with their Prefaces,* Vol. 2 (London, 1971), p. 47.

2. Stanley Weintraub, "The Avant-Garde Shaw," *Bernard Shaw's Plays* (New York, 1970), pp. 341–355.

3. Christopher Norris, *Deconstruction: Theory and Practice* (London, 1982), pp. 24, 31.

4. Bernard Shaw, *The Quintessence of Ibsenism* (New York, 1957 [1913]), pp. 185–6.

5. Jonathan Cullers, *On Deconstruction: Theory and Criticism after Structuralism* (Ithaca, N.Y., 1982), p. 213.

6. *The Quintessence of Ibsenism,* p. 157.

7. *The Bodley Head Bernard Shaw,* Vol. 2, p. 781.

8. Ibid.

9. *The Quintessence of Ibsenism,* p. 171.

10. *The Bodley Head Bernard Shaw: Collected Plays with their Prefaces,* Vol. 3 (London, 1971), p. 16.

11. Proof that the intent was not always realized is to be found in Richard M. Ohmann's

Shaw: The Style and the Man (Middletown, Conn., 1962), where, although Ohmann correctly identifies overstatement as a favorite device, yet in judging Shaw (p. 38) he strangely neglects to treat such overstatements as figures of speech. Taking Shaw literally, Ohmann falls into the old wheeze of denouncing him for his "perverse enthusiasm for Mussolini, Stalin, and Hitler."

12. Norris, pp. 24–25.
13. Ibid., p. 32.
14. For a discussion of the extent to which Saussure presents language as determining and determined, see Catherine Belsey's *Critical Practice* (London, 1980), pp. 44ff.
15. *The Quintessence of Ibsenism*, p. 39.
16. See my article, "Shavian Psychology," *The Annual of Bernard Shaw Studies*, Vol. 4 (University Park, Pa., 1984), 149–171.
17. *The Bodley Head Bernard Shaw* Vol. 2, p. 788.
18. See Albert Bermel's "Jest and Superjest," *Shaw Review* (May, 1975), 57–69.
19. Belsey, p. 132.
20. *The Quintessence of Ibsenism*, p. 7.
21. Ibid., pp. 7–8.
22. Ibid., p. 8.
23. Cullers, p. 213.
24. For a discussion of the role of hierarchies in deconstruction, see Cullers, pp. 18, 131, 147, 213.
25. Norris, p. 61.
26. Ibid., p. 88.
27. Cullers, p. 157.
28. *The Quintessence of Ibsenism*, p. 33.
29. Ibid., p. 31.
30. Ibid., p. 33.
31. For an account of how Shaw increasingly identified thought with passion and embodied that identity in his plays, see M. Meisel, *Shaw and the Nineteenth-Century Theatre* (Princeton, 1963), Chapter 16.
32. Stanley Weintraub, ed., "The New Theology," *The Portable Bernard Shaw* (New York, 1977), p. 305.
33. Bernard Shaw, *Our Theatres in the Nineties*, Vol. 1 (London, 1932), v.
34. *The Bodley Head Bernard Shaw*, Vol. 4, p. 465.
35. Ibid., p. 459.
36. Ibid., see especially pp. 564–5.
37. John Fowles, *The French Lieutenant's Woman* (New York, 1969), p. 285.
38. *The Bodley Head Bernard Shaw*, Vol. 4, p. 577.
39. Norris, p. 106.
40. Ibid., xii.
41. Ibid., p. 128.
42. *The Bodley Head Bernard Shaw*, Vol. 4, pp. 565–6.
43. For one of the latest and most ingenious attempts to find a unity in the Bible transcending the disintegrations of scientific analysis, an attempt kindred to Shaw's, see Northrop Frye's *The Great Code: The Bible and Literature* (New York, 1982).
44. William E. Cain, "Deconstruction: An Assessment," *College English*, Vol. 46, No. 8 (Dec., 1984), 811–820.
45. Ibid., 820.
46. See Shaw's "The Illusions of Socialism," *Selected Non-Dramatic Writings of Bernard Shaw*, ed. by Dan H. Laurence (Boston, 1965), p. 423.
47. Cullers, p. 200.

Index